Please return/renew this item by the
last date shown to avoid a charge.
Books may also be renewed by phone
and Internet. May not be renewed if
required by another reader.

www.libraries.barnet.gov.uk

BARNET
LONDON BOROUGH

Call of the
OUTBACK

The remarkable story of Ernestine Hill,
nomad, adventurer and trailblazer

MARIANNE VAN VELZEN

ALLEN&UNWIN
SYDNEY·MELBOURNE·AUCKLAND·LONDON

All attempts have been made to locate the owners of copyright material. If you have any information in that regard, please contact the publisher at the address below.

First published in 2016

Allen & Unwin
83 Alexander Street
Crows Nest NSW 2065
Australia
Phone: (61 2) 8425 0100
Email: info@allenandunwin.com
Web: www.allenandunwin.com

Cataloguing-in-Publication details are available
from the National Library of Australia
www.trove.nla.gov.au

ISBN 978 1 76029 059 7

Set in 13/16.5 pt Garamond Premier Pro by Post Pre-press Group, Australia
Printed and bound in Australia by Griffin Press

10 9 8 7 6 5 4

MIX
Paper from
responsible sources
FSC® C009448

The paper in this book is FSC certified.
FSC promotes environmentally responsible,
socially beneficial and economically viable
management of the world's forests.

For Leonardus van Velzen
and
Maria Johanna Meijer
in loving memory and gratitude

They dared to lose sight of the shore.

'Man cannot discover new oceans
unless he has the courage to
lose sight of the shore.'

André Gide

Contents

Prologue: Alice Springs, 1933   xi

1   The Foster-Lynams   1

2   Child genius   9

3   J.F. Archibald and *Smith's Weekly*   15

4   Robert Clyde Packer   23

5   Tasmania   31

6   On the road, 1930   39

7   M.P. Durack   47

8   Victoria Downs and Darwin   57

9   Land, sea and 'Blue Moon'   66

10   Adrienne Lesire   73

11   Daisy Bates   80

12   Jake and Minnie   89

13   Gold fever   98

14   Eric Baume   106

15   Borroloola   114

16   Perth   120

17   The *Silver Gull*, 1934   126

18   Adelaide   133

19   From Alice to Dumas   140

20   Writing books   152

21   The silver river   157

22   Radio star   163

23   Exemption   172

24   Travels with Bob   181

25   Henrietta Drake-Brockman   188

26   A dog and a caravan, 1947–48   196

27   *The Territory*   203

28   Eleanor Smith, 1952   213

29   Art and age   220

30   Mary Durack   226

31   Bob   231

32   Disasters and grandchildren   238

The lady in the blue dress   248

Epilogue   254

Author's note   257

Notes   261

Bibliography   289

Acknowledgements   305

Prologue: Alice Springs, 1933

In the late afternoon of 7 January 1933 a crowd gathered along the railway line, clustering together on the small platform at the station in Alice Springs. The sand-beaten *Ghan* came to a quivering halt. As the doors opened and people started spilling out, the men and women at the back of the crowd craned their necks, trying to catch a glimpse of the travellers.

They had come to see a particular group of medical scientists. An article in the Adelaide *Advertiser* had drawn attention to the arrival of a group of men who were to camp out in the desert for six months. According to the newspaper, the scientists would carry out tests on Aboriginal people to 'ascertain how [they were] able to exist on small supplies of water in arid areas'.

Among the scientists were the young doctor John Antill Pockley and the artist Arthur Murch. The latter had been invited on the trip to paint the 'dead heart' of Australia and lend a hand where necessary. After boarding the train in Adelaide, the young men had acted like schoolboys on an outing but disembarking in Alice Springs and realising that the crowd had gathered merely to see their strange troupe, they suddenly felt somewhat self-conscious.

The seven men were going into the outback, braving temperatures of more than 50 degrees Celsius. They set out for the Hermannsburg Mission to meet anthropologist Theodor (Ted) Strehlow, the son of the first administrator of the mission post, Reverend Carl Strehlow. There they planned to live among the Aboriginal people and their task for many weeks would be to measure how much water these locals drank against water lost in their urine and sweat. It meant heat, dust, flies and, for the young doctors, an adventure like no other. Pockley nervously plucked at his three-day-old moustache as he disembarked. He and Dr Hugh Barry had decided to grow moustaches and beards on the trip.

As he turned to the crowd, Pockley's eyes caught the outline of a frail lady in the background scribbling away in a notebook. 'The culprit,' he thought. This lady reporter was no doubt responsible for the articles in *The Advertiser* that had attracted the unwanted crowd.

His attention refocused when he noticed a tall man making his way through the sea of inquisitive heads. It was his friend, Dr David Brown, the only medical man in Central Australia. After a quick hello, Brown led the party away from the curious gazes and into the blistering sandy streets of the Alice. 'I suppose you men would like a drink?' he asked as he led them on. 'I live next to the Stuart Arms, the oldest pub in town.'

The pub was reasonably cool and the party positioned themselves around the bar, where they were handed cold beers by a scrutinising barmaid. 'You blokes the professors?' she asked haughtily. 'Thought as much.' Her eyes showed she had already passed judgement, no matter where they came from.

As the bar began to fill, the men were introduced to a solicitor, the bank manager and the lady reporter, whose name was Ernestine Hill. Pockley was somewhat surprised and a little disappointed when the lady told him she was in town to cover the gold rush at the Granites rather than the scientists' arrival. The promise of gold had turned into a disaster, but now the town was buzzing with the news of a murder. A body had been found near the Granites diggings and suspects were being held at the police station. There was a flicker of excitement in Ernestine Hill's large faun-like eyes as she lit a cigarette.

Two of her fingers were the colour of egg yolk. Too much smoking, the doctor in Pockley thought. The young man also noticed that what he had mistaken for a frail posture earlier on, when he had caught a glimpse of her in the crowd, was actually wiry toughness. She was small and thin with inquisitive eyes and a pronounced mouth. A superficial observer could easily mistake her for quite a harmless soul—'What a great asset for a journalist,' Pockley thought. Dressed in trousers and a blouse, she blended in nicely with the outback crowd but, as soon as she opened her mouth, she betrayed herself. Her speech gave away an elite schooling. A little nervously, the reporter suddenly excused herself and sat down at a corner of the bar.

She wrote in quick spasmodic jolts and would only tear herself away from the notebook to light up yet another cigarette. Hugh Barry nudged Pockley some time later and flicked his head towards the writing journalist. 'Have you ever seen anyone smoke that much? She reminds me of the bloody *Ghan* on a run, all that billowing smoke.'

After a few rounds had been drunk, the barmaid thawed and told the young men her name was Edna. She wondered aloud to Hugh Barry if the reporter was a spy. 'You seen her writing? It's all squiggly, like someone chopped the letters up. Not like any writing I've ever seen before. It looks I-rabic. She's spying for the Afghans, I reckon.'

'Some really strange people visit Alice, you know,' she added after a moment's thought. 'Take you blokes. I nearly peed my pants when I heard that all these professors were coming thousands of miles into the desert just to measure Aborigine piss.'

The Foster-Lynams

Ernestine Hill's grandparents, Thomas and Catherine Foster-Lynam, were Irish Catholics. Her grandfather, Thomas Foster-Lynam, arrived in Australia on 26 June 1844 on the *Briton*. He was nineteen years old and according to his immigration papers could read but not write. Like most Irish immigrants, Thomas almost certainly arrived in Australia hungry and poor. He had fled his homeland as a free passenger to a land where too many of his countrymen had years before been dropped as convicts. Except for this fact, most Irish immigrants knew very little about their new country; they were simply happy to leave behind the bleak desperation of their lives in Ireland. Reasoning that nothing could be worse than living under English rule in their own country, the Irish, in great numbers, left their country in search of freedom. And although most Irish Catholic migrants regarded the English-ruled colony with some degree of suspicion, they adapted well and their political views tended to mellow over the years. Most were urban workers who experienced less official discrimination than they had in Ireland.

Thomas Foster-Lynam was married twice. His first wife was Elizabeth Kennewel, who lived in New South Wales, and they had a child, Elizabeth, who died in infancy. Travelling up the coast to Rockhampton, Thomas met Catherine Ryan, who was twenty years his junior. They married, although it is unclear whether Thomas was divorced or a widower at the time. For the rest of his life he continued to travel periodically up and down the coast. His marriage to the young Catherine soon produced a child, Mary, who died when she was only two years old, but in the same year, 1862, their second child, Margaret, was born. Nicknamed Madge, she would later become the mother of Ernestine Hill. Another seven children were born into the Foster-Lynam family: Ann, Thomas, Daniel, the second Mary, Denis, Katherine and Michael.

In the second half of the nineteenth century hundreds of thousands of Irish came to live in Australia, and today many Australians claim an Irish ancestor. At the time, three-quarters of Irish land was owned by the English Protestant conquerors, who leased it back to the Irish. If the rent wasn't paid, livestock and furniture were taken and families ultimately faced eviction. For most of their existence, the Irish people had endured poverty and famine; Australia could give them a new future and especially hope. Thomas loved his new country and always placed Australia first and the Empire second.

The European history of the area where the Foster-Lynams settled began in 1853, when the brothers Charles and William Archer, who were seeking grazing lands, visited the district that would become Rockhampton. They were acting on information from earlier expeditions by Ludwig Leichhardt and Thomas Mitchell, who had explored the area in 1844 and 1846 and thought it suitable land for grazing. The Archers founded Rockhampton on the Fitzroy River, which provided a convenient waterway to ship supplies for those who followed.

The town's first shop was built in 1856 and its first inn appeared six months later. The discovery in 1858 of gold at Canoona, about 50 kilometres to the north-west, resulted in a sudden influx of miners and prospectors. The rush was short-lived but the population increased dramatically. There was work to be found on the surrounding cattle properties but also in Rockhampton, which by now had grown into a town. Cattle was its main source of income and it became the beef capital of Queensland.

The Foster-Lynam offspring were probably encouraged to learn to read and write, as most of them secured reasonably good jobs in their adult life. Religion was a big part of Irish life. Irish priests and bishops were arriving in Australia all the time with the intention of keeping the faith alive, and most Irish migrants were socially and politically aware.

There was outcry and rage among the Irish whenever one of their countrymen was attacked by the authorities, or seemed to suffer discrimination. Madge was nine years old when Ned Kelly was roaming Victoria, his outlaw life becoming an echo of 'old Ireland'—the common man struggling against oppression. But Ned was homegrown, and the police who finally captured him were as Irish as the outlaw himself. A romanticised version of his story spread throughout Australia and young Ned became a legend.

By the time the Foster-Lynam children were adults their father, who had always had poor eyesight, was going blind.

Thomas may also have suffered from mental issues. Whatever the cause, he became estranged from his family. He saw less and less of them, and finally cut himself off completely. Suffering from dementia and blindness, he eventually appeared on the streets of Brisbane as an organ grinder.

He became a well-known figure in and around Brisbane, where he greeted the Queen Street pedestrians with the words: 'Remember the music, ladies and gents.' Old Tom was considered a nuisance by some Brisbanites, who claimed that the tunes he ground out on his 'wheezy old organ' were monotonous, but others appreciated his melodies and his 'admirable disregard for the "eternal fitness of things"'.

During this period, Thomas's family saw very little of him, although one of his sons, also called Tom, did help him from time to time. Thomas Foster-Lynam died in Brisbane at the age of 76. Presumably because they had lost track of him and no one knew his next of kin, his family did not claim his body and, as a result, his death certificate was compiled by a stranger and included one or two errors. Before his death, Thomas had acquired a considerable amount of property in Rockhampton. He owned a half-acre allotment at the corner of Fitzroy and West streets upon which two cottages had been erected. One was let and the other was occupied by his family. Thomas also owned a piece of land on William Street just opposite the show-ground. Nevertheless, he was buried in a pauper's grave at Brisbane's Toowong Cemetery on 7 July 1897. In an article in *The Queenslander* dated 17 July 1897, he was remembered as a Brisbane icon. Just one year later, in July 1898, his wife Catherine passed away, at the tender age of 57.

For a woman in those days there were limited options in choosing an occupation. Madge had become a schoolteacher, a very respectable job for a woman at the time, and she taught at the state schools in Rockhampton and later in Brisbane and in Townsville.

Madge, at the beginning of her teaching career, might have preferred to teach within the Catholic school system, which was established in 1860 in opposition to the state-funded schools, because of both her faith and the Catholics' different approach to education. Catholic schools were run and taught entirely by nuns and had no funds to employ professional teachers. Madge would therefore have been able to work only in a state school. She must have thought highly of the Catholic school system, however, because she sent her daughter, Ernestine, mainly to Catholic schools and did teach at a Catholic school later in life.

Madge remained single into her late thirties. This was not uncommon at the time, as the country was only sparsely populated and the men often worked on settlements and cattle stations. Two of her sisters were also unmarried; one of them, Mary, had become a nun and was living in a convent.

It must have come as a surprise to everyone within the family when Madge introduced her fiancé, Robert Hemmings. He was a widower with a daughter, Ray. Madge and Robert met in Townsville, when Madge taught at the Ross Island State School.

Robert had migrated from England as a child on a free passenger ticket with his parents, who now lived in Melbourne. He was a tailor by trade and involved in the Australian Natives' Association (ANA) in Melbourne, so called because many of its all-white members had been born in Australia. The association played a leading role throughout the 1890s in the movement towards Federation; it also provided work, medical and funeral insurance for its members. The ANA claimed to avoid party politics, so some were surprised when they chose the prominent Victorian politician and ANA member Alfred Deakin to represent them in the Federation movement.

Robert had been engaged in business for many years and had also worked as a freelance writer, publishing articles in the Melbourne *Age*. He later moved to Sydney for business and then to Queensland. He was working for Finney, Isles and Co. and G.R. Ryder Ltd as a commercial traveller when he met Madge. Being both English and Protestant, he initially must have represented the enemy to her family, but it would have helped that he was well known and highly respected in the Townsville area. Mixed-religion marriages could not be performed at the Catholic altar, an exclusion that some felt was a humiliation, but the couple married on 6 July 1898; Robert was 45 and Madge 37.

Seven months later, on 21 January 1899, their daughter Mary Ernestine Hemmings was born. As a mix of English and Irish, Protestant and Catholic, she must have found her life, even in infancy, filled with contradictions. Before she could talk, her parents thought she showed signs of great sensitivity and intelligence, and she was much loved and pampered by them both. Her literary talent emerged early and, as young as six, she wrote poetry with the help of her father. Robert and Margaret were both lovers of poetry and literature, so there was no lack of encouragement.

Madge's younger sister, Katherine, who became Ernestine's Aunt Kitty or Kit, also indulged in the arts, writing poems and composing music. One of her poems, dedicated to Nellie Melba, was published in the Rockhampton *Capricornian* in 1909. The previous year, Katherine had written a waltz dedicated to her two nieces, Ray and Ernestine, called 'Rayernie'. Aunt Kitty would play an important role throughout Ernestine's life.

Ernestine turned into a very shy little girl, softly spoken and with an imaginative mind. For her first years of schooling she attended the state schools in Brisbane and Cairns, but when she was nine and her parents left Cairns for Hermit Park, a suburb of Townsville, Ernestine was sent to St Joseph's Convent School, located on the Strand.

She was happy in Townsville, she later wrote. There was a mango tree in the garden that she and Ray climbed, pretending to be pirates as they looked out to sea. Her mother planted palm trees in the backyard, and when Ernestine visited the house in later years she noted how immense they had become, describing the sound of their large leaves rustling overhead as soothing whispers in the soft breeze.

Their lives took a sad turn for the worse when Robert died suddenly of heart failure on 3 October 1910, just eighteen months after the family had moved back to Townsville. Their marriage had lasted less than twelve years. Although his death was sudden, it was not totally unexpected. He had been ill during the previous twelve months and had recently consulted a heart specialist in Brisbane.

Robert had returned to Townsville from Brisbane and, on the Wednesday evening, gone to his usual lodgings at

Townsville's Central Hotel, where he often stayed when he returned late from a business trip.

On the Friday, the hotel clerk noticed Hemmings, seemingly quite well, reading a paper in his room with his door open. Just a short while later the proprietor of the hotel, a Mr Goyle, passed his room and found him stooped over and apparently in great pain. The local physician, Dr Parkinson, was called, but it was already too late. The post-mortem described the death as due to 'fatty degeneration of the heart'—what we today would call heart disease.

After the death of her husband, Margaret sent Ray away to live with an aunt. No one seems to know why. As Ray was in her teens, Madge perhaps foresaw trouble in rearing her, but there was also a question of money—Robert had not left them any substantial amount. Whatever the reason for her mother's decision, the result was that Ernestine never saw her stepsister again.

Affected by the death of her father and deprived of the company of her much-loved sister, Ernestine retreated into poetry. Every free moment of the day she escaped into a world of her own. She was good at poetry, so good that a few years after her father died her teachers encouraged her to send her first poetic contribution to the *Catholic Advocate*. Titled 'A Kiss for Peter Pan', it was an entry in the Peter Pan Playing Pitch of June 1914, a contest run by the paper for the best verse or essay about Peter Pan. When *The Advocate* published it, it became her first newspaper publication.

Although young Ernestine seemed destined for a life as a poet or writer, no one of course had any idea how great her fame would one day become.

2

Child genius

Ernestine's first vivid memory was of watching her father write. The magic of words coming out of a pen or a pencil and forming squiggly lines, like crazy heartbeats on a white sheet, was to her like watching a Houdini illusion. She had no idea at the time that the squiggly lines were recording thoughts but, had she known, it would have enhanced the wonder of the act. Later, as she gradually learnt how to turn her thoughts into words on paper, it became her very own gratifying escape act.

After acquiring the skill, she wrote almost constantly, mostly poetry at first, but her parents also encouraged her to write prose. From the start she loved the rhythm and colour of the words, and the limitless world she could create using them. Writing so much on a daily basis improved her skills to a point where she even began to wonder where the words were coming from; she assumed for a while that her writing extended beyond her own imagination and was sent to her from some kind of cosmic, universal library.

The night Dr Parkinson came to the house he looked exactly as a doctor should—his glasses slipping to the tip of his nose, his impeccable dark suit pulled straight and his doctor's case hanging at his side. When Madge opened the door and his outline emerged from the twilight, she wondered who was sick. He peered from the doorway into the hall and frowned when he saw Ernestine, together with Ray, standing behind their mother.

Reluctant to come in, he looked stern and thoughtful, pushing his glasses up to the bridge of his nose so that Madge could see his eyes. Manoeuvring himself into the hallway, he whispered to her, the sound of their voices so soft that Ernestine could only catch the words 'life' and 'death'. But at these words her mother brought a hand to her mouth and turned to her young daughters with a confused expression.

That evening, after the doctor had left, Madge explained to Ray and Ernestine that their father had died and they were on their own. Madge assured them they would be fine. Their father had been away on business for long periods of time and they were used to coping on their own.

Ernestine was ten years old and her father's demise left a more heartfelt gap than her mother imagined. Madge's decision to send Ray away only added to the younger child's grief. Writing gave her a refuge, a safe private place where she could keep her sadness and at the same time escape from it. She invented a world where all was well, without loss or hurt. Creating a romantic haven on paper, and letting others read it, also gave her confidence. Her poems attracted the attention of teachers and her fellow students; she was showered with praise.

After her father's death, financial problems soon arose. Madge realised she would need to take up teaching again to secure some kind of income. It would mean moving back to

Brisbane, because Madge had left her previous teaching job at St Joseph's after a dispute with the headmaster. Aunt Kitty now stepped in to help her sister take care of Ernestine, who in later years noted that she always felt like she had two mothers.

Ernestine was sent to the Sandhurst Convent School in Brisbane but Madge had more ambitious plans. With faith in her child's ability, she coached Ernestine thoroughly and, when she thought she was ready, took her to apply for a scholarship at All Hallows' School in Brisbane, which some considered the best school in Queensland.

The all-girls All Hallows', founded in 1861 by the Sisters of Mercy to provide the less fortunate in colonial society with an education, was the first Catholic high school in the state. Many of Queensland's poorest residents at this time were of Irish Catholic immigrant stock. The nuns provided a curriculum that they felt would offer girls an opportunity to become accomplished, financially independent women of deep faith and sound learning. The nuns enjoyed a certain degree of autonomy and managed the convent and its finances independently, with no interference from male clergy.

This approach must have appealed enormously to Madge. With two unmarried sisters, she had always believed that women should not confine their options to marriage. In All Hallows', she recognised an educational system that she believed would widen her daughter's life options. To her great joy and relief, Ernestine was awarded a scholarship and was enrolled at All Hallows' Convent School in 1913.

For Ernestine herself, the school was somewhat of a disappointment. She felt the sisters were not at all interested in her writing and did not encourage her in any way. It was only after she won first prize in a 1914 essay competition run by the Queensland Society for the Prevention of Cruelty to Animals that the sisters started to take note, but she suspected that positive publicity for the school might have been their main incentive. She later wrote to her cousin Coy (Catherine), the daughter of her Uncle Denis, that the nuns 'had tried to take the credit for my writing career but that [they] both knew it had been Mother who had been my best critic and stimulation'.

The Catholic archbishop of Brisbane, James Duhig, did notice her, though. The Foster-Lynams had become acquainted with him during his term as archbishop of Rockhampton. Duhig had acquired a somewhat dubious reputation for his grand construction projects both there and later in Brisbane, and people jokingly called him 'The Builder'. He seemed to have borrowed huge sums of money to invest in his business plans for the diocese of Rockhampton, but he had an unconcerned attitude about repaying his debts. In fact he was quoted as joking that if he had not been an archbishop he would have been in gaol. Duhig liked to travel and he liked to build. On the hills of Brisbane, convents, schools and churches were constructed while he was archbishop.

Brisbane's archbishop was also particularly interested in the education of young Australians. His attention was attracted by Ernestine's poems, published in the *Catholic Advocate*, and he was impressed by her talent. To her amazement, he came by the school one day to meet her and started to recite by heart one of her poems, 'The Song of the

Curlew', which had appeared in *The Queenslander*. His booming voice filled the schoolroom with her words. Duhig praised her, saying he thought she was very gifted.

Ernestine Hemmings' first book was published in 1916 by the Hibernian Newspaper Company (which published the *Catholic Advocate*) with a preface by Archbishop Duhig. Titled *Peter Pan Land and Other Poems*, it included entries in the 1914 Peter Pan Playing Pitch. Although the greater part of the volume consisted of poems and essays by Ernestine, a few other contestants contributed as well.

After it was published, the newspapers applauded her as an unspoilt genius and the new star in the literary firmament. Journalists described her as something more than a mere composer of verse; they praised her as a true poet who would one day inevitably rank among the notable figures in Australian literary history.

All this praise rather frightened her. She was only sixteen and felt an expectation she was unsure she could fulfil. The Melbourne newspapers described her as a shy, modest girl, way too young for her age in both appearance and manner; they noted that her hair hung around her shoulders and that her skirts were short enough to 'permit ankles being seen'. A journalist from the Sydney *Sunday Times* portrayed young Ernestine as 'as shy as a Wonga pigeon', with a rather wistful and sad face.

There were also words of caution from the press. One reviewer found the claim of genius somewhat extravagant considering her age. Another found Ernestine's poems weak in original thought and advised her to confine herself to a simple expression of simple things. The same reviewer accused the budding poet of 'smudging her muse with banality', a criticism Ernestine found unfair and untrue. Her mother scoffed at the reviewer, telling Ernestine the man must be mad and was probably jealous. The tabloids described Madge as an overfond and proud mother.

During her time at All Hallows', Ernestine constantly scribbled verse. Annoyed by this distraction from her studies, the nuns ordered her to stop wasting her time and to focus all her attention on her schoolwork. She revealed in a later interview that the nuns' attitude towards her writing had made her feel as if they were trying to crush her ambition as well as her imagination. Discouraged by the lack of interest in her writing at school and praised on an almost daily basis by the newspapers, she gave up all idea of going to university and decided to develop her literary talent instead.

Her mother was not pleased, but Ernestine would not let anyone tell her that her writing was rubbish. To her, writing had always been very worthwhile. It was the one thing she excelled in. Her ultimate dream at the time was to become a journalist on a metropolitan paper.

3

J. F. Archibald and Smith's Weekly

Stott & Hoare's Business College, a highly regarded and prestigious institute founded by Sydney Stott in 1885, was where Ernestine wanted to study. The college had originally been established in Melbourne but soon after branches were opened in Sydney, Adelaide, Perth and Edward Street, Brisbane. On Edward Street the students were tutored in lofty and spacious rooms fitted with electric fans, lights and modern seating, and equipped with Remington typewriters. Each student had to pass eight grades before reaching the senior division in the shorthand department.

Ernestine must have realised that, given her aspirations to become a journalist, typing and shorthand might come in handy. She was admitted into Stott & Hoare's Business College in 1917 and proved a diligent pupil, passing the course in advanced shorthand after only five months. The Pitman shorthand she learnt proved an invaluable skill in later years.

Topping her year meant Ernestine gained immediate employment in the Queensland public service, initially as a typist at the Stamp Duties Office. For the young and imaginative Ernestine, working there soon became boring and tedious, so when a vacancy arose for a librarian at the Department of Justice in Brisbane, she applied for the job. She would at least have the chance to work surrounded by books, and reading them would afford some kind of distraction. It was a new position; as the department had no librarian, books were being borrowed willy-nilly then lost. Ernestine's sole duty was to ensure that the borrowed books were returned. She earned 30 shillings a week.

Brisbane was still a small city at this time and Ernestine, who had seen her poems published in newspapers and a book, was a figure of public interest. Every now and then her name would pop up in a newspaper. In 1918 she confessed to a journalist from the *Cairns Post* that life at the library had turned out to be a deadly monotonous affair. There was too little to do and nothing exciting ever happened. The only diversion from the mind-numbing day-to-day work was meeting the frequent visitors who admired her work and discussed poetry with her. Ernestine's poems were still regularly published in the *Catholic Advocate*, *The Tribune* and the *Australian Worker*. People would come in for a chat; sometimes they gave her advice or tried to cheer her up. Although she had at first claimed that working at the Justice Department 'was just the thing', it soon turned out that she found it increasingly difficult to conceal her growing discontent.

Her confidant there was Timothy Keleher, who also wrote poetry and later became a magistrate. They became good friends but, to Ernestine's dismay, Keleher was transferred to Toowoomba only a few months after she arrived, although the two kept in touch. In her letters to Keleher, Ernestine showed signs of an interest in politics, scoffing at the right-wing newspapers that denounced the Ryan Labour Government and accused it of wasting taxpayers' money: 'Queensland would be a great deal worse off in these bad times if it weren't for Ryan's Government . . . In a new country like Queensland one must be prepared to spend money to develop things . . . These are stirring times as the teaspoon said.' Timothy wrote that he might give up studying law to perhaps chase a career in writing. And when Ernestine's essay 'Sea Thoughts' was published in the *Australian Worker*, Keleher seemed just as excited as she.

By now it was obvious that her job at the Justice Department would not last a lifetime. With her lively imagination, sitting in an office all day must have felt like prison to Ernestine. She wanted to be on the move, to meet people and explore new horizons. She was almost twenty years old, but she must have felt she had not even glimpsed life yet. Her urge to move on (something that became especially evident later in her life) was the inevitable consequence of a persistent longing to experience new possibilities.

The office staff undoubtedly considered her very shy, although she always described herself instead as self-conscious. As a young woman she had a long face with wide dark eyes, a long nose and full lips. Most of her colleagues would not even have suspected her need for adventure, so it must have come as a shock when, one day in 1918, she tendered her resignation and announced that she would be moving to Sydney. Her cousin, Coy Foster-Lynam, was to go with her; together they would be joining the founding staff of a newspaper called *Smith's Weekly*.

Smith's Weekly was being launched as an independent tabloid. The new paper's main financier was Sir James Joynton Smith, who had been a prominent Sydney figure during the First World War. Its two other founders were theatrical publicist Claude McKay, who was to be the editor, and journalist Robert Clyde Packer, who went on to become the founder of the Packer media empire. The aim was to create a lively mix of sensationalism, satire and controversial opinions, together with sport and financial news.

Coy was taken on as a typist and junior journalist while Ernestine was appointed secretary to the new literary editor, Jules François Archibald. Ernestine was intelligent enough to realise that this might be her chance to become a journalist, but the thought of the two of them living in the 'big smoke' must also have seemed an exciting prospect.

When she first applied for the job, her chances of actually getting it were probably slim. After all, she had gone straight from a Catholic girls' school into a few years of business training, then had only worked a few months as a librarian. But she was given the position. And so she bade the Justice Department goodbye and headed for a job that would change her life in ways she could never have imagined.

Ernestine and her mother spent the Christmas holidays with her family in Melbourne, and on their way back stopped in Sydney to visit the office of *Smith's* and meet some of the staff. Although in later years Ernestine came to dislike Sydney—always feeling sad, intimidated and overwhelmed in the booming city—as a young girl she probably saw possibilities for herself there. Brisbane was fine and quiet—its old trams making their way along palm-lined streets—but at that time Sydney, like today, was very much a vibrant city, bustling with people, with everyone who was anyone living there.

Although he was now an old man, J.F. Archibald was little less than an icon. He had co-founded *The Bulletin* in 1880 and was later its sole owner. *The Bulletin* was a hugely popular magazine that mixed politics, sensationalised news and literature. As its legendary editor, he had provided such illustrious writers as 'Banjo' Paterson and Henry Lawson with a platform for their work. The 'Bushman's Bible', as people affectionately called *The Bulletin*, had always maintained a high standard of prose and poetry, and had introduced a more populist style of journalism to Australia. It was still the country's best-known weekly.

People wondered why Archibald had ended up at *Smith's*. Rumour had it that, after selling his interest in *The Bulletin*, he had found himself at a bit of a loose end. In March 1919 he had entered the office of *Smith's Weekly* and offered his help. Packer, McKay and Smith accepted; Packer especially realised it might be good for the brand-new weekly to have a famous and respected name on board.

Now and then the *Smith's Weekly* staff had been known to make snide remarks about Archibald's name. 'Jules François' had been originally just plain 'John Feltham'. The man loved to play the bohemian and had even given his country of birth as France, but there wasn't a French hair on his balding head. Archibald was born in the Geelong suburb of Kildare. Nobody really knew where his love of all things French had originated, but one day John Feltham had transformed himself into Jules François and even furnished his mother with a Jewish–French identity to justify his adopted first names.

Stepping into the old man's office, Ernestine must have felt both awed and intimidated. The twenty-year-old was entering the domain of a legend.

With his metal-rimmed glasses perched on a hooked nose, Archibald had the demeanour of a librarian, and Ernestine may have wondered if working for this very old man would be any different to working at the Justice Department. She was always very aware of his significance, of what he had meant to famous writers and how he had coaxed them into fulfilling their literary potential. Because he had always avoided any personal publicity, Archibald was also somewhat of a mystery. No one really knew anything about his private life. He may have looked old and finished, but he had been welcomed onto the staff of *Smith's*, so at least Packer must have believed he still had some life in him. Ernestine might have simply hoped he would teach her the art of journalism.

Ernestine discovered, as they settled into a routine, that the old man could be impatient, demanding and at times somewhat absent-minded, but he was also gentle, open and responsive. He appeared to like her and they got on quite well. Archibald was a tactful editor who had learnt over time that encouragement, rather than bullying, could help a budding talent evolve. His tactfulness had undoubtedly helped a young Henry Lawson find his own easy and superb prose style and, given time, it might help a young Ernestine Hemmings find her own voice.

Those who knew Archibald claimed there was also a sad side to the old man. His wife Rose had died in 1911 and he still grieved her loss. The office had more or less become his home. It was rumoured that he practically slept there.

The Bulletin had been his life in the past and now *Smith's Weekly* gave meaning to his existence. Archibald wasn't one for parties but sometimes, when the staff went out for a drink or a meal, he would join them and surprise everyone with his skill as an entertaining conversationalist.

Aside from all this, it was obvious he had been unwell. He had spent several years in Rozelle's Callan Park Hospital for the Insane, a period that had been marked by depression and mania—what we now call bipolar disorder. Many people had written him off in the past, and although he appeared to be fine at this stage of his life, he was always afraid the bad times would return. His surprise at Packer accepting his offer had been as great as everyone else's, but he also realised that Robert Clyde was a shrewd businessman with a keen eye for marketing. Packer wanted a piece of the legend.

From the start, the old man must have realised that young Ernestine showed potential. He advised her, once again recognising talent when he saw it, and eagerly discussed with her the journalistic needs of postwar Sydney. He told Packer that he thought his secretary could become a good journalist if given enough opportunity.

Archibald must have been distinctly aware that no one could fail to notice Packer—larger than life and self-assured, booming down the hallway into the office every morning, he was everything young Ernestine was not. Archibald, who looked much older than his 63 years, may have warily shaken his head at this incredibly energetic man who never failed to impress the young ladies working for him.

Archibald took his subediting work very seriously, and for some months seemed to have regained some of his former zest and energy. He described himself as 'the soler and heeler of paragraphs' and would sometimes entertain—he was an excellent cook—at his weekend cottage at Cronulla.

This didn't last long, however, and his career at *Smith's* turned out to be his finale. Archibald became very ill in August 1919 and his health deteriorated swiftly. Just before his death, Ernestine visited him in St Vincent's Hospital. She thought a lot of her editor and it must have been a sad affair for both of them, but the frail old man wrapped under the stiff white sheets managed to lighten their spirits with a 'chuckle at the world he was about to leave'. *Smith's* received word of his death on 10 September 1919. The staff had barely had enough time to get to know him.

After the funeral service they went for a drink, finding it appropriate to toast the great man. On one of the rare occasions Archibald had accompanied the staff for a drink, he was remembered to have said: 'If I must die, then let me die drinking in a pub.'

J.F. Archibald was buried in the Catholic section of the Waverley Cemetery. Ernestine had worked for him for just five months.

4

Robert Clyde Packer

After Archibald's death, Ernestine might have feared she could lose her job. But Robert Clyde Packer, who had a keen eye for talent and had listened to Archibald's recommendations, made a very young Ernestine a subeditor at *Smith's*.

Robert had been a thorough newspaperman since arriving in Sydney from Tasmania in 1902. After a couple of jobs as an apprentice on some provincial newspapers in New South Wales, he was offered a position with the *Sunday Times*, where he worked his way up to editor. In the partnership that launched *Smith's Weekly*, Packer managed the paper, including the recruitment of staff. He was not an easy man to work for and he drove his staff hard, but they were rewarded with good salaries.

Packer was twenty years Ernestine's senior; her admiration for him was obvious. Although he was old enough to be her father, she later told Coy that he was the love of her life. He was the epitome of everything most women looked for in a man. Good-looking, intelligent, entertaining, robust and energetic, he had a very good singing voice to boot—he was a tenor and sometimes performed in amateur productions. His father had played the organ back in Tasmania and the Packers were well known in music circles on the island. He had once flirted with joining a film company and becoming an actor, but he soon gave up that idea and returned to journalism.

Packer and Ernestine had long conversations, but there was nothing personal or secret about their talks. Mostly they discussed matters concerning the newspaper, and spoke about the way to turn news items, however mundane or boring, into copy that would amuse and interest a general public. It became Packer's personal objective to find a way to portray news so that everyday people would feel the need to read it. He encouraged his staff to write about sport, crime and human-interest stories.

From the very first edition of *Smith's* there was controversy, and it even resulted in a couple of defamation suits. Although this cost the founders money, it also brought *Smith's* a lot of publicity, and the circulation skyrocketed. One of the first things Ernestine would have learnt is that controversy gets people talking and that it's not always a bad thing to be the centre of debate. Packer seemed to know what he was doing.

He had his bad points. If he was upset or one of the staff let him down, he would tear through the office like a discharged bullet, hunt down the unfortunate guilty party, yell mercilessly at them and then fire them without hearing them out. His big burly frame would then pound back into his office, leaving the stunned and silent staff to deal with the aftermath. But he was also an unexpectedly charming man, and could behave with surprising flair and sophistication.

Despite their age difference, Ernestine seemed to be developing a 'schoolgirl crush' on him. For her, this would not have been a problem. Ernestine's father had been nine years her mother's senior and her grandfather had been twenty years older than his wife. She would have had few male role models because, since her father's death, it had always been her mother, Aunt Kit and her. As a travelling salesman, her father had been absent for long periods anyway. Robert Clyde Packer was probably kind to her, flattering even. But he was also married.

His wife, Ethel Maude Hewson, was the daughter of the Anglican Archdeacon Frank Hewson. She and Robert had a son, Frank, born in 1906 and a daughter, Kathleen, born in 1910. Coy may have warned her cousin in some way, but as her early poems attest, Ernestine was a romantic and probably failed miserably to see what lay ahead.

When a dashing young New Zealander stepped into the *Smith's* office one day in 1922, Coy forgot all about Ernestine's confused feelings for her boss. Charles Henry Bateson, or Hank as he liked to be called (Ernestine called him Harry), knew Claude McKay, who also hailed from across the Tasman. Bateson had written to the *Smith's* editor to let him know he wanted to come to Australia, and McKay had offered him a job. He was only nineteen, and was appointed to the younger staff section, where he worked with both Coy and Ernestine.

From the start, Coy was impressed by this serious young man—and he appeared equally impressed by her. Harry seemed older than his age; he had gravitas. They were both young and ambitious journalists and they had a lot in common. On 27 August 1923, Coy Foster-Lynam became Coy Bateson in St Peter's Anglican Church, Darlinghurst.

Some years later the couple left *Smith's* to join the staff of Ezra Norton's Melbourne newspaper, *The Truth*. Hank became the leader writer there and also turned out to be a talented administrator, at times managing and editing the paper.

Ernestine no doubt felt lonely after her cousin married. She seemed to have few friends outside the office and certainly did not appear to have a boyfriend. Ernestine must have been well aware that people sometimes ended up alone: her aunts, Mary and Katherine, were not married, and her mother had never re-married after her father's death. In later life and probably also as a young woman, Ernestine was not a very open and outgoing person. She always found it difficult to reveal herself. Although she could be amiable, talkative and appealing to others, and sometimes to men—she had a very friendly relationship with Timothy Keleher, for example— only one man, she believed, always brought out the best in her.

Soon Ernestine was pregnant. She had always been skinny, so as she started to fill out, she probably didn't take much notice. Turning from a slight girl with long hair and a shy smile into a slightly chubby woman was no reason for concern, just a sign of maturity. At first she might even have been pleased that her breasts were filling out instead of disappearing among the folds of her dress.

How soon did she begin to suspect she might be pregnant, as she filled out more and more? At some stage she must have realised it wasn't just fat and tried to reassure herself. After all, she was a child prodigy. Keep an eye on young Ernestine, the newspapers had predicted. This girl was going to go far, this girl held a promise for the future. They had predicted that she would someday become a famous poet: 'This charming, unspoilt, gifted daughter of a very proud mother.' It wouldn't have been easy for her as she stared at the growing bulge in the mirror and her suspicions slowly matured into frightening knowledge.

During those first months she probably asked herself how she could have let it happen and how she could have been so reckless. It had not all been his fault. She herself had been so eager—eager to please, eager to experience life. He had not been the first man ever to take any notice of her, but he had been the finest.

She must have decided at some point that she would have to tell Robert Packer; it had become an undeniable fact. However they discussed the matter, she no doubt hoped for a brief moment that he would choose her, run away with her, that they would sail into the sunset together. She was 23 years old, and although she always remained a romantic at heart, she was also a realist. Falling pregnant at such a young age, with no prospect of marriage to the child's father, brought home to her how overwhelmingly harsh life could be. Sydney changed her: she would always be self-conscious, but she now acquired some toughness.

After she had told him, Ernestine may have watched Packer calculate the possibilities in his mind, ticking them off one by one. Looking up at him, perhaps she tried to hold back tears. She realised that he had a lot to lose. She could not be saved, she may have reasoned, so there was no need for them both to suffer. Did they turn their backs on each other, realising they would never find a solution?

It must have been very difficult to tell her mother and her aunt of her pregnancy. Madge was proud of her daughter, but she was a strict woman who could hold order in her classes with a mere glance. In her school reports she was praised for her authority and precision. Madge was no doubt disappointed—she'd had such high hopes for her daughter—but she did not abandon her as some mothers at the time would have done. Ernestine probably felt ashamed because, despite all that had happened, she still loved Packer and may well have believed that he loved her.

Madge had shown that she was a strong woman from the moment her husband had died. She had dusted herself down and stood up as a woman who could solve her own problems. Ernestine undoubtedly observed the strength and resilience of both her mother and her Aunt Kitty, and took them as her model.

Madge was never the type to let her only child become a fallen woman, whispered about behind her back. And neither would she allow her grandchild to be torn from its biological mother and grandmother, and adopted out. It is difficult to know when exactly they hatched their ingenious plan, or if everything just fell into place by chance.

Madge probably realised that her daughter needed to leave Sydney, to have her child elsewhere. When she told her what they must do, Ernestine at first felt torn. She did not want to be forced to go away; it felt like a rebuke, a rejection. By pulling a few strings and executing an intelligently formed plan, however, they could ensure that the child would not have to bear the stigma of illegitimacy.

Whoever made the arrangements, a few weeks later

Ernestine boarded a train for Melbourne. Her mother promised to join her soon; she would tell the family and friends in Queensland and Sydney that her daughter was spending a well-earned holiday in Melbourne and, after that, she would be travelling to Tasmania, where she had been offered a new job writing for a Launceston newspaper. The last part was true. Given Packer had grown up in Tasmania and his family still lived there, it is tempting to imagine that he was instrumental in securing Ernestine a post there.

On a windy day on 24 October 1924, Ernestine's son, Robert David, was born in Melbourne. Robert had been her father's name, her lover's name and was now her son's name (although the baby's birth was never officially registered). Ernestine later claimed that the day her son was born was by far the happiest of her life. Her mother came down from Brisbane, together with Aunt Kitty, and for the time being the two took care of mother and child.

Not long after the birth, Ernestine visited a hairdresser. She no longer wanted to look like an innocent child. All the fretting she had experienced over the past months had left dark shadows under her eyes so, to distract attention from these smudges, she adopted a fringe that fell just above her eyebrows. It was a distinctive hairstyle she wore to the end of her life.

Despite her new look, she retained the shy and timid gaze that gave her the appearance of a frightened deer. She would always remain self-conscious about her appearance and never developed a sense of being beautiful. Asked at one stage to give a description of herself, she told a journalist she considered herself 'skinny and sinister'.

Her pointy features soon returned and the curves disappeared back into her body. As she nourished and nursed her baby, she fell hopelessly in love with this small wonder of new life. She knew it would be hard to take up a job and be separated from him, but she also realised that she would need some kind of income to support a baby.

A short while later, a sum of money began to appear in her bank account every month. It was not enough for them to live on, but it did provide some form of financial security, and it was meant for the child. It was perhaps sent on condition that she keep quiet about the boy and who his father was. Ernestine never revealed that information herself, and her son was never openly acknowledged by anyone.

A few months later, mother, child and grandmother left for Tasmania, where Ernestine Hemmings took up a post on the Launceston *Examiner*.

5

Tasmania

Ernestine met Iris Reid the day she stepped into the *Examiner* office. At first the staff hardly noticed the unassuming and quiet newcomer.

The Examiner was located in an imposing three-storey, Edwardian-style building, constructed in 1911. The paper was owned and managed by William Rolph and his sons. Iris, a junior journalist at the time, thought the new girl looked even younger than she was, so it came as a surprise when Ernestine was introduced to the staff as the new editor of the women's pages.

The women's pages were being launched as a new feature section in *The Examiner*. Up to that point, newspapers had been mainly directed at male readers, but now there was a rising demand for articles that would be of interest to the growing number of female readers. Ernestine's job was to organise and edit these pages.

From the start, the new editor set about her task with considerable vigour and determination, although her colleagues may have considered her ideas of what women would like to read much too progressive. The chief editor and the manager, no doubt with advertisers in mind, wanted her to publish articles about the latest fashions and handy kitchen utensils. Ernestine, on the other hand, wanted to write about ladies who were important to Tasmanian society, and about the island's countryside and history.

In Sydney she had been taught how to write for a broad public, spicing up her articles with her imaginative turn of phrase. She wanted to buy a camera and enliven her articles with photographs. At that time it was rare anywhere for photography to complement a journalist's copy, but in Tasmania it was unheard of. She must have been very disappointed that most of her ideas never made it into print.

It was Stephen Spurling who sparked Ernestine's enduring love of photography. A prolific landscape and commercial photographer who at the time owned the largest studio in northern Tasmania, Stephen was also a third-generation photographer, his grandfather having established a studio in Hobart in the 1860s. Stephen took staggering shots of the caves at Mole Creek and was the first to take photographs on the snow-shrouded summit of Ben Lomond. He liked to go on expeditions, and his photos were often published in *The Examiner* as well as in professional journals. He had photographed Lord Kitchener, who had been the figurehead for the war effort, as well as the Prince of Wales, and in 1919 had even taken a series of aerial photographs of Launceston.

Ernestine bought her first camera, a little foldable Zeiss Ica, from Stephen and he gave her lessons in photography, including how to develop her own film. She proved an able student and learnt a great deal from him.

She remained a very private person, keeping mainly to herself, never going out for a drink after work but instead hurrying home. The staff knew she had a child and that her husband was 'away' and not coming back, leaving her a single parent. They must have sympathised with the young girl raising a child on her own, although some knew that she did sometimes have help from her mother and an aunt. Kitty now lived primarily with her youngest brother, Michael, in the Brisbane suburb of Ashgrove. A horseriding accident when he was a young jockey had left him with a disabled leg. It was later, when Ernestine left Tasmania, that Kitty joined her on the mainland to help take care of her child.

Although she looked so very frail, Ernestine was not as fragile as everyone imagined. She could become adamant when she thought she was right or was expressing her personal opinion. She would never press the point, but retreat into herself if she didn't find the dispute worth pursuing to the limit.

Knowing that Ernestine had once worked for *Smith's Weekly*, the staff must have wondered why she had left to come to Tasmania—most aspiring journalists would have given the world to work there. Ernestine claimed that when Archibald died, her job as his secretary died with him, so she had left. But Ernestine left Sydney four years after the old man died, and it was also clear that she had learnt a lot about how to write articles in the meantime.

She did seem to love Tasmania, though, and travelled all over the island during her holidays, her camera her constant companion. Although Tasmania had been Iris Reid's home for years, the images Ernestine showed her looked as if they had been taken in another world; Iris had not realised such breathtaking vistas existed. This young woman had an eye—not only could she take a good picture with her camera but she could also paint one with words.

Ernestine, on occasion, would stare through the office window, a cigarette smouldering between her fingers, looking as if she desperately wished to be elsewhere. It was obvious that Tasmania would soon become too small for her, but it was no time for a single mother to simply give up her job. Ernestine stayed where she was, but it would only be a matter of time before she moved on. After a few years the novelty of her new job slowly began to wear off.

When she was asked if she might not want to move back to Sydney, Ernestine replied that this wasn't an option. The child's father lived there, and living in Sydney would be too close for both their liking. She wanted to travel, she said. Not abroad, but in Australia—on the mainland of the country she would so intimately get to know and learn to love. Her ambition was to discover who was living out there and to paint their stories with her pen, as Henry Lawson had done.

She discussed the classics with her colleagues, confessing that she loved the 'bush poets', Henry Lawson and Banjo Paterson. Lawson had died in 1922 but the unforgettable images he created of barefoot children and gaunt, penniless mothers and fathers would live on forever. Although Ernestine loved Lawson's prose, she must have realised that his bleak characters were in dire need of updating.

Ernestine had an elaborate, almost flowery poetic style, nothing like Lawson's dry, spare voice. She wrote articles like a poet, filled with romance and colour, easy to read and appreciated by readers. In such uncertain times the public wanted to read about beauty and success; they wanted to read stories that were bright and full of promise. She would go on to write about good-natured, wholehearted people with an inner drive strong enough to make their lives a success. Stories that could give Australians what they were looking for. She spoke about her ideas with so much passion and optimism that Iris told her she should follow her heart and write about the people and the land.

Ernestine's decision to leave *The Examiner* came one Monday morning after she opened a letter to the paper from the Inland Mission Sisters at Halls Creek in Western Australia. She loved to read letters from remote areas and they always kindled her inner fire. This long missive included a short narrative about a mission boy who had visited a city for the first time in his life and had approached it as darkness fell. He was amazed at the view of the city lights from the hills. Writing back to his mother, he captured those first impressions with the words: 'Fancy, Mum, the lights in the city look just like the lights of the blacks' camps over the ranges.'

For the editor of the women's pages, these words must have conjured a picture of a world beyond the city lights, beyond straight outback roads and far beyond her own experience. It was the final push she needed to pick up her family and her belongings and head for the mainland. In that instant it became clear to her what she wanted to write about and what she wanted to do with her life.

As Iris Reid watched her in thought, mesmerised by the letter, with cigarette smoke meandering from her mouth, she asked her if there was anything wrong. Ernestine looked up at Iris with those big oval eyes and said, 'Do you realise that in Australia there are still blacks' camps sufficiently big to look like the lights of a city on the hillside?' Iris shrugged, not really grasping what she was on about. Looking back down at the letter, Ernestine said, 'I'm going to go and see them. I'm going to see them before they're gone.'

She would become a travel writer. She would write stories that would distract people from their poverty and shabby future prospects. Ernestine undoubtedly understood the need, when one's outlook was dismal, to find escape in another place—her unplanned pregnancy must have taught her that.

Before she could leave and pursue her ambition, however, one of the worst floods in Tasmanian history hit Launceston. It was April 1929 and weather stations in Burnie predicted extreme rainfall in the north-east of Tasmania. In three days more than twenty inches (508 millimetres) were measured and the next day it was hard to reach the *Examiner* office as the streets began to flood. On 4 April the new Briseis Dam broke and the already flooded streets started filling to alarming levels. As Ernestine and Iris took the bus home that evening, they watched in horror as the waters of the North and South Esk rivers broke their embankments and swept cars, mud, boulders and uprooted trees along in the surge.

The next morning the *Examiner*'s presses began printing thousands of leaflets with evacuation instructions. The staff called upon the senior students of the Wellington Square School to distribute them, especially in the low-lying areas of the city. Iris and Ernestine were sent to attend a meeting convened by the mayor to prepare for evacuation. The mayor, screeching like a parakeet, could not make himself heard above the din of the constant downpour, and the two journalists did not hear a word.

The next day the Duck Reach Power Station was destroyed, plunging the city into darkness and stopping the presses. Everyone finally fled when the post office bell began to toll at 2 a.m., signalling an evacuation. The city was badly damaged, and Ernestine and her family barely survived crossing the Tamar Street Bridge over the North Esk. Watching the town's destruction unfold as they looked back across the ferocious river, it must have dawned on Ernestine that it would take Launceston years to recover.

In October 1929, as Launceston was slowly picking up the pieces after the devastating flood, the New York Stock Exchange collapsed. Australia was hit hard and mercilessly by the Great Depression that washed over the world in the wake of that catastrophe. Australia had flourished in the 1920s, but now there was widespread collapse; Tasmania suffered even more than the mainland.

For poor Launceston it meant a double disaster. Unemployment skyrocketed and the rates of bankruptcy doubled. Those men and women who had been evicted or had lost their houses in the flood were left to roam the streets with no means of survival. A life of eating out of rubbish bins, queuing for the dole, and tramping the countryside in search of work was all that was left to them. For the working man it was hard to believe in a better future. Destitute people yearned for good news.

Ernestine was still working for *The Examiner*, but she made no secret of her unwillingness to sit and wait for good news to arrive. She wanted to be the deliverer. It came as no surprise to the office staff, therefore, that before 1929 came to an end she announced she was quitting her job. She told Iris she had been offered a position as a feature writer for the Sydney *Sunday Sun* (one of the Associated Newspapers group, of which Robert Clyde Packer had been appointed general manager), which wanted stories about the remote areas of Australia. Ernestine was heading west and would finally fulfil her long-time dream. People asked her if she was afraid, a woman going alone into unknown country. 'Goodness no,' she replied, 'What is there to be afraid of?'

On leaving Tasmania she not only left her job and her friends on the island, she also left behind her surname. Hemmings transformed into Hill on the boat back to the mainland. Her co-workers had by now assumed there was no husband—no one had ever seen him and she never discussed him, except in vague terms. Changing her surname before landing on the mainland could have been a means of gaining respectability for herself and legitimacy for her child.

It was December 1929 when she returned to the mainland with her mother and child as Ernestine Hill. It was the name she would keep for the rest of her life.

6

On the road, 1930

Landing in Melbourne, Ernestine felt freed from the confines of the island. While in Tasmania she had longed for the openness and varied countryside of the Australian mainland, where she hoped she might stumble upon interesting stories just past the last signposts. She was excited at the prospect of roaming those outback roads, meeting the inhabitants of remote Australia, visiting tiny towns and stations, and listening to stories told around a campfire; calling on the inhabitants of faraway outposts, to write up their unusual lives and recognise their existence. She had been guaranteed the *Sunday Sun* would publish everything she sent. So right from the beginning she was assured of a large readership.

Little Robbie was now five, a wide-eyed chubby little boy, and Ernestine hated to leave him for any stretch of time, but as a single mother, she was forced to make a living. Her first obligation was to write features for the *Sunday Sun*, but she would also try to peddle other copy she wrote to the Western Australian newspapers on a freelance basis. It was mainly her Aunt Kit who minded her child while Ernestine hunted for copy, but Madge would also come along at times. Ernestine tried to see as much of her family as possible, taking them along on her journeys whenever she could. The monthly payments from Sydney served as a safety net and provided some leeway.

When she left Melbourne, friends asked her if she contemplated packing a gun. Ernestine hated weapons and anything to do with killing or hurting a living creature, so she decided against it—all she took with her were sharpened pencils. Some scorned her for this, arguing that her naivety prevented her from recognising the brutality to be found in Australia's remote areas, but she refused to be scared out of something she dearly wanted to do. Her sharpened pencils would bring Australia's hidden outback to life, she told them.

In 1930s Melbourne, the Depression hit hard: Ernestine observed the wretchedness all around her. Poor and deprived people spilled from cold houses, roaming the streets, looking for a job or food. These people would not want to read about failure and poverty—it was what they had to endure daily. Ernestine quickly understood that they would want and need stories about hardworking people who prevailed. She still had to find her own particular voice, but she soon built upon an appealing style that was unique to Australian writers: a strange mix of popular journalism, scientific inquiry and social anthropology. Ernestine Hill did more than just pick up this way of writing; she managed to give it her own sensually evocative touch. Her stories, spiked as they were with romantic notions, are a very vivid and imaginative account of the outback.

At the beginning of 1930, Ernestine and her family travelled by boat via the Great Australian Bight to Perth, where her adventure began. Because of the discovery of gold in nearby cities, Perth had not suffered so greatly during the Depression as had Melbourne and Sydney. Ernestine sensed a feeling of optimism and confidence on Perth's tranquil streets. She found lodgings in a guesthouse called the Mansions, and in an effort to introduce herself to the Perth newspapers, wrote a story she sent to the *Western Mail*. On 7 February 1930, that paper published a story by Ernestine Hill about a man taking a photo of himself against a backdrop of the Swan River, his camera perched on a tripod. It appeared under the title 'This week's best tale'.

This man must have caught Ernestine's attention because of her interest in photography. Although she had been unable to use photos as part of her journalistic arsenal during her years in Tasmania, the *Sunday Sun* was now ready to publish them and she hoped the other newspapers would follow suit, so she could give readers not only a written account but also a visual glimpse of the outback. The small Zeiss Ica turned out especially handy for travelling, as it folded into a flat rectangle and easily fitted into a bag.

In the 1930s the newspapers were dominated by articles about an unlikely racehorse and an Australian cricketer, both of whom were symbols of hope to a country engulfed by the Depression. Donald Bradman, who as a young boy had swatted golf balls against his parents' water tank with a single stump, became an inspiration for those who hoped life would reward them if they worked hard enough. But Bradman had a rare talent that most people queuing for the dole did not possess.

He was just eighteen when he became a first-class cricketer, but he soon became a legend. During the English summer of 1930 Bradman scored 974 runs in only seven innings over the course of the five Ashes Tests, the highest individual total in any Test series before or since. The story of this remarkable boy sparked the imagination of a nation. Stories of people who, against all odds, could secure a better life for themselves inspired Australian readers. In the public mind Bradman was a boy who had worked hard to become a hero.

Surprisingly, his popularity was surpassed at the time only by that of a racehorse. A big, plain-looking chestnut, Phar Lap was an underdog and loved by all. Trained by the poor but confident Harry Telford, who leased the horse from his American-born owner, David J. Davis, the horse soon began to attract attention as he won race after race. Here again a poverty stricken public identified with both horse and trainer. Regarded as battlers and unlikely heroes, Telford and Phar Lap were adored and admired.

As Bradman hit Australia into never-ending glory on the cricket field and Phar Lap ran his unforgettable circuits of racecourses, Ernestine Hill was probably mapping out her trip with a fair idea of what readers would appreciate. She would go out and find those battlers and unlikely heroes of the outback, and she would return with their stories in her note-books. At that time she had no real idea that 'out there' she would find the mother lode of yarns.

As well as writing her regular piece for the *Sunday Sun*, Ernestine began contributing to the Western Australian newspapers, and the Perth editors gradually became acquainted with the dark-haired, husky-voiced lady. On 7 June 1930, the *West Australian* published her article about a

Greek school in Perth. They also published some of her poems. She still wrote poetry, albeit sparsely; her urge to do so would never completely disappear, but over the years it would be displaced by poetic descriptions of a remote and unknown Australia.

By the end of July 1930, Ernestine decided it was time to leave Perth. She, Kitty and Robbie flew with Western Australian Airways from Perth to Carnarvon. She was thrilled to be up in the air, watching the Australian landscape pass below her 'like a tapestry'. In a state of excitement she took out her notebook and scribbled away in shorthand. Her words flowed across her notebook almost as quickly as the aircraft crossed the land. The lavish language she used to describe the terrain below reveals her exhilaration at finally being on her way. The landscape east of Perth looked 'laughably like a clipped poodle', Ernestine wrote, then described the 'fragment of a rainbow that hangs vivid as a chevron' just beyond the plane's wing. Her Pitman shorthand proved an invaluable asset.

After they arrived in Carnarvon, Ernestine was so eager to find copy that she left her aunt and Robbie and set out almost immediately on the government steamer, the *Koolinda*, to the small settlement of Shark Bay. It anchored eleven kilometres from the shore of the little settlement, so the passengers had to be lowered in a basket and taken to land in a smaller boat. Forgetting to check the departure times for her return journey was her first big error. She soon discovered there was no road out of the tiny town—she was stuck. When she moaned about her stupidity, the people of Shark Bay reacted kindly, saying she had made a rookie's mistake and that under the circumstances it was entirely excusable. Any 'townie' might assume that outback towns would have scheduled services, but Ernestine learnt the hard way that visiting remote areas would require planning and patience. Buses sometimes got bogged and did not come, and captains kept their boats in safe ports for months during the wet to avoid being wrecked by hurricanes. Ernestine was stuck in this small pearling settlement for more than a month.

Gathering copy there proved no easy task. The slumbering little town had 'a broken-down store, one hotel and one beacon on the sandhills for the fishermen at night'; it was not an example of the adventurous and exciting outback town she had hoped for. A local divorce was about the most breath-taking occurrence during her stay.

The necessity of bringing in the money needed to support her aunt, mother and child forced her onward, making her determined to succeed. The stories had to be out there, she knew.

A boat that could take her out of Shark Bay finally came, and Ernestine travelled to Cossack, where she wrote articles that were her first to be published in the *Sunday Sun* from this trip. The cemetery there held the graves of many of those who had been shipwrecked along that cruel coast; it was only by looking at the inscriptions that she realised with some surprise that the Australian north was a melting pot of cultures and nationalities. It was a far cry from the all-white Australia of the bigger cities in the south and east. Here whites mingled with Malays, Malays mingled with Japanese, Arabs mingled with Chinese and Aboriginal people mingled with everyone else. Like some other writers of her time, she thought of the 'Aboriginal race' as some sort of pure species that was dying out and needed to be preserved.

It was almost the end of 1930 and Ernestine decided to spend Christmas and New Year's Eve in Broome. She pushed on, picking up Kitty and Robbie in Carnarvon and hopping by plane via Roebourne and Port Hedland to Broome. They stayed at Broome's Continental Hotel, and from that small port came Ernestine's first significant flow of copy.

Sitting on the hotel's verandah, she wrote about the riches of the pearl industry while in the southern cities thousands were on the dole. She also drew attention to the terrible fate of many of the pearl divers, who lost their lives while retrieving these rare and valuable gems. Most of the divers were Malay, Chinese or Aboriginal men; imprisoned in heavy rubber suits, they always had the odds stacked against them when disaster struck. Pearl divers regularly faced the threat of shark attack as well as the dreaded crippling effects of the bends. Some sources say that the death rate for divers was 50 per cent. In addition, whole pearling fleets were sometimes shipwrecked in a single cyclone. Between 1908 and 1935, four cyclones hit the Australian pearling fleet at sea, destroying about 100 boats and killing more than 300 men.

Ernestine loved Broome from the moment she arrived, and in the years to come it was often a haven when big-city living became too oppressive. On the road, she more than once had to live rough, sleeping in cars or on an outback route with nothing to curl into but a swag, so Broome's laid-back pace and lazy luxury appealed to her. She stayed there for most of 1930, collecting enough stories to keep her editors happy for a while. Robert, now old enough for school, was enrolled at Broome's St Mary's Primary.

But when the Broome copy began drying up, Ernestine realised she would have to leave her child and aunt behind and visit remoter areas in search of material. Her friends in Broome had told her of strange people living in even stranger places, so in February 1931 she took a plane from Broome to Derby.

In Derby she hitched a ride with the mail truck. While living in Broome, she had been invited to stay in Halls Creek with the local policeman and his wife. To visit them was the best decision she could have made. Police Sergeant Archibald and his wife, who hadn't had the chance to speak to another white person for months, spilled stories by the dozen and Ernestine provided a very willing ear. Sometimes their stories were sad, sometimes horrific and sometimes tall, but they all came with enthusiasm and in abundance. This is what had drawn Ernestine into the wilderness: the stories, the people, their fears and their hopes.

But the best piece of luck was yet to come. When she later took the postie's truck from Halls Creek to Wyndham, she happened to bump into one of the most famous and esteemed pastoralists of the north, one Michael Patrick Durack. She had no idea that this encounter would, years later, result in her most ambitious work, nor that this introduction to the Durack family would have extraordinary long-term consequences for both her and her son.

7

M.P. Durack

At 65, Michael Patrick Durack—or MPD as most people usually called him—was still a tall, slim and attractive man. Although his hair had turned from orange to white, it was a full crop. With his well-kept beard and moustache, the elderly pastoralist looked almost French, and around the area people regarded him as a bit of an aristocrat. As the richest and most influential pastoralist in the area, he was admired by most, but also feared and loathed by others.

Since the Duracks had left Ireland, their source of income had been cattle. The business had brought the family wealth in Queensland, but MPD's father, Patrick 'Patsy' Durack, had been eager to expand his empire. One of Patsy's brothers, who had headed into the north of Western Australia to seek out good grazing land, had sent back a positive report, so Patsy decided to drove a herd of some 7000 cattle through the Northern Territory and into the Kimberley. It turned out to be quite a trip.

MPD, his brothers and uncles had left Queensland in 1883, and it had taken two years to cross the 4800 kilometres of treacherous country. On the way they lost half their cattle and a number of men, as their party was plagued by disease and other hardships. Local squatters disliked them and were displeased with the arrival of such an enormous cattle herd into their territory. The Indigenous people were also hostile to these invaders of their traditional lands.

The local Aboriginal people relied on their traditional lands for food and water, and realised that their livelihood and independence were threatened by the arrival of white people and their cattle, all drinking from their waterholes and forcing them off their land. The Duracks were by no means greeted with open arms.

They finally reached their destination and settled on the banks of the Ord River in September 1885. Among them they leased and managed 3 million acres. The distraught Aboriginal inhabitants initially put up a fight and, in an attempt to drive away the unwanted intruders, speared the Durack cattle and two Durack men. If they could not roam over their traditional lands, they, their women and their children faced disease and hunger. But the intruders were there to stay. It took the family the better part of a decade to put down roots and build a sufficiently good relationship with the local Aboriginal people to feel relatively safe.

The Duracks gave the local men no other option than to work for them or keep out of their way. They hired any Aboriginal man who was willing to work and, although there were disputes and rumours of maltreatment, the Duracks were regarded by their workers as better than average bosses. The stations were supplied with sugar, tobacco and occasionally alcohol to keep the hired hands happy, but if these pleasures ran out, the station managers would often experience difficulties. No manager wanted dissatisfied and grumpy hands doing the mustering, so that was the main reason for MPD's visit to Wyndham on that particular day in 1931, to pick up an enormous load of supplies in his truck.

The day was turning out hot as usual, and MPD took off his hat and swatted at the flies that were after a drop of his sweat. The load packed onto his truck was chiefly for one of his border stations called Auvergne, near Timber Creek, where he would be travelling with his eldest son, Reg. The caretakers of Auvergne were Harry Shadworth and his wife. Harry had sent MPD the message that sugar and tobacco were running low and that he was finding it hard to keep the workers under control.

That morning, MPD had decided to drive up from his home at Argyle Downs Station to Wyndham to get the supplies. He would take his own supplies back to Argyle first and then, after picking up his son Reginald, would make a dash up to Auvergne, staying overnight before heading back the next morning. It was the end of October and MPD knew there was probably only one month left before the wet would make almost any means of transport impossible.

Just to make sure there was no prospect of rain for the moment, he searched the sky, shading his eyes with his hat. It was best to get rations in before the rains threw his stations off the map. If the rains held off, it would be a swift drive of 160 kilometres to Auvergne, just across the Territory border, but if the rains came early, they could be marooned. Luckily, all now looked well.

As he wiped the sweat from his brow with his shirtsleeve and replaced his hat, he noticed a slight figure in trousers and pith helmet arguing or negotiating with the local policeman across the street. At first glance MPD mistook the figure for a boy. Four Chinese men, who were standing beside the road waiting to be loaded into the policeman's paddy wagon, were looking on with some amusement. MPD was rather surprised when the 'boy' turned from the wagon, crossed the street, started heading towards him—and turned out to be a lady.

She greeted the tall pastoralist in a soft raspy voice, a cigarette nonchalantly perched between her fingers, averting her eyes slightly as she spoke. She told him she was a newspaper reporter looking for a lift, that her name was Ernestine Hill and that the constable had suggested she might be able to hitch a ride with him. MPD, taken aback by the lady's unexpected request, was at rather a loss. 'All depends on where you need to go,' he replied.

Her problem was, Ernestine said, that she wanted to go to Darwin but her options were limited. She could travel with the mailman, Piggy Williams, on a packhorse, but bumping up and down for days on a horse over harsh terrain didn't really appeal. Or she could go with the constable, but he had four Chinese men under arrest for smuggling opium and was not very eager to have a lady he might have to keep safe. Ernestine told him she was quite desperate and was more than happy to travel with a well-known pioneer. She was always looking for copy, she told him, and she thought he might well be good for a story or two.

But MPD was not travelling to Darwin, nor even as far as Katherine. 'I'm heading for Auvergne, one of my stations, 100 miles down the road, just across the border.'

Ernestine was dismayed—she had been hoping to get to Darwin before the wet. She had a son and an aunt waiting for her in Broome and she wanted to get back there. MPD twirled the ends of his moustache as he contemplated her plight. 'The Victoria River Depot Races will be held soon,' he finally replied. 'If you drive to Auvergne with me, there is bound to be someone who will take you to Victoria River Downs, and from there you could easily get transport across to Katherine and hop on a train to Darwin, though you might want to stay for the races at Victoria River. It's quite a spectacle and lots of people with a good story about. It would make good copy.'

He explained that he would be going back to Argyle first and picking up his son, but that she was welcome to accompany him. If all went well, they would head for Auvergne the next morning.

It was almost noon when the two drove out of the town and the temperature had soared. Wyndham lay boiling under a tropical sun—it was all lakes, desert and mudflats. The landscape around them was mostly beautiful, but very inhospitable for white people. Ernestine offered MPD a cigarette and, although they had only just met, they soon found common interests and felt quite comfortable with each other. MPD told her he had been sent to the most elite Queensland schools; being a good scholar, he had hoped for a life as an academic and politician. His father, Patsy, however, had expected him, as the eldest son, to follow in his footsteps. So here he was in the Territory, battling crocs, mosquitoes, rain and heat, when he would much rather have been a member of parliament.

For a moment Ernestine must have doubted what this outback man was telling her, but the tone of his voice and the serious look in his eyes must have convinced her he was telling the truth. He made no secret of his lack of love for the land he had inherited. It was getting harder by the year to make ends meet, he confessed. The family was already in debt and the prospects for the coming year were not good. It was a hard life.

He himself considered outback life too harsh for his wife, Bess, and had sent her to live in Perth with their five younger children. He advised Ernestine to look them up when she returned—his eldest daughter, Mary, had literary aspirations and would undoubtedly love to meet her. His children seemed to love station life, but he thought it best for them to grow up in 'civilisation'.

MPD was highly regarded in Perth, and this gave him access to the elite of its business and political community; he always looked forward to the intellectual discussions and challenges city life offered him. He visited Perth during the wet season because nothing could be done on the station and the Aboriginal people returned to their traditional life as soon as the rains came. He told her he always looked forward to seeing his wife and children, and he always took gifts with some link to the station up north—'a baby croco-dile, a pony or a galah'. She told him about her son and aunt in Broome, and she left his inquiry about Mr Hill unanswered.

The road to Argyle took them through grey bush and flat windy desert. Dry sand began to blow through the windows as they drove through the flatness and, even though the heat inside the truck was stifling, they had to wind the windows up to keep the heat and sand out. Ten minutes later the wind suddenly abated and all was fine again, the sandy gusts a thing of the past as they drove around a beautiful bend in the Ord and caught sight of its stunning gorge. Argyle was situated on the banks of the river, which was fringed with bamboo and pandanus palms. A large baobab stood guard in front of the house, like a helpless fat monster paralysed between the graceful gum trees.

The house was constructed of limestone blocks and of mortar made from crushed termite mounds. With some pride, MPD told her they had built it with their own hands. It had been designed as an open and airy structure, funnelling cool air through its gun-barrel-straight hallway. It was never a grand building, with cockroaches making their homes in every nook and cranny, but it was dignified if sparsely furnished; surprisingly the living room housed a showpiece grand piano. The Duracks had transported it from Queensland in a lorry but no one could play it because the cockroaches had become stuck in the strings at the back. They had to get in a specialist every year to remove them and retune the instrument.

After he set the station hands to work unloading the supplies, Reg welcomed them into the kitchen for homemade cakes and cold lemonade. Like his father, Reginald was a scholar, although he had been unable to carry on to university because the Duracks were not as wealthy as many people supposed and the ever-practical MPD also needed someone he could rely on at Argyle.

He hoped his twenty-year-old son would soon become manager of Auvergne. It was one of their most problematic stations because the Aboriginal workers were becoming increasingly discontented with the current managers. There were rumours of ill-treatment and exploitation, and MPD had no wish to come under public scrutiny. He was sure that Reg would see to it that the workers' wants were met; Reg had already questioned him about the social injustice of Aboriginal labour.

Ernestine pondered the fates that had befallen the elderly pastoralist and his son, two men whose intellectual aspirations had been frustrated by family obligations. It was evident, however, that Reg, unlike his father, thrived on station life; he loved the land, he said, and always met the challenges it presented head-on. Although he regretted not finishing his studies, he loved Argyle and his life in the saddle. Reg could speak so enthusiastically about being a station manager that no one would ever imagine this young man was also versed in Ancient Greek and Latin.

During her visit, Ernestine spoke with Reg about his philosophical outlook and later wrote jokingly to his sister Mary that she believed Reg 'was rabidly communist'. He was always reading and his choice of books was taking him towards socialism and Marxism. He entertained Ernestine with his youthful abundant energy and constant chattering, and the two ended up talking until the early hours of the morning.

Later that morning they headed off early, the cliffs that framed the river turning from grey to purple and then to orange as the sun threw ever more light upon them. The Territory border was marked by a single string tied around a tree, which was hardly discernible to anyone not looking for it. Newry, with its suspension bridge dangling above the

Keep River, came and went as they pressed on, the truck chewing away the last 110 kilometres to Auvergne.

Set on the bank of the Baines River, Auvergne Station was a pretty home. Mrs Shadforth came out to greet them when they arrived. She had managed to grow roses, carnations and English wildflowers in the garden, having set her heart on it, she said, after an agricultural adviser told her it could not be done.

They had hardly sat down before a young Aboriginal boy ran into the sitting room to announce another visitor. 'There's dust on the road,' he simply said and ran out into the yard again. The visitor turned out to be the surveyor-general of the Territory, William Robert Easton. He had been surveying the countryside for the past few months and was now scurrying back to Darwin in his car before the wet set in. Ernestine was over the moon when he offered to take her as far as Katherine, where he would need to stay for some time on business: 'So you'll have to take the train from there.'

That evening they discussed the Northern Territory and the role of women there. Ernestine thought more women would be willing to stay in the Territory if homes could be made more attractive for them. Young Easton, however, disagreed. He was adamant that the Territory was no place for a white woman to live and that he would not think of asking one to live there.

MPD would later write how fascinated he had been with Ernestine, impressed by her keen interest and lively conversation: 'It takes a great measure of courage and initiative for a woman to set out on a journey such as she has undertaken.'

After spending the night at Auvergne, Easton and Ernestine Hill left for Katherine early the next morning.

As they shook hands, MPD and Reg thanked her for being such entertaining company.

'You might write about the Territory one day,' MPD added.

'I know I will,' she replied curtly then, turning to Reg, urged him to take up writing too. 'Write about how it all was in the beginning, about those fascinating big rivers. Tell people what you have seen.'

They left as life on the station began to rouse and the first lazy sunrays of dawn crept from behind the gum trees.

8

Victoria Downs and Darwin

Ernestine's travelling companion, Robert Easton, as he was known, had been appointed the first surveyor-general of the Northern Territory in 1926. He was quite a small man, but his views and deeds made up for his size. He had been a lieutenant in the army during the First World War and had trained Australian engineers in Perth and Sydney. He had also served in France and England, returning to Australia in 1919.

In 1921 the Western Australian government had appointed Easton to lead an exploration party to the Kimberley to discover suitable places for new ports along the coast between Broome and Wyndham. During the expedition, rations began to run out because of a bushfire that swept through their camp. Due to the rough terrain three of their horses became lame and had to be left behind. On top of all that they were supposed to meet a boat at Swift Bay, but about ten kilometres south of their destination the party came upon a line of impassable cliffs. Realising their predicament, Easton and another member of the party set off on foot to meet the boat; it took them two and a half days to reach the bay with nothing to eat but snakes. He chatted about their findings—the North Kimberley region possessed quite a few good and promising harbours, but the strange rock formations that fringed the coastline made them difficult to reach and almost inaccessible by both land and sea.

Easton truly liked the Aboriginal people he had encountered on his trips and found that other whites judged them too harshly. He had written: 'The ingenuity displayed by the Aboriginal in hunting and obtaining his food proves that he is not lacking in mentality and initiative. Some of the methods are a little short of wonderful . . . They [the blacks] are primitive, but . . . far from being a degraded race, although the two terms are sometimes confused.' Easton explained this point in an analogy for white men: 'It is primitive to travel by horses in these days of flying, but certainly not degrading.' At the time, Ernestine's notions differed from his, although she later accepted some of his ideas. She described him as 'a very well-spoken and charming companion'.

On the way they were flagged down by a bushman who suddenly appeared from the scrub, wild-eyed and wild-haired, with a £5 note in his hand.

He wanted them to place a bet for him. 'You going to the races?' he asked.

When Easton told him they were heading for Katherine the man seemed relieved and told them it was practically on the way. Easton frowned, and the bushman started to look a little desperate. Driving into Victoria Downs wouldn't take up much of their time, he urged, and 'they'd be doing an old dingo hunter a great favour'.

Seeing the concern on the bushman's face and perhaps finding the idea of spending another day or two in the company of his travelling companion an appealing prospect,

Easton agreed to place the bet. The bushman, visibly relieved, asked them to give the money to Jim Maloney, a bookie, and tell him to put it on Shotgun. He told them that Easton would easily recognise Jim Maloney: 'He'll be the bloke shouting the odds from a beer case.' And with that he disappeared back into the scrub, leaving his £5 note in the hands of a somewhat bewildered Easton.

'Looks like we might get held up at the races,' Easton said, turning to Ernestine.

He had told her that his fiancée was waiting for him in Katherine, so she asked him if making the detour wouldn't be too much of an inconvenience, but they were both game for a day at the races and he thought his fiancée could wait a day or two.

The Victoria River Depot race meeting was renowned in the area, even though its location, the Victoria River Racecourse, was not the most pleasant of places during the November heat. Spread over flat red soil, dotted with ant hills and patches of withered grass, Victoria River seemed a bleak outback settlement. Hot winds swept in from the desert, twisting and twirling in dusty spirals on the baked and cracked earth. Debris danced around in crazy circles as it caught in the flurry of coiling air. Up the road the mudflats of the mighty Victoria River played host to quite a few crocodiles. But the baobabs stood like proud and majestic chubby giants in their magnificent yellow November foliage.

Racing enthusiasts had come from everywhere, travelling on any kind of available transport. There were drovers, station hands, dog trappers, cooks and wanderers; they came into town on foot, mules, packhorses, in trucks and cars. Unable to resist the hustle, excitement and stories, Ernestine felt at ease and talked to the bushmen and station hands. Her self-consciousness disappeared almost completely when she was on the road. This may have been due to the lack of decorum, or the lack of competition from other women, or just the absence of judgmental people. Despite her educated vowels and her conspicuousness as a woman, Ernestine felt very much at home in remote Australia.

Nobody out there gave a toss if she dressed in trousers and shirts, smoked like a chimney and wore a pith helmet to keep off the sun. Here she became one of the crowd, laughing and joking along with them. Her ability to listen to everyone with intense and genuine interest may have been what made her so popular with the outback and bush people. She made them feel they were being heard.

The Victoria River Depot Races was a yearly event at the beginning of the wet and an opportunity for those tucked away in the remoteness of the outback to meet old friends and new, although it did not attract many women—only about six that day. Ernestine did not regret the detour. There is nothing that animates men more than a bet at the races. Their faces light up and their features change. Old men become young dogs, barking commands and cursing across the track.

Soon after the races, she left Victoria Downs with the surveyor-general, who delivered her to Katherine as promised. To get to Darwin, she had no other option than to take the uncomfortable *Sentinel*, a mixed passenger and goods train hated by travellers. Ernestine had been warned by people in Katherine, who mockingly referred to the train as the 'Leaping Lena', about what she would be in for. She would never forget that horrific journey on those hard and inhospitable wooden benches that bumped her up and down all the way to Darwin. She was filled with anxiety every time the train had to climb a hill; its wheels would squeal as it laboured to reach the top, sporadically falling back when its efforts failed. The sheer madness of the descent that followed left her shaken and uneasy.

The rains set in as the train arrived in Darwin, but Ernestine was so pleased to get off the Lena that she walked to the Victoria Hotel with her luggage in the pouring rain, hardly able to believe she had survived. Drenched and making puddles on the floor, she checked herself into the hotel, where a compassionate receptionist handed her a towel. She made a promise to herself, right there in the lobby of the Victoria, never to travel on the *Sentinel* again.

Her visit to the capital of the tropical north resulted in a much longer stay than she had originally intended. Ships came in to Darwin once a month from Singapore, but the *Koolinda*, the steamer she had intended to take back to Broome, had stopped running. Stuck for the time being, she felt ever more confused by this northern city, finding it both a jewel and a horror. The kaleidoscopic combination of people, flowers and smells, set against the oppressive heat, evoked mixed feelings: 'Darwin is hell and heaven and good copy.'

In Darwin, different peoples mixed and intermingled, becoming indistinct as a result. Ernestine was slightly horrified by this and found the result baffling and disturbing. Her contradictory feelings about the tropical north—a reaction to both its exoticism and its lack of what she considered to be morality—left her confused.

Her opinions about racial purity would these days be considered bigoted and discriminatory, but at the time her views tallied with those of most people in the southern and eastern cities. There was a good deal of racial discrimination in northern Australia, and this became especially evident at the 'talkies'. Everyone holding a ticket was seated according to 'race', with the Aboriginal people seated in the worst spots.

It was the mixing that bothered Ernestine the most. She was surprised and dismayed, for example, to stumble upon a white boy who had been adopted by a Chinese couple. The boy spoke and thought in his Chinese dialect and could also speak pidgin English. She discovered that his birth mother lived somewhere in the north-west but did not want him. He looked well cared for and happy enough; his foster mother, a bright, intelligent Chinese woman, seemed to love him. And yet Ernestine could not help picturing him as a tragic figure, lost in a Chinese world that was not his own, halfway between heredity and environment. She thought the church and state should have 'saved' this boy from the 'yellow people' his countrymen held in contempt as alien immigrants.

After her article about the boy was published in the *Sunday Sun*, the paper was bombarded with indignant and angry letters. Some were upset that the journalist could prefer an indifferent white mother to a loving Chinese one, while others shared Ernestine's concern and were alarmed by what they considered an abomination.

Although many articles bearing Ernestine's name were published that year, she found it difficult to gather copy in Darwin and often even harder to get it out. The rains forced her inside for large parts of the day but, whenever the downpour let up for a few precious hours, she would attend court cases, football matches and mixed weddings. In the oppressive heat she wrote until the early hours of the morning, sweating profusely over her typewriter while a silver sheet of rain poured persistently from the heavens. Then, in the early hours of the morning, she would topple into bed. She was often unable to sleep and would lie there sweating some more. 'Darwin is not a good place for sleeping,' she wrote.

It soon became impossible to travel anywhere, and even getting her copy to the post office turned into a hazard. After wading through knee-deep water, she was informed that the train that would have carried her copy to the outside world was stranded miles down the track. So she would sit smoking and waiting for hours in the hotel's vestibule.

It was there that she met Gerhardt Laves, to whom she devoted four lines in a newspaper article, describing him as 'a philologist from Philadelphia University collecting blacks' languages on a gramophone'. The poor man's equipment had become badly waterlogged in Darwin and she wrote that she thought he had 'lost heart'. Gerhardt Laves, as it turned out, had been a student at the University of Chicago, not Philadelphia. He studied six Aboriginal languages while in Australia and proposed that all Australian languages belong to a single language family. Laves had made eleven cylinder recordings of Karajarri speech and song at La Grange Mission (Bidyadanga Aboriginal Community) earlier that year. He seems to have abandoned his Aboriginal language studies later in life, so perhaps Ernestine's suggestion that he had lost heart was right.

Anyone could lose heart marooned in Darwin's wet. Slouching on the hotel verandah, smoking cigarette after cigarette, desperately wanting to return to Broome, Ernestine hatched a plan to visit Borroloola, an outpost on the Gulf of Carpentaria. It was in the opposite direction from Broome but she hoped there might be a ship or lugger going that way. It seemed a silly plan, hatched out of monotony, but it gave her something to do. Her fellow guests at the Victoria could not understand why Ernestine would want to go to such a place. At the post office she heard that they hadn't seen a white woman there for six years; she later described her fascination for the place: 'It was a place where the roads turn back, the last, lost outpost of the Territory.' She scurried to the harbour every now and then to find out if a lugger was going that way, but all the ships were tied up waiting for the rains to abate.

Borroloola was tiny, surrounded by tropical rainforest and wetlands; its only road was just a few miles long, leading from the coast into the township. Some old cattle hands told her that if she wanted to travel by road, the best option would be to journey all the way back to Katherine by train, then try to hitch a ride with Norman Stacey, the postman who made his way down the Roper and the McArthur rivers with 30 pack-horses every few weeks. As it stood, the postie hadn't been heard of for weeks, so some people thought he might have become bogged and was probably waiting out the rains on some distant cattle station. To Ernestine, taking the Leaping Lena back to Katherine was not an option, so she went back to waiting and hoping for a boat. The rains, however, would just not subside, and in the end she had to let the Borroloola idea go. She stored away the plan for a later date, feeling certain she would make the trip one day.

By now she was badly missing her aunt and especially her son, so as soon as the ships started sailing again, she booked a passage to Broome, taking with her a wealth of stories. It was enough copy to last almost a year, and it gave her time to enjoy the company of her family and take up her responsibilities as a mother once again.

9

Land, sea and
'*Blue Moon*'

Ernestine left Darwin for Broome on 27 March 1931. There she picked up her aunt and son, and set off by plane to Perth to be reunited with her mother. It was just short of a year since she was last there.

During the rest of 1931, Ernestine and her family lived at the Mansions on Mounts Bay Road in Perth. Ernestine loved the west and was comfortable financially, working principally for Associated Newspapers, and particularly for its *Sunday Sun*. Local Perth papers, such as the *West Australian*, also bought and published her articles.

The *West Australian*, whose offices were located in Newspaper House on St Georges Terrace, across the road from the Palace Hotel, was especially keen for her articles. Its new editor, Charles Patrick Smith, saw the potential of her travel stories, and he appreciated the feedback they elicited from readers: they were always widely read and would provoke either anger or enthusiasm. They were so popular that sometimes the *West Australian* would announce one of Ernestine Hill's articles the day before its publication.

For quite a few months after she settled back in to life in town, Ernestine set to work sorting her notes and turning them into printable copy. Her articles were not specifically related to the news of the moment and could be published at any time. This made it possible for her to sell an article to one newspaper months after it had already been published in another. The editors had noticed a gradual shift in what the public wanted from a newspaper. Sport, crime, political scandals and human-interest stories were being added to the day-to-day reporting, giving newspapers an entertainment component. Associated Newspapers, under the business leadership of Robert Clyde Packer, had been steadily setting the trend.

Ernestine's use of poetic and descriptive prose to turn local stories into appealing narratives caught the attention of everyday readers. At last people in the city were developing a hunger for learning about the country, although the stories they wanted had to be thrilling and sometimes sensational. Ernestine almost constantly stumbled across this kind of copy and, to make the mysterious outback world come to life, her photographs were often published alongside her articles. Her images—of Aboriginal men in corroboree, of the Darwin Chinese community, or of a pearl lugger with its hardy crew of father, mother and son—brought to ordinary city folk a world of which they had not been aware. Most people in big cities never encountered Aboriginal people, and many had never even seen them.

In some instances Ernestine did overdo it, though. She often wrote up as news things she had merely heard, and some of her stories provoked readers into taking up their pens in mocking disbelief. In one slightly exaggerated account, for example, she reported that a swaggie named Bullocky

Johnson had told her, among other things, that his donkeys would eat anything and that he had in fact seen them fighting over a bite of *Smith's Weekly*. Bullocky's stories were just tall tales of the outback, from a lonely man who had at long last found a patient ear. She was ridiculed for writing up this story, and her readers accused her of naivety. Ernestine herself had been seeking only to amuse.

A sarcastic attempt by W.J. Carey to surpass her unlikely tale was published as a letter to the *West Australian*. Carey, who lived in the north, thought that dear old Bullocky may have not only pulled Ernestine's leg but also have left out a few facts. In his letter to the editor, Carey described how he once witnessed a thrilling spectacle when a local cook tried to catch a fish. Up north, he wrote, when fish see you, they leave the water and try to fly past you, so the cook tried to lasso the fish with a quick flick of a piece of rope he had on him. Failing in that attempt, he drew one of his trusty Colts. Firing from the hip, he proved a good shot and the fish fell at his feet, cleaned and ready for cooking, as they often do in the north. Carey concluded: 'Numerous other remarkable happenings have occurred, but I'm afraid your correspondent was not in the north long enough to hear them all.'

Ernestine never replied to the letter; she seldom did, realising that this might well result in more letters and more criticism. Nevertheless, this teasing must have affected her. Her craft was writing descriptive prose to capture life and she did perhaps bend the truth slightly now and then to create a narrative her readers would enjoy.

She expressed her personal views on specific subjects on only a couple of occasions. An article in which Ernestine voiced her preference for the poet Henry Kendall over Adam Lindsay Gordon infuriated Gordon fans all over the country, just as she predicted it would at the beginning of her piece. She took her position against Gordon, she explained, because he was 'an adopted Australian with a mind that was singularly un-Australian', and she openly declared her absolute preference for the 'patriotic and truer' Kendall. Kendall found inspiration in his environment, she wrote, depicting Australia's rich but largely hidden beauty in wonderfully lyrical verse.

This opinion resulted in an explosion of letters to the editor. Although she had expected a modicum of controversy, she was rather shocked by the malicious tone of some of the feedback. As a result, she became a little more circumspect about expressing her opinions, but she still managed to create the odd storm in the years to come.

Having acquired an appetite for outback tales, readers remained hungry for new stories, so it wasn't long before Ernestine began making plans for a new trip. It was her own restlessness as much as the readers' demands that drew her out into the wide open spaces. She had an impatient need for 'spasmodic travelling', as she called it. Staying in one place for any length of time compelled her to smoke endlessly and become irritable.

As soon as she started organising her new trip, she felt revived and excited. Her plan was to follow the railway tracks from Perth to Kalgoorlie, then almost in a straight line across the Nullarbor to Port Augusta, and then northwards to Alice Springs. She would visit the goldfields, the opal mines and the unknown heart of the country.

But she had to attend to a few outstanding tasks before she could set off. During her year in Perth she had started to make notes and work out the storylines for two books. One would be a fictionalised account of Matthew Flinders' life, and the other a compilation of her travel narratives, with annotations that had not made it into the newspapers.

For the story of Matthew Flinders she felt she needed to experience life at sea. Except for sailing on a few luggers and steamers, her knowledge of the ocean was non-existent. So when she was asked to write an article about Beatrice Grey and her husband, Captain Jack Reginald Grey, for the *West Australian* in 1932, this unexpectedly presented the possibility of joining a real seafaring voyage with an experienced crew.

The Greys were in Perth awaiting the completion of their boat, *Silver Gull*, the hulk of which was then being built in Fremantle. Ernestine had already met the Greys during her stay in Broome, when having their own yacht built had been merely a dream. Beatrice was a marine biologist and her husband a scientist. They had been hired by the British Museum to collect marine specimens and scientific data in the waters off north-western Australia. The money they earned had finally made it possible for them to have the yacht built. When it was finished, they planned to take a maiden voyage to the north using a Chinese crew.

Jack Grey was a retired English naval officer and Beatrice, like Ernestine a Queensland girl, was foremost a scientist, but also a keen photographer and a writer to boot. Beatrice and Ernestine had a lot in common, and they got along wonderfully, talking about books, writing and sailing. Ernestine told

Beatrice of her intention to write a book about Matthew Flinders and that she was on the lookout for a chance to experience life on a ship. Both Jack and Beatrice, without hesitation and very generously, invited her to join them on their maiden voyage to the north-west and back to Perth. Ernestine was over the moon. While sailing with them she could turn out copy for the newspapers; their expedition, as a result, would receive plenty of publicity.

The voyage was being planned for 1933, but quite a lot of work still needed to be done on the interior of the ship and the Greys were not sure when they would leave, but they hoped to be able to avoid the wet in the north. Wanting the yacht to become a very luxurious home, Beatrice supervised most of the interior carpentry. Although the yacht was far from finished, she and her husband lived there on a temporary basis to protect it from vandalism. Little Robert and Ernestine were regular guests.

Beatrice and Ernestine discussed the possibility of writing something together, and one night while they sat on the yacht's deck they contemplated a film script. They had no experience whatsoever in writing anything remotely like a film script, so they joked and laughed about it. But their initially frivolous discussions turned quite serious. Why not, they thought? It wasn't as if they had no experience in writing, although Beatrice's had only been for scientific work. For a few weeks they diligently worked together on their story, sometimes at the Mansions and sometimes on the boat. In April 1932 they finished a dramatic film script and called it 'Blue Moon'. To safeguard their copyright, they even registered it at the registrar's office.

10

Adrienne Lesire

Désirée Lesire met Ernestine Hill in 1932 and introduced herself as Adrienne Lesire. A Frenchwoman, Adrienne went under a number of names at the time—among others, Désirée, Violet Debreuil and Miriam Bebe, as she was known in the camps. When Ernestine came looking for her she was living in an Afghan camp at Farina, north-west of Andamooka, between Lyndhurst and Marree.

Ernestine had been having an awful trip with the local mailman. Food supplies had been low and she had been stuck in the front of a truck with her typewriter and camera for a few days. She had already had to sleep in the truck for one night. On the second night, an Arab boy gave her the fright of her life.

During the night, Adrienne's son, Sher Ali Mahomet, had found the vehicle and, thinking it was possibly marooned in the desert, had taken a closer look to check the passengers were all right. Ernestine, awoken in the middle of the night, had looked up to find a phantom straight out of *Arabian Nights* peering into the front window of the truck. Sher was half-French and half-Afghan, with green eyes and olive skin; he was dressed as usual in a caftan and turban. The camel he had been riding stood behind its master, grumbling in the night.

The mailman tried to reassure the somewhat startled Ernestine, telling her he knew the boy and that he was the son of a Frenchwoman who had wed an Afghan. The reporter in Ernestine was immediately intrigued by this story and she asked to be taken to the camp.

Adrienne was delighted by her visit and Ernestine was surprised to find more than one white woman living there. Adrienne told her the Afghans considered the Australian environment too harsh for their own women, so they often married white or sometimes Aboriginal women while still having a partner in their home country.

As Ernestine walked through the gates into the high-walled camp, she was awed by its camel yards, date palms and minarets. She thought the camp beautiful, and she later described the 'balloon pantaloons and curved slippers' worn by the men. She stared in amazement at the tents, some of which were furnished with pianos and wireless sets. She'd had no idea of the comfortable existence these people enjoyed; she had expected something from the Stone Age but their encampments, with their magnificent tents and their tin minarets blinking in the midday sun, were quite luxurious.

Ernestine wanted to know about this exotic woman's life and how she had ended up married to an Afghan. Adrienne told her that her husband's name was Gool Mahomet and that he was quite respected by his countrymen. Gool could speak, read and write English as well as Arabic, which made him a kind of spokesman for the other Afghans. The Afghan cameleers did not all come from Afghanistan but from countries all over the Middle East—it was the Australians who collectively labelled them Afghans.

Adrienne was well aware that some white Australians would look down on her for marrying an Afghan, but she had always loved Gool, and he had been a good husband to her, more courteous and loving than any white man she had ever met. Adrienne told her that she found white Australians often ignorant about how the Afghans had benefited their country.

The Afghans had, to some extent, she said, made it possible to open up the interior. Together with their camels they serviced communities, towns, mining establishments and pastoral properties—places that could not be reached by cars and trucks. With so much desert and so few means of transport, the camels and their riders had become invaluable. Early explorers could not have gone through the centre of the country, nor the Overland Telegraph and railway lines been built, without help from the cameleers. They did not get much credit for it, though.

When they first came to Australia, the Afghans had lived tucked away in the dusty Territory and were hardly even noticed. If a journalist stumbled upon them, it was usually the camels that captured the spotlight, receiving more publicity than their hardworking owners.

The first camel arrived in Australia in 1840, just two years after the first Afghans. It was the only one of six to have survived the horrific boat trip from the Spanish island of Tenerife off north-west Africa, and when the ship landed at Port Adelaide, the camel had to be hoisted off the deck by crane. The spectacle of the animal dangling in the air above the dock, frightened out of its wits, drew quite a crowd.

Six years later the animal was accused of killing the explorer John Horrocks. This wasn't really the camel's fault— it had lurched while Horrocks was on its back, and his gun had discharged, the bullet hitting him in the mouth. In reality, of course, Horrocks had shot himself. He initially survived, but died of gangrene a month later in his home at Penwortham, in South Australia's Clare Valley. Horrocks' dying wish was that the animal be 'executed'.

No other camels were imported into Australia for some time after that, until Samuel Stuckey travelled to Afghanistan in 1866 and returned to Port Augusta with a hundred camels, all hauled from the boat by crane. During the years that followed, hundreds of camels and cameleers were imported into the country.

The story Adrienne Lesire told Ernestine about how she ended up marrying a cameleer was not the whole truth. Adrienne may have been ashamed of her past and bent the truth somewhat. She told Ernestine that she had been a French governess travelling around Australia with a rich family and had bumped into an Afghan nobleman called Gool Mahomet. It was love at first sight and she had since travelled the desert with her Afghan 'king' and his string of camels for 30 years, giving birth to six children in the process. This was the story Ernestine wrote at the time for the *Sunday Sun*.

Having the six children was true, but the rest of it could be called an 'outback' version of the truth. It started with her name, which was neither Adrienne nor Désirée Lesire but in fact Violet Debreuil. Before marrying Gool, she had worked in the brothels of Kalgoorlie for a wealthy French madam who called herself Blanche D'Arville. The brothels on

Brookman Street were popular among station hands, Afghans, miners and lonely bushmen. Adrienne was Madame D'Arville's favourite, but hated the work. As a foreigner without a trade, however, Adrienne realised it would be difficult to give it up.

Gool, who was born in the Afghan town of Ghazni, became Adrienne's client when he was about 29. One day he offered to take her with him and marry her. The other girls advised Adrienne against it, believing it stupid to even contemplate life with a 'coloured' man. They warned her she would live a life of slavery, and predicted all manner of terrible fates should she surrender herself to such a man.

But Adrienne accused the girls of jealousy. She was tired of the prostitute's life, and Gool had always been courteous and civil to her, so in March 1907 Violet Debreuil ran away with her Arabian prince, changing her name to Désirée Lesire in the hope that Madame D'Arville would be unable to find her and take her back to Brookman Street.

The couple were married at a friend's house in the Afghan camp in Coolgardie. It was a typical Muslim wedding, with music, magnificent food and a large crowd. Adrienne wore a caftan and Gool wore his best pantaloons, a colourful turban perched on his head.

Regrettably, the whole event had a surprising and unpleasant aftermath. Apparently Dowd Khan, the man who married the couple, was not actually authorised to do so under Australian law. Khan was accepted as an imam within his religion, but Gool did not know that by Australian law the imam also had to be officially registered. After the marriage, the couple and their imam were summonsed to court to sort the matter out. In the end, Dowd pleaded guilty and had only to pay a fine. It was a test case, Western Australia's registrar-general claimed. Gool paid the defendant's fine of £10 and also the £6 4s costs of the court. The couple went home somewhat bewildered but happy that things had been resolved.

After the marriage, Adrienne's name changed again and in the camps she became known by her Muslim name of Miriam Bebe. Gool and Adrienne travelled quite a bit during the early days of their marriage and she gave birth to their children during this nomadic life. Adrienne described them as 'beautiful, green-eyed, olive-skinned children'.

Gool had always been a cameleer, but the way of life in the camps was by then already fading. The camels were being rapidly replaced by trucks, and many of the Afghans were starting to make a living as shopkeepers. At some stage Gool and Adrienne decided to settle down with their six children and bought a market garden at Leonora, north of Kalgoorlie. That had not gone well, so they had moved back to Farina.

Gool still kept camels, as they were a cheap means of bringing in wool from the isolated stations, but he knew it was only a matter of time before the animals would become redundant. Adrienne told Ernestine in 1932 that a camel was then worth no more than £5 when, only a few years before, you would had to have paid at least £100.

The consequence was that many camels were let loose to roam the outback because their owners could not cover the cost of feeding and watering them. Being desert animals, they thrived in the Australian heat and sand, and they bred quickly. Eventually they became a pest, munching away at the grass meant for livestock, and were shot in their hundreds, greatly to the relief of the pastoralists. Even today they are culled periodically to keep their numbers down and protect the native vegetation.

Gool was a good man, Adrienne said, and she had never regretted marrying him. Like most white Australians at the time, Ernestine probably viewed Adrienne's relationship with Gool as marrying 'down'. Ernestine also wrote about Rebecca Forbes, a white woman who had married an Aboriginal man. Her attitude towards these women, who had chosen to live by their husbands' beliefs and rituals, was strangely inconsistent. On the one hand she would praise them: according to Ernestine, Rebecca had an above average intelligence and could write a good letter, while Adrienne's children were bright, intelligent scholars. But she always had difficulty accepting their chosen way of life and would often add a belligerent note to her articles. When describing Rebecca's love for reading thrillers, for instance, she noted that Rebecca was 'unaware that she was the most hair-raising thriller of the lot'.

Later she wrote to her cousin Coy: 'I have so much respect for our black people—the real ones.' To Ernestine, people like Adrienne and Rebecca may have represented a threat to the purity of race. She no doubt thought of them as causing the 'real' Aborigine or Afghan to vanish.

Gool remained well respected among the Afghans and later became the mullah of the Adelaide mosque. Ernestine's article made it into print, bringing the lives and customs of these 'alien' people to her readers. Adrienne Lesire, in remote Australia, had managed to change her name and occupation, and become the wife of an Aghan sheik.

11

Daisy Bates

The Trans-Australian Railway had taken Ernestine from Perth to Kalgoorlie, where she had visited the goldmines and Adrienne Lesire in the Afghan camp, and then she continued along the line to Ooldea Soak, stopping there to meet a woman who lived in a tent. Although she had no invitation and had in no way announced her impending arrival to Daisy Bates, Ernestine hoped this old lady, living among the Aboriginal people at the soak, would consent to meet her.

Three days before, Ernestine had sent word to the Ooldea stationmaster that she would be arriving, and his wife had graciously invited her to sleep on a camp stretcher on her verandah for the duration of her stay. If Daisy turned her down, she would at least have a place to lie down for the night.

Ernestine first heard Daisy's story at the Karrakatta Club for women in Perth. The women talked about books and debated current affairs. Daisy Bates had been invited there a few times to discuss her newspaper articles about Aboriginal people, each time leaving the ladies with confused opinions about the somewhat strange and eccentric woman they had met. Some found her a scatterbrain with far-fetched ideas about Indigenous people, while others considered her a very able and devoted researcher.

Although she was not educated as a scientist or anthropologist, Daisy had devoted many years to studying Aboriginal life; she had travelled along the northern coast to such places as Port Hedland and Beagle Bay. She had researched and written millions of words on the history, culture, rites, beliefs and customs of the Aboriginal people she met. While studying them she had written tirelessly to newspapers, anthropological and geographical societies, and anyone else willing to listen, until eventually people started to take note. In 1912 she became the first woman ever to be appointed 'honorary protector of Aborigines', at Eucla.

In 1917 Daisy had first settled on the fringe of the soak at Ooldea, which lay on the edge of scrub country towards the eastern end of the Nullarbor Plain, with spinifex country sprawling to its north and north-west. It had for a long time been a busy meeting place for Aboriginal people coming in from the desert—somewhere they could drink and eat. If she were to study these people, she decided, this would be an appropriate spot to do it.

For centuries the soak had been an abundant source of clear and clean water, but the arrival of the Trans-Australian Railway had meant the end of all that. The railway's steam engines and the houses along its track had relied heavily on Ooldea water, but the railway pumping station had brought up close to thousands of litres a day, so by 1926 this water source was completely exhausted. This had had a major impact on the lives of the Aboriginal people who had relied upon it.

The loss of water also meant the destruction of traditional bush foods found around the area. Robbed of their only means of survival, the Aborigines were left empty-handed.

Roaming along the railway line, they also fell victim to the diseases the Trans-Australian passengers brought with them and to which they had no resistance. When the people of the southern Central Desert came looking for water and food, they found nothing but a railway line that brought them illness, alcohol and prostitution.

The Aboriginal men and women Ernestine saw along the Trans-Australian line were the poorest and most neglected Indigenous inhabitants she had ever encountered. When she arrived at Ooldea, she was shocked by what she saw. Up north the Aboriginal people were beautiful—physically fit and athletic—but these lost souls living along the railway line and begging for food were thin, sickly and dressed in nothing but rags.

From her camp at the soak, Daisy Bates had witnessed the gradual decline of the local Indigenous people. She was described as a benefactor to the Aboriginal people, providing them with food, water and simple medical care while no one else seemed to care. The train conductor had told Ernestine that some people had their doubts about the old lady's charity. Daisy had no money and, as far as anyone could see, she could not cook and knew nothing about medical matters.

According to earlier newspaper articles about Daisy Bates, she was hard to miss. They described her as a throwback to the Victorian era—a saviour of the destitute local Aboriginal people who looked like the old Queen herself and lived under appalling conditions in a small tent. Who was this lady,

Ernestine wondered, who had given up 35 years of her life to sit with these nomadic peoples, handing out food and water to men she described as 'futureless', tending to the sick with no more than a bottle of olive oil and a bandage? It was a mystery Ernestine was determined to unravel.

In the beginning, she was somewhat apprehensive, because she had been warned at the Karrakatta Club that the old lady was quite wary of publicity. This was one reason she had decided, against her normal procedure, not to announce her arrival. Showing up on someone's doorstep without prior notice could have its drawbacks—being sent away was a not unlikely consequence—but Ernestine hoped the element of surprise might catch Daisy Bates off guard and confuse her into inviting her in.

The stationmaster's wife came to greet Ernestine as she disembarked from the train. She told her that Mrs Bates would be coming shortly to pick up the mail and, sure enough, ten minutes later the shimmering outline of a woman with a parasol emerged from the scrub. Her first sight of the 'lady who lived in a tent' took Ernestine's breath away. This mirage from the Victorian era was baffling in appearance—gloved hands, an immaculate, albeit old dress that enveloped Daisy Bates' petite frame as if it had been moulded to fit her, and a striking hat with a green fishnet veil attached to keep out the flies.

Ernestine's own sensible outfit—trousers, shirt and a pith helmet—made her feel and look totally unfeminine next to this daintily dressed old lady. There was a moment of uncomfortable silence between these two seemingly contradictory individuals before Daisy broke the ice. She had read some of

Ernestine's articles and was enthusiastic about them. Ernestine was surprised and slightly confused by this unexpected compliment, but then Daisy invited her to walk with her to her camp about a kilometre and a half from the town.

Like many bush women, Daisy evidently seized any opportunity to talk to another woman for a while. She insisted that Ernestine stay for the night at her camp in the 'spare room', a small separate tent equipped with a camp stretcher. This was for the exclusive use of female visitors, because any men staying overnight could have damaged the reputation Daisy had so painstakingly cultivated. To 'her people' she must always be 'Kabbarli', grandmother. Ernestine's stay lasted much longer than intended—four nights and five days.

During that time, Daisy showed Ernestine her trunks full of notes. This massive jumble of jottings, scribbled on whatever she could find to write on, was the unique and obscure record of her years with various Aboriginal peoples. She showed the younger woman all her belongings—the death bones, medicine stones, quartz knives and kurdaitcha (executioner's) shoes—and during the evenings, by the light of a campfire illuminating the night, she told Ernestine an embroidered version of her own life. In spite of their age difference—Daisy was some 40 years older—she and Ernestine got on incredibly well. They talked for hours about writing books and about their nomadic existence so far from the cities.

Daisy had written a number of articles for different newspapers and was considered an expert when it came to Indigenous matters. Ernestine was very impressed by her aristocratic manners and soft Irish brogue, her ability to live with so little means, and her self-sacrifice. She warmed to this woman and felt they had known each other for years. To anyone who encountered them sitting outside their tents by the small campfire they must have made a strange-looking couple—the chain-smoking journalist, continually scribbling into a notebook, and the prim Victorian guardian.

In those days Ernestine, like Daisy, thought Aboriginal Australians would not and could not survive progress, and would inevitably be wiped out. It was commonly assumed at the time that Aboriginal people were destined to disappear, and the 'collection' of 'mixed-race' Aboriginal children (many of whom became part of the Stolen Generation), with the intention of eventually 'breeding them white', was a direct result of this assumption. Ernestine had seen the plight of Australia's Indigenous inhabitants on her travels. Fearing that they were doomed, she, like Daisy, felt that the only way to save them was to give them their own space and exclude all whites from that space to protect them from 'civilisation'. They became advocates of trying to 'save' Indigenous people in this way.

Like Adrienne Lesire, Daisy told Ernestine a very glorified version of her life. It was only many years later that biographers discovered the true facts. Daisy Bates was born Margaret Dwyer in Ireland in 1859. After her mother died when she was three and her father died on his way to the United States just a few years later, she was raised by relatives. In 1882, aged 23, she migrated to Australia after a sexual scandal, changing her name on the boat to Daisy May O'Dwyer. Daisy settled in Townsville and married poet and horseman Harry (Breaker) Morant. Still married to Morant (who died in 1902), she met Jack Bates in New South Wales and also married him. After her son was born, she left Bates and her child and travelled to England, only to return in 1899.

By the nightly fires that intimately enfolded them after the sun disappeared, Daisy told Ernestine about the birth of her only child, her son Arnold, which had been a traumatic experience, and how she had distanced herself from the boy for years. Ernestine, for whom pregnancy and birth had been equally traumatic, could not imagine never seeing Robert again—the very thought filled her with dread and anxiety. The boy was her delight, and she tried to see him as much as possible.

Daisy told Ernestine she had left her boy with her husband's relatives when she decided to travel to England and make a new life for herself. Arnold was well looked after and she now never saw him. Ernestine wrote of feeling a pang of compassion when Daisy showed her a faded photograph of a toddler with ringlets. It was Daisy's only reminder of the boy who must now be well and truly a man. Arnold had moved to New Zealand, Daisy said; he had suffered shell shock during the war and, as a side effect, could hardly remember his mother. It is not clear if Ernestine ever found out that Arnold never wanted to see the mother who, he felt, had abandoned him.

To some it might seem strange that Daisy Bates and Ernestine Hill got on so well, but it was actually very predictable. Both had suffered a mortifying sexual experience that had forced them to leave their homes, both had changed their names on the boat that took them to other shores, both had a son and neither had a husband, and both were writers of some kind. Daisy had found her vocation as the caretaker of the people of Ooldea; Ernestine had found hers by writing about people like Daisy—outback people leading unusual, even unique, lives.

In her articles about Daisy and her later book *Kabbarli: A personal memoir of Daisy Bates*, Ernestine reflected on marriage and how Daisy had felt that hers 'had become an impediment, a frustration, a subjugation of her temperament and will'. Did Ernestine feel that she herself had been spared a life of duty and obligation by not having a husband? She may well have had herself in mind when she wrote of Daisy that 'marriage must have seemed an anticlimax to her education, her aspiration, a sad awakening from her girlish dreams'. When Ernestine decided to go into the outback to seek true stories and tall, she had regained her life, her respectability and her career.

Daisy 'reigned' over 'her people' and nurtured them. It gave her life significance and it gave her self-esteem. Without this act she might, in public opinion, have been reduced to a mere homeless, eccentric and lonely old lady. As Kabbarli, their 'grandmother', she had a title she could wear with dignity.

These two women would in time become household names, each on their own merit. For now they were two strange women sitting and talking softly together at the Ooldea campsite.

At the end of Ernestine's stay, Daisy told her something horrific. She claimed to have witnessed cannibalism among the Aboriginal people, and she took Ernestine to watch a young mother she thought was about to eat her offspring. Daisy had made such claims in articles a decade earlier but had been openly challenged by anthropologists and scientists such as Theodor Strehlow, who accused her of wild exaggeration of what she thought she had seen and an overactive imagination.

As the two women watched the unsuspecting mother from behind a bush, nothing happened. Yet because Daisy and her stories had made such an impact on Ernestine, she did believe that such a thing could be true. After all, she reasoned, Daisy had lived with these people and seemed to know them very well.

As the young mother walked away, talking and singing to her child, Ernestine came to believe that she had been spared a horror. She admitted later that she had been slightly disappointed to have been robbed of some sensational copy.

The day after their spying adventure from behind the bush, Ernestine packed her belongings and bade Daisy farewell. She had a date with an old Dutchman down the line in Kingoonya.

12

Jake and Minnie

Minnie Berrington was one of the first female opal miners in Australia. Her brother had emigrated from England in the early 1920s and often wrote letters home about his exciting life digging for opals in Coober Pedy. Minnie was working in London as a typist at the time but, finding her life boring, in 1926 decided to follow her brother. She wanted 'to prove that women could go down holes just as well as men could'.

Apart from digging for opals, Minnie had for a time looked after Jacob (Jake) Santing's shop in Coober Pedy while he was away. She had since moved on to Andamooka in search of new fields to work but came back to Coober Pedy every Saturday evening. Jake was the local postie and outback supplier, on Saturdays bringing the mail and supplies into Coober Pedy from the Tea and Sugar Train. It was the social event of the week in the area, and Minnie would come over to share a drink with her old mining mates.

On one of those Saturday evenings she bumped into Ernestine Hill, whom old Jake had brought into town after picking her up at Kingoonya railway station. A small weather-beaten man, Jake was originally from the Netherlands and had for some years been a camel driver, carting much-needed water to remote areas. Driving his camels into Alice Springs one day, he had noticed quite a few cars about and wondered if this new means of transport would start to replace camels. It took him hours to get to certain locations with his camels, and he reckoned that a car would get him there a lot quicker. It was an advantage that a car didn't have a strong will and was not subject to moody tantrums. And, not to be overlooked, a car didn't bite.

So at some point Jake gave up water carting and bought a truck, obtained a mail licence and became Coober Pedy's link to the outside world, bringing in supplies to the opal miners living underground and also supplying a number of the surrounding station homesteads.

The Tea and Sugar Train, as the locals called it, serviced isolated Australian towns along the Trans-Australian Railway. The train was a lifeline, providing almost every necessity for townsfolk, graziers and fettlers. It made a weekly journey from Port Augusta to Kalgoorlie and back.

Ernestine had sent Jake a telegram from Kalgoorlie a couple of weeks earlier, but when the stationmaster first told him there was a telegram waiting for him in the station office, Jake almost had a fit. He never received any mail addressed to him. Minnie had asked him once if he still had family in Europe and he'd answered, 'Yeah, probably,' but he thought his family had most likely forgotten all about him by now or assumed he must be dead. Mail was something others received, and old Jake didn't think he was important enough to justify a letter, let alone a telegram.

When he returned to Coober Pedy, he went straight to Minnie with the telegram. She didn't really know if he could read English. She told him the telegram had come from a Ms Ernestine Hill, informing him of her arrival at Kingoonya the following Saturday and wanting to know if it would be convenient for her to travel around the area with him in his truck. Minnie helped him with a reply—he told her to just write 'No worries'. They hadn't heard from the lady since.

Jake always felt quite uncomfortable around women, even Minnie, who was considered one of the blokes. He was a good sort, but not much of a communicator. The thought of this lady sitting right next to him for his whole run—320 kilometres to be exact—filled him with dread. They would stop at Bon Bon, Mount Eba and the Twins, all stations accessible only by dirt tracks pocked with potholes.

Jake was worried about his truck. He didn't know what the lady was expecting as a means of transport, and the men of Coober Pedy had a good old laugh when they watched him doing some running repairs with tape that morning. Jake's truck would never have garnered high scores in the fancy department. The bonnet and mudguards were held together by fencing wire and it was badly dented here and there; the upholstery was torn and spotted with stains of indeterminate origin.

After he loaded the supplies from the train, the old truck would be stacked to the limit with diesel, petrol, sheep dip, groceries and meat. Its speed would climb to about 40 kilometres an hour on a good day. It would be a long bumpy ride and Jake knew it. He told Minnie he hoped the lady would be up to it.

Kingoonya was a railway support town, so it didn't have a huge population, but it did have a pub. It also claimed to have the widest main street in Australia. Jake had seen quite a few cricket matches played by locals in the main street while they waited for the train to arrive, but there was no cricket the day he picked up the newspaper lady—the constant wind was the spoiler, dragging buckets of red sand in its wake. Everyone waiting for the train was huddled in their cars or had taken refuge from the scalding sand inside the station or the pub.

When Jake arrived at the station that day, he too sat in the shelter of his truck, scratching his two-day-old beard and absentmindedly checking if his wallet was still in his back pocket, as was his habit. He tended to lose his wallet from time to time.

He probably had to squint to make out anything on the sand-blurred horizon, as his vision was deteriorating due to trachoma. By now all the locals were at the station—usually, whoever saw the train first would yell out 'Here she comes', and people would start moving around all at once.

At last the train came shuffling into town, then jolted to a standstill beside the platform. Its doors made a terrible noise when they opened as the sand constantly crept into the hinges, making them squeak distressingly. The station came to life as passengers started to alight and board, and the cries of merchants and buyers went up.

Jake made his way to one of the carriages, but he didn't see anyone who looked like a newspaper lady. He'd asked Minnie before he left what they looked like, but she had no idea.

A sixteen-year-old Aboriginal boy called Dig rode the train and helped people with their luggage for a few pennies. You could always recognise him by his chewed Havana hat an

American passenger had once given him. He helped Jake haul three drums of diesel onto the loading platform of the truck. Three more of petrol came next, and then a drum of sheep dip. Jake and Dig then visited the train's grocery wagon, coming back with two large canvas bags full of fruit and vegetables. When all the supplies were loaded on his truck, Jake paid the boy and went to get the mail at the post office inside the station.

Ernestine was sitting on the bench outside the station; Jake told people later that he at first took no notice of her because he thought she was a boy. She was skinny, with cropped hair, and was dressed in a shirt and pants. Her dark eyes peered from under a straight fringe. When she stood and asked if he was Jacob Santing, she extended her hand and Jake gave it a quick, bashful shake. He pointed to his battered truck and mumbled something about 'the mail inside and you can sit in the passenger seat', then he wriggled through the station door like a shy dog, leaving Ernestine staring after him.

When he returned with a heavy mailbag clutched in his hands, he saw Ernestine sitting in his truck, comfortably perched on the passenger seat, her suitcase neatly tucked between the oil drums on the tray.

'You all set?' Jake asked, getting in while propping the mailbag between the two of them.

Ernestine offered him a cigarette. He usually rolled his own, employing only one hand—friends could never figure out how he did it—but he wouldn't turn down a free smoke so, as the truck coughed and hiccupped into life, they sat silently smoking together. They couldn't have talked much anyway—once the truck did start, it rattled and jogged and hissed and jerked, making an awful din.

After they'd smoked another cigarette, Ernestine coaxed out his story—how he had left home when he was sixteen, working as a deckhand aboard a boat that took him to Brazil. His memories of working in the Brazilian saltpetre (potassium nitrate) mines weren't happy ones but the money was 'beaut', he told her. After a while he had boarded another boat and it had taken him to Australia.

People who knew Jake wondered how Ernestine had extracted so much information out of this usually laconic man. Without alcohol, Jake's conversation was normally reduced to only the sentences and words that were strictly necessary. They would have been surprised to know that this woman, just a few years earlier, had been herself described by other journalists as shy and self-conscious.

Jake wasn't the world's best reader in English, but he could recognise words and write them if need be; what this lady was scribbling down in her notebook, though, was like no writing he had ever seen. Ernestine explained that it was Pitman shorthand. Jake asked Minnie later if Pitman was a language and which country spoke it. Being a typist, she knew about shorthand and tried to explain it to him. He reckoned it looked somewhat like the 'Arab scribbles' he had seen during his time as a camel driver.

Jake always stopped along the way so that Fred Matthews, a stockman on a remote station, could pick up his mail. To Ernestine it seemed like a random stop in the middle of nowhere. Jake sat there shuffling through the mail as if it were a deck of cards, looking for Fred's weekly letter.

That day Fred was in a joking mood and gave Ernestine the fright of her life by popping up unexpectedly at the rear window and shouting his usual 'G'day, mate!' When he saw how terrified she was, he gave her a wink and asked if Jake was transporting ladies nowadays, along with the goods and post. Jake just blushed and handed Fred his letter. The stockman, in his turn, produced a couple of bottles of beer and the two men stood for a while talking and smoking and drinking together.

After twenty minutes Ernestine suddenly appeared in front of them asking if there was a Ladies' anywhere nearby. Fred pointed one finger south and another one north, saying, 'Take your pick—about 500 miles in either direction.' Ernestine wasn't fazed by this in the slightest; she had been in the outback long enough to know what was what, and surprised the men when she resolutely disappeared into the scrub to do what she needed to do.

Jake's supply truck was always enthusiastically greeted at Bon Bon sheep station by the owner and his wife. Happy to have another woman to talk to at last, the lady of the house invited Ernestine inside. She called Jake's truck a biscuit tin while they drank tea. Ernestine seemed exhausted after being jiggled about, but she explained that she was used to travelling rough. 'Last week I spent four nights sleeping in a lean-to at Ooldea Soak,' she said.

After all the formalities had been completed, Jake started up his truck again. It misfired a few times before it sprang to life, then they headed to Mount Eba and the Twins.

Ernestine noticed that the road sometimes disappeared and wondered how Jake kept on track. He explained that the wind blew the road away sometimes, so you had to follow your gut. But from time to time his gut feeling could be wrong and he'd be out there groping through the outback for a couple of days. He said he was never afraid of getting lost as he had all the groceries in the back and enough fuel to get him to Darwin if need be.

That Saturday evening, as night started to fall across the outback hills, Ernestine and Jake finally drove into Coober Pedy. Ernestine gave him a blank stare when he announced that they had reached their destination. 'There's nothing here,' she said.

Coober Pedy was indeed a strange place, and above ground you wouldn't have known anyone lived there. Everyone lived below ground, like a town of the living dead. It is way too hot during the day to live out in the open and much cooler down below; since most people worked in the shafts every day, digging for opals, they were used to being underground.

The Dutchman grinned as he left the truck; Ernestine must have been startled as people emerged from the lifeless hills like zombies from their graves. Twilight feathers marked the sky as the sun died into the hills, making the scene even more mysterious. But the Coober Pedy zombies were a friendly bunch. As one of the only women in the town, Minnie introduced herself and took Ernestine straight to the pub. She thought she could use a beer.

Later that evening, as they left the pub, Ernestine stumbled on something lying in the road. Suspecting it was a snake or a small animal of some kind, she let out a sharp shriek. Minnie picked the thing up, already suspecting what it was:

Jake's wallet. He tended to lose it after he'd been to the pub, but all the locals knew whose it was and the wallet was always returned in one piece.

Minnie knew where to find him, because he always crawled back into his truck to sleep off the booze. Sure enough, old Jake lay sprawled over the seat, snoring comfortably in a drunken stupor. Minnie tucked the wallet into his pocket.

Minnie offered Ernestine a place to sleep in her old dugout and told her she could make use of it for as long as she liked. Pointing to Jake, she told Ernestine she might have to drive herself around the next day as it always took Jake a while to recover. But Ernestine replied that she didn't drive. Minnie wondered how she got about without her own transport. 'I ride with whatever comes along,' was the answer.

13

Gold fever

In August 1932, Ernestine took the train to Rumbalara, close to the South Australia–Northern Territory border. It was a one-man town—the stationmaster was its sole inhabitant. A man named Harvey, who owned a yellow-ochre mine 30 kilometres up the track, was there to meet the train. Harvey drove Ernestine to Horseshoe Bend, where she was to meet up with mailman Harry Tilmouth and his Aboriginal camel driver, Okey. They ran the only camel mail run left in Australia at the time, the 260-kilometre route along the Finke River to Hermannsburg. Ernestine wanted to join them for a week, the time it took to deliver the mail to the settlements along the river.

After she met up with Tilmouth at Horseshoe Bend, he introduced her to Midgeree, one of his majestic but moody camels, which for a week would become Ernestine's mobile throne. As they set out, trudging in a leisurely fashion along the water's edge, she felt a little like the Queen of Sheba.

It is often claimed that the Finke River is the oldest in the world. It springs from the MacDonnell Ranges and runs like an ancient artery through the land, 600 kilometres to the western edge of the Simpson Desert. But although Ernestine was awed by the river's landscape—its soaring cliffs banded in purple, white and red, and the slightly stooping red gums and the odd palm cast against the brilliant blue sky—she gradually found herself regretting that she had agreed to join the trek.

When she later recalled this particular trip, she often wondered which was worse—riding the Leaping Lena or travelling on the back of Midgeree. For what began as a journey on an exquisite throne ended six days later with her feeling dirty and sand-clad, with aches and pains in every muscle. She rejoiced when their destination—the Hermannsburg Mission (Ntaria)—finally appeared in the distance.

Old Midgeree first drew her attention to the collection of small mission buildings shimmering in the heat. He or she—Ernestine could not quite determine which—snorted and moaned at the sight of them and suddenly picked up the monotonously slow pace that had not changed all week. The camel appeared as happy as its rider that the ordeal would soon be over.

At the mission, Ernestine 'hooshta-ed' Midgeree down and for the first time during the whole week the animal did what it was told without the slightest sign of disobedience or haughty arrogance. When she bade it goodbye with a pat on its hump, however, its answer was a loudly ungracious 'bah'.

The Hermannsburg Mission, about 100 kilometres west of Alice Springs, was founded by German Lutheran missionaries in 1877. Harry Tilmouth's little band was met by a small man who warded off the sun with a green umbrella. Reverend Heinrich was the mission's present superintendent, filling in for Reverend Albrecht, who was away. Without wasting many words, he ushered Ernestine into the cool main building, where she was greeted by his wife and a bed, bath and cup of tea.

After Ernestine had bathed and rested, Reverend Heinrich and his wife invited her into their living room for a chat. The pastor had worked at the mission for fifteen years and had known the famous Reverend Carl Strehlow. Strehlow had come to Hermannsburg in 1894 and had learnt Arrernte, the local Aboriginal language. By 1919 he had translated the New Testament into Arrernte, an almost impossible feat. When he fell ill in 1922, Heinrich had set out with the sick man on the 550-kilometre journey to the nearest doctor. After 260 kilometres by buggy, Strehlow died and was buried at Horseshoe Bend.

Ernestine told Heinrich that had she known Strehlow was buried at Horseshoe Bend she would have visited his grave. The pastor shook his head as he recalled how his friend had died and toyed with the green umbrella that stood by his chair. Ernestine asked him about it. Before he came to the mission, he said, he had been advised by his friends to buy an umbrella to shelter him from the harsh sun and rains. The green umbrella had provided shade as Strehlow lay dying in the buggy and Heinrich had become very attached to it over the years.

Both the minister and his wife taught in the mission school for Aboriginal children. They found the task rewarding and said that most of the children were bright and eager to learn, although mathematics posed a problem. 'After counting "one, two", they slip into the vague numeration of "big mob",' Mrs Heinrich claimed.

In the days to come, Ernestine found getting a lift out of the mission problematic. There was supposed to be a daily truck service from Alice Springs, but she was told the Alice was jam-packed with prospectors because gold had been discovered about 560 kilometres north-west of the town, at a location called the Granites. The minister had been told that the daily truck was busy taking prospectors and their luggage to and from the site. So Ernestine found herself marooned.

A week later, Wallis Fogarty and his truck picked her up. On the way back to the Alice he talked of nothing but gold. *The Ghan* had been rechristened 'The Gold Express'. He said people in the town thought Lasseter's lost gold reef might finally have been found.

Just a few years before, in 1929, Harold Bell Lasseter had announced the discovery of a fabulously rich gold deposit in a remote corner of Central Australia, but his explanations of the whereabouts of the reef had been confusing. He claimed that, after his discovery, he had experienced difficulties and had to be rescued. A passing camel driver found him wandering in the desert and had taken him to the camp of a surveyor, Joseph Harding. Together, Harding and Lasseter had tried but failed to relocate the reef. In 1930, Lasseter had managed to secure funds for an expedition that left Alice Springs that July, but it soon became apparent that Lasseter had no idea where he was headed.

The other members aborted the expedition, but Lasseter had pressed on. When he did not return, people assumed he perished in the desert—bushman Bob Buck found his body in 1931. But the story of the 'lost' reef continued to spark the public imagination. Some, however, claimed that Lasseter was a charlatan and the reef no more than a figment of his imagination.

On a Saturday evening at the beginning of October 1932, Ernestine Hill arrived in Alice Springs. Very isolated from the rest of the country, it was then no more than a small outback cluster of buildings with a population of about 200. The land surrounding the town had been home to the Arrernte people for thousands of years but, with the promise of gold and the arrival of a railway line in 1929, the town had begun to expand as more Europeans trickled in.

Gold. The word crackled in the Alice Springs air like an electric storm, making people dizzy with excitement. When three or four old prospectors claimed to have unearthed in three months more than 8.5 kilograms of gold at the low ridge of rocks called the Granites, word quickly got around.

This was what the whole of Australia had been hoping for—new goldfields that would rekindle the hope of a nation still suffering through the Depression. Australia wanted and needed a gold boom, a new Coolgardie or Kalgoorlie, and Ernestine was soon covering the story for the outside world. Joe Kilgariff of the Stuart Arms Hotel had, in the alleyway next to the bar, showed her his fist full of gold. It sparked a fever in her.

There were warnings during those first weeks. Some said the site was too remote and the circumstances too harsh, with no drinking water for miles. But as men and women flocked into the Alice the excitement grew. Mark Twain wrote, 'There comes a time in every rightly constructed boy's life when he has a raging desire to go somewhere and dig for hidden treasure.' As far as Ernestine was concerned, the same applied to girls.

The Advertiser had already run a headline, 'Gold boom: Granites field trading at fever pitch', written by one of its correspondents at the site. Ernestine had hoped to be one of the first newspaper reporters to cover the story, but there was a scramble as papers from all over the country sent their journalists out.

It was frustrating for her to find that most of the trucks leaving for the site were filled to the brim and would not take an extra passenger. After biting her nails for four days, she was finally able to secure a ride with a group of geologists and set off in search of a good story—which to Ernestine was as good as finding a nugget.

It was an arduous two-day drive over rough terrain, and when the party reached the site she appeared to be the only woman there. She knew of other women who had arrived earlier but, appalled by the very harsh conditions, had left again in a hurry. With no water except for what the miners took with them, the men were forced to wash gold with their drinking water. At the Granites, Ernestine found out what a hard thirst was really like.

It was hot and sticky at the site, and swarms of flies hovered over the men and their meagre water supply. Although Ernestine hated the place, she was also enthralled by its prospects. That same evening she managed to get a story out, sending it by wireless at the 'post office' operated by David Laws, a 23-year-old young man sitting under the shade of a tree, sending telegrams and copy.

Laws was an amateur who'd had a small experimental transmitting station in Brisbane. Now he was responsible for keeping the Granites in touch with the outside world.

Sending out hundreds of messages, he enabled wives, daughters and other loved ones to contact the men working at the site. In fierce temperatures and with myriad flies causing irritation and distraction, Laws worked calmly and devotedly at his small transmitter. This young man's logbook eventually became the official record of the Granites gold rush.

Ernestine's first article about the rush, sent out from the Granites site, was headlined 'Granites is gold city in embryo' and continued 'with the faith of Australia and £1,000,000 behind it'. She wrote about 'a police station, post office, store and a hotel established'.

This was an exaggerated and far too optimistic account of the actual situation at the Granites site, as the police station, post office and hotel were yet to be built. Although there was no doubt in her mind that it would be only a short time before they were established, at the time there was no water supply and very little food, the store was no more than a tin shack and there was nothing to suggest anything as civilised as a hotel. A couple of men took her into the fields and aroused her enthusiasm as they pointed out the site for a future railway station. She became so caught up in the excitement that she reported on what she hoped would materialise in the future rather than the mundane truth.

She headed back to the Alice the next day on a nonstop day-and-night journey. A few days later she came upon Eric Baume, her editor at the Sydney *Sunday Sun*. He was accompanied by the geologist Cecil Madigan and a photographer, Franz Marcard. They had come to determine whether newspaper stories and testimonials about the gold rush were reliable. It became apparent that this was no ordinary expedition, and Ernestine was puzzled by it, especially given Baume already had her there to report on the rush.

Right at the end of October a man called Paul Johns approached Ernestine at the Alice's ice-cream shop. A dingo shooter, he was the last person to see Harold Bell Lasseter alive. When Lasseter had managed to secure sufficient funds to undertake an expedition, he hired Johns, who owned a string of camels. But after they had been on their way for a few days they quarrelled and parted company. Ernestine had heard the gossip that Johns had murdered Lasseter. Now Johns wanted her to write up his story.

The story Paul Johns told her at the ice-cream parlour the next day disappeared into her trunk for almost 30 years before it was published.

14

Eric Baume

Eric Baume found the Granites episode a most unfortunate affair, a fiasco. But then none of the newspaper correspondents had known beforehand that it was a bubble rather than a boom, even though that did become obvious fairly quickly. Some brokers on the Melbourne Stock Exchange had looked with disfavour upon the boom very early on, at about the same time the newspapers were running overheated headlines about the new goldfield.

The *Sunday Sun* had already run a few dispatches from Ernestine, telling stories from the old prospectors. Her first reports were feverish accounts of the lure of gold.

After those first articles appeared, F.B. Stephens, a former director of the Stawell School of Mines in Victoria, had written to Melbourne's *Argus* newspaper to say he had inspected the area on behalf of a few mining companies based in Melbourne, Adelaide and London on his way to the Tanami fields in 1929. Baume rang Stephens, who said he had spent half a day looking over the field. He had found 'indications that it was a gold area, and that some prospecting and shaft-sinking had been carried out by other parties, but the site was devoid of water—the nearest known supply was about 240 kilometres to the north-west. Stephens thought there was little justification for speculative interest in the field, and advised that an adequate water supply would need to be definitely proved before he could recommend the field as a practical proposition'.

By then the articles that were being published about the new gold rush in Central Australia were spiced with optimism and hope. Ernestine had been encouraged to write about the exciting news by her bosses, who were in the business of selling newspapers, and she knew that stories about gold always sell.

Ernestine was R.C. Packer's preferred journalist and, although Baume had a certain aversion to her, he could understand why her copy always had to be published above and beyond the rest. 'Her stories had a punch to them that gets news editors where news editors should be got,' Baume wrote later in his book about the Granites rush, *Tragedy Track*. There were rumours doing the rounds about why Packer really wanted her copy to be given prominence. Nevertheless, her articles were always widely read and her copy generated sales, no doubt about it.

For some reason, those people who could and would make history flocked around her. Men and women sat on the stone porch outside Joe Kilgariff's pub at Alice Springs telling her their stories. Baume supposed she was the most trusted woman in the far north, where her name was almost sacred. The men of the desert adored her, so it was no surprise that she was the first to hear the tales directly from the men who had wandered in from the Granites with gold. Perhaps it wasn't for her to question their stories, Baume thought. She simply turned what she heard into news reports.

But by now Baume, who had picked up on the negative reports coming in from different sources, started to fear that the newspapers might be blamed if it became clear that hundreds of people would lose every penny, leaving them destitute at the Granites with no more than rubble for their money.

Baume discussed the telephone conversation he'd had with Stephens with R.C. Packer's son, Frank. The main man had been intermittently ill for a while, so Frank had more or less taken over his father's job by then. It was no secret that Baume's relationship with R.C. was now somewhat strained, even though Baume often described himself as Packer's 'devoted servant'. The older Packer, who was under the impression that the sharp-witted Baume had betrayed him in boardroom intrigues, did not trust him.

Frank Packer quickly understood the implications of what Stephens had told Baume, and together they considered solutions. They did not want the public pointing the finger at them, but they also agreed that it would not be easy to turn the tide. Publishing Stephens' assessments, they believed, would not be enough to convince anyone; they would simply be publishing facts that had been known three years earlier. They needed something more compelling.

By now the view that the Granites rush might well be no more than a bubble was coming in from several sources, and the warnings were sounding ever louder. They would have to move fast and come up with a convincing plan of action. The rise in value of the Granites shares on the stock market had been way too swift, so they decided on an independent inquiry.

No one really knows who came up with this brilliant idea, but it might have been a collective plan. After discussions with Keith Murdoch, then managing director of the Melbourne Herald and Weekly Times group, Frank Packer decided they would undertake a joint effort on behalf of the public. The Packer company, Associated Newspapers, together with the Herald and Weekly Times, would send well-known geologist Cecil Madigan to investigate the Granites gold rush.

Madigan had a degree in mining engineering and a sound reputation and, moreover, was independent. He had flown over the site a year earlier and had seen no evidence of gold, but he could not be certain at that altitude. Now he would get the chance to assess the site on the ground, accompanied by Baume as the representative of Associated Newspapers.

It may seem strange to send Baume, given Ernestine Hill was already there, but perhaps they thought this would enhance their credibility. Who could argue against their sincerity if their own editor was out there verifying the stories sent to them by one of their journalists?

The next day they released a nationwide article stating that 'a party consisting of Mr Baume, Mr Madigan and a photographer will be sent out on an expedition to the Granites site to ascertain whether the large amount of capital invested by speculators was justified by the prospects of the field'. The proprietors of various Melbourne and Sydney newspapers, the article said, felt 'that the investing public is entitled to a better and more authoritative description of the field than could be—or would be—given by any individual mining company'.

'In short, if the Granites proved a good find, they would tell Australia, but if there was no gold—and Madigan would soon know—they could warn the public, so that people who could ill afford to gamble would be stopped in time and lives would not be endangered in the desert outside Alice Springs.' It would make no difference to the newspapers whether the news they brought back was good or bad; they could not lose. A few days later the party set out to uncover the truth about the Granites.

They left Adelaide railway station for Alice Springs in mid-October. Frank Packer waved them off, making sure photographs were taken and later published. Nothing was left to chance. The party was excellently funded and very well equipped for the job at hand, taking two buckboard trucks, three 200-litre drums of petrol, 45 kilograms each of flour and meat, 90 litres of water, two tents and camp stretchers. They also took gold dishes, dolly pots, sample bags, picks and shovels, screens, explosives, drilling steel, compasses and a surveyor's chain. All of this equipment was unloaded at the Alice.

When Baume ran into Ernestine Hill in Alice Springs, she seemed surprised to see him there and thought it strange that he should have come to write copy too. She told Baume that she thought: 'They [the *Sunday Sun*] must be desperate for copy if they sent you all the way out here.' She seemed not to have read of the latest fears for the people investing in the Granites and to have no idea of the expedition's real objective. Baume did not enlighten her at the time.

After they had taken a few days to rest and Madigan had gone over their supplies, assuring himself they would be sufficiently well stocked for the trip, the party set off. Simon Reiff and George Underdown, who had been prospecting in the area for more than 25 years, drove them. It took five days to get to the site with their heavily laden trucks in the oppressive heat, and the trip became a nightmare for the fussy and pedantic Baume. It was a strain from beginning to end.

The isolation of the Northern Territory, with its heat, flies and dust, made the trip especially trying. Once they were bogged for hours when one of their heavy and very large trucks got stuck in the mud of a creek bank. The temperature rose to about 49 degrees Celsius in the shade, and the ironwork on the truck burnt their hands as they tried to manoeuvre it out of the mud. Naked Indigenous men stood silently in the scrub with their spears, yam sticks and boomerangs, looking on with surprised indifference. 'They showed no sign of violence', but Baume wrote that they made him feel 'quite uncomfortable'.

The party had enough supplies to last them the best part of a month; this compared favourably with most prospectors, who went into the fields with very little means, poor food supplies and hardly any water. The well-equipped Baume found the ordeal almost unbearable, so he could well imagine what a harrowing experience it must have been for the many poor prospectors. Baume wrote that 'every ounce of gold gleaned from The Granites was earned in sweat and flies and sickness'.

As Madigan assessed the potential of the field it soon became evident that thousands of acres had been pegged out with no reasonable justification. Gold had been found there, no doubt about it, but 'People could find a handful of gold only to discover that was all there was.' There was no gold in quantity at the Granites—and that was the alpha and omega of the matter, Baume wrote.

The whole gold rush was a tragedy and, while Baume was there, he witnessed much suffering. He wrote about one man from Adelaide who collapsed near the tin shed that served as the store, worn out by flies and dysentery, half-starved and unable to buy food because he was penniless. He was unable to borrow from the others because they were short of rations themselves. Baume feared the man might well have died there.

In the end, the Madigan report destroyed any hope of finding a substantial amount of gold at the Granites. In the five days Madigan spent there, he had been anxious to find the field a success. He realised how important a gold find would be to Australia but, as time went on, hope gradually sank to despair. People were told to stop coming, that the rush was the quintessential flash in the pan. There was not enough water to wash gold and nothing to drink, and although a well had been dug a few miles from the site, the water it produced was too brackish to drink.

After the publication of these conclusions, the Granites shares plummeted and the hopes of thousands were shattered. People returned from the site destitute and begging for lifts, sometimes for food. Every penny of those unfortunate souls had gone into securing a site—a worthless site, it now appeared. The bubble burst just as suddenly as it had risen.

The newspapers received a collective pat on the back for their part in preventing more suffering and for carrying out an objective investigation. A year later, Baume wrote his book about the expedition and his experiences at the Granites, rather blatantly blaming 'little Mrs Hill' for causing the rush in the first place.

Ernestine ultimately paid dearly for her optimism. The public tended to blame her for causing the tragedy. She admitted that the tone of her copy had been way too optimistic, but she reminded people that she was not the only reporter 'who was turning gold fever into headlines at the time'.

The public, as always in these matters, wanted a scapegoat and Baume gave them one.

15

Borroloola

After the Granites gold rush, Ernestine lingered in Alice Springs with Robert and her aunt and mother. Ernestine loved the town as it lazed in the summer sun, with its wide sandy streets and huge ghost gums towering over high-roofed bungalows with wraparound fly-proof verandahs, and Kitty and Madge loved it too. The summer heat was less stifling there than in the coastal areas up north, and the evenings cooled down wonderfully. There were nights when they needed a coat to go out and a blanket to sleep under.

So they spent Christmas and New Year together, delighting in the beautiful surroundings of the Alice. Alice Brown, the wife of Dr David Brown, took them to Emily Gap to see the Aboriginal rock paintings of the Caterpillar Dreaming; they also went to Simpsons Gap and Jessie Gap, and in the evenings they marvelled at the lights of the Arrernte camps flickering on the hillsides of the MacDonnell Ranges. It was just as she had imagined when sitting at her desk back in Launceston three years before. The lights from the Aboriginal camps danced on top of the distant ranges, like fireflies in the charcoal night, and the stars throbbed along with them like so many lighthouses on an endless cosmic sea.

Ernestine's son was already well grown at eight. He had been a big baby and was tall for his age. Madge had started calling him Bob. He was turning into an enterprising child. Ernestine and her Aunt Kitty had laughed when one day he came in carrying a cat and her four kittens, proudly announcing that he had bought them for one shilling. She tried not to miss out on his life too much, and would take him on her journeys whenever possible. She knew he was well cared for when she was away, and she comforted herself with the thought that he would soon be old enough to accompany her on her trips all the time.

She strolled down to the railway station in the afternoon of 7 January 1933. *The Ghan* had just arrived and now stood wheezing breathlessly; smoke, like a smouldering bushfire, still trickled from its pistons. She waited for the passengers to disembark, then caught sight of the group of men she was looking for. From their demeanour she assumed they were the scientists she had already written about. Their strange quest, to take samples of Aboriginal urine and sweat, was the talk of the town, and she had announced their imminent arrival in a small article published the week before. She did secretly wish them luck, even as she felt fortunate that it would be their task and not hers to take those samples in the desert near Hermannsburg.

By now a large crowd had gathered on the platform to see the scientists, curious to find out what kind of men would undertake such an odd mission. The young men looked self-conscious as they disembarked, plucking at their beards and hesitantly looking around for someone to rescue them from all the inquisitive stares. Rescue came in the form of

Dr Brown, who hauled them away from the crowd and marched them and their luggage to their quarters. Ernestine made a note to try the pub or ice-cream parlour later, to attempt to elicit a story.

A few days later, wanting to leave the town in search of copy once more, Ernestine arranged to head out on the mail truck driven by a Mr Johanssen. She did hesitate to leave, though, because for the past few days the town had been filled with talk of a murder. A man had been found dead near the Granites site and the police, suspecting foul play, had made an arrest. Ernestine had visited the murder site herself, but there was nothing left to see except a few old prospectors left over from the rush. Given that the trial would be held in Darwin and not for many months, she decided to let it go. The Alice was wonderful, but she had already stayed for four months and the wet was setting in up north.

So she clambered onto Johanssen's truck, leaving the Alice, the Granites and the murder trial behind her. The mailman's route took her across the border into Queensland and on to Birdsville, then up again to Katherine, where the skies clouded over and sudden downpours stranded them in the town.

Once again her thoughts turned to Borroloola. There was no logical or sane reason to go there but its location, 50 kilometres from the Gulf of Carpentaria, had continued to fascinate her since she sat on a Darwin verandah waiting out the wet. It was a place that literally marked the end of the road; beyond it lay a vast rainforest and the unknown. Blank stares and fearful warnings were the only reactions from friends to whom she revealed her plans. She knew she would be heading for a town where the only road was a short track to the coast, with no one but the Aboriginal people, a policeman and his wife as residents.

The policeman's wife had not seen another white woman for many years, so Ernestine was sure she would stumble upon stories galore near the shores of Carpentaria; if not, she would at least be providing a little company for this isolated woman.

There were two ways of approaching Borroloola: via Mataranka by way of the Roper River, enduring 800 kilometres on a packhorse, or sailing 1600 kilometres around the shores of the Gulf of Carpentaria from Thursday Island, most of them by lugger. Ernestine had wanted to hitch a ride across to Roper Bar and try to get to Borroloola on a packhorse from there but, after waiting for days for the rain to stop at Katherine, she reluctantly booked another trip on that 'glorified string of cattle trucks' they called the Leaping Lena, even though she still had vivid memories of her bruises from the year before.

After a long and uncomfortable journey, Ernestine found herself back in Darwin. It was 18 February 1933 and rain greeted the train as it bounced into Darwin railway station. She didn't stay long because just a few days later the steamer *Maroubra* took her from Darwin to Thursday Island. She loved the island but she was eager to get to her destination.

At Thursday Island word came that the little lugger she intended to take to Borroloola, *Noosa*, was reported missing. They advised her to take another lugger to Burketown in Queensland and await the *Noosa* there. She boarded the *Porpoise*, and slept on the deck in a tin shack for three days.

When she finally arrived in Burketown, she was grateful to be able to book into a decent hotel room at last.

The *Noosa* finally arrived, albeit three weeks late. Its crew—no more than the captain, his wife and their son—had been delayed due to very bad weather while taking a mother and her stillborn baby to hospital. The vessel's crew appeared very disheartened and affected by this tragedy, and the storm they'd had to endure had sapped them of their energy. When Ernestine presented herself to the captain, he was somewhat irritated and refused to take her. 'They'd had a frightful time, he explained, and he had sworn he would never take a woman on his lugger again.' She eventually changed his mind, although she had to invest what she later described as 'all my innocence and naive earnestness' to persuade him.

Her persistence did pay off handsomely—the trip resulted in five or six feature articles—but reaching Borroloola was not easy. The *Noosa* could not approach any closer than eight kilometres off the settlement, and Ernestine and the captain's son had to row the dinghy to the shore in the dark. The Hotel McArthur of Borroloola, when they reached it, was dilapidated and dusty, 'hung with cobwebs and lined with broken windows'.

The next day, however, her trip to that obscure place was rewarded with an extraordinary discovery. She stumbled upon an unlikely find tucked away in the dense surrounding tropical rainforest—a hidden library. Three thousand books had been collected by a mounted policeman called Cornelius Power and stored in the old police lockup. Ernestine stood marvelling at the volumes by Lytton and Twain, Shakespeare and Gibbon, tenderly turning their crumbling pages that were yellowed and stained by time and damp.

She could not believe her luck. Mrs Bridgeland, the policeman's wife, told her the little library had once been the centre of cultural life in the area and the police station's inmates had boasted they were the best read in the Territory, reciting poems when you least expected it. Ernestine's stay in that fascinating little settlement would last just one day, but what a day!

The captain of the *Noosa* was anxious to leave and so was she. She wanted to visit Roper Bar and the waters of Arnhem Land before returning to Perth at the beginning of April.

16

Perth

By the beginning of autumn 1933, Ernestine was back in Perth as she had planned. Knowing where she would sleep at night was a luxury. Of course she had her notes to sort through and articles to write, but she also had time to relax. She wondered if people understood how stressful a life of travelling could be. She seemed to be constantly arranging transport, places to stay and places to eat, and these necessities were by no means commonly available in the faraway places she visited. A feeling of pressured uncertainty grabbed her by the throat as soon as she had to move to another location, but she felt the same way if she stayed too long in one place, so her life seemed full of contradictions. She often suffered from nervousness; cigarettes were her dubious cure.

Out there, traversing those outback roads, she really had no idea how her copy was being received in the major cities, but when she returned to Perth in the middle of 1933 she noticed a change in the way people approached her. During her trips her articles had attracted the attention of many readers. Suddenly, everyone seemed to know her name.

The name Ernestine Hill had become so famous, in fact, that it attracted imposters. Although she in no way perceived herself as famous enough to be imitated, it did happen. In 1933 Ernestine was informed by police that one Frederick Hopkins had been telling people he was Ernestine Hill and that he wrote articles under that name for *The Advertiser*. Hopkins was apparently under the impression that she was a man. He got away with the scam for a while, receiving food and lodgings from unsuspecting farmers, until a few people started to become suspicious. Quite a few did know that Ernestine Hill was a woman.

The police were informed and they caught up with the man, arresting him in the Ceduna area of South Australia. The poor soul had just one penny to his name when they took him in. He was sentenced to three months' imprisonment with hard labour at Port Lincoln Gaol, a punishment far too harsh for such an offence. The man had not really done much harm, although he had abused the trust of those who had given him food and lodging. Ernestine had no say in the matter, however; it was the law.

She knew there were many more con men out there, and she had run into quite a few on her travels—men who traded claims they reckoned were near Lasseter's Reef, or who sold a few acres of non-existent pine forest, or even sold unsuspecting farmers their own cattle or horses back. Some enterprising young men in an old car had even sold building lots below Port Phillip's high-tide mark. There was the story of a man who sold a brand-new, but still empty, station-master's house at Emungalan to a couple of unsuspecting Greek migrants who wanted to run a bar there.

Some of these outback confidence men looked to earn money from their scams while others just hoped for a bed and a meal. Ernestine found them a shrewd lot, but in the end she feared they would spoil the good-hearted and kind outback people she had encountered on her travels, making them suspicious and less willing to welcome a stranger into their homes. She always believed in the good of people, but her aunt and her mother both warned her that they believed 'there was definitely a force of evil out there'.

In Perth, Ernestine was invited to many social events, but although she did accept invitations these events were not a high priority for her, as she always fared badly in front of large groups. She did, however, speak to the Western Australian Society of Women Writers on 24 September as its guest of honour, using the opportunity to emphasise the responsibility of the nation to Indigenous people, especially those who lived along the Trans-Australian Railway. She was applauded for her compassionate plea, but nothing came of it.

Perth was not a big city back then, but it was home to a substantial group of authors promoting Australian literature—such as Katharine Susannah Prichard, J.K. (Keith) Ewers, Alexandra and Paul Hasluck, and Henrietta Drake-Brockman. Because of Western Australia's goldfields, Perth suffered less from the Depression than the other major Australian cities at this time and this attracted many writers and artists.

Writers in the other states imagined Perth to be a sleepy grey mirage of a city, but in 1933 it was developing a lively artistic scene. A scheme to promote education in remote towns had been set up by Walter Murdoch, an academic and influential essayist. He sent some of the academic staff from the University of Western Australia out to country centres to give lectures, and also established a reading circle that distributed boxes of books to various centres to stimulate reading.

Ernestine noticed that there was hardly any Australian literature in the boxes. Even though Murdoch had been a Professor of English at the university since 1913, he preferred the English classics. Ernestine, a staunch advocate of Australian writers and books about Australia, was surprised that no place could be found for such works in the reading boxes. She urged Murdoch to include them but her plea was barely noticed.

Radio had established itself in Perth at this time and was broadcast from His Majesty's Theatre, mainly dispensing market news for farmers and household hints for their wives, but there were also programs with an educational flavour. In 1932 the Australian Broadcasting Commission (ABC) took over this radio station and placed greater emphasis on broadcasts that would not only entertain but also educate.

There were a number of theatres, although they housed mainly amateur or semi-professional companies. In 1932 the *West Australian* had agreed to make space on the top floor of Newspaper House for use as a private gallery, giving Perth residents a space to view works from local artists. Developments like this enlivened Perth's artistic scene considerably.

Quite a number of Perth writers travelled overseas, seeking inspiration and new ideas—Prichard, the Haslucks and Ewers among them. Ernestine, in contrast, never left the country of her birth and always wondered why those writers didn't travel around their own country. Whenever she said this, fellow writers would often reply, 'But there's nothing out there.' They were wrong, she knew, and she suspected they had never read her articles.

Katharine Susannah Prichard and Ernestine had been introduced by Henrietta Drake-Brockman, but they differed considerably in their points of view. Prichard was extremely political, a member of the Communist Party of Australia who used her writing to present the communist ethos to the reading public. When Prichard asked Ernestine what party she supported, and Ernestine told her she was not involved in politics, Prichard seemed horrified.

They did not speak much, but did occasionally exchange letters. They admired each other's work and appeared to like one another, despite seeming to come from different planets. Later on, Prichard travelled with Ernestine for a few days, but for the time being both were very much caught up in their own interests and lives. Henrietta Drake-Brockman remained a good friend to them both.

Drake-Brockman and Prichard were both members of the Sydney Fellowship of Australian Writers. 'Too much fellowship and not enough writers,' Ernestine later complained of the Sydney branch. 'Members seem to specialise mainly in organising and speaking.' Ernestine preferred Perth, Broome, Darwin and Adelaide, where she had made her home and she had friends.

By now Baume's book, *Tragedy Track*, had appeared and people had started pointing the finger at her as the instigator of the human disaster on the goldfields. In a letter to Coy, she revealed her dislike of Eric Baume: 'I like quiet natures who realise their littleness in life. People forever absorbed with their own reflections in the mirror make me tired.' Keith Ewers told her not to worry; Baume's book had been written in a great hurry and it did not charm the reader as a fine piece of writing. But she feared that *Tragedy Track* would always be held up as the definitive record of a gold rush that ended in tragedy, and that her name would always be associated with it.

As 1933 turned into 1934, she finally received word from Beatrice Grey that the *Silver Gull* was nearing completion. The wonderful 26-metre motor yacht was anchored at Perth's Crawley Bay. Western Australian timber had been used for the keel, stem and sternposts. Beatrice said the fitting was almost complete and soon the boat would be taken to Fremantle to prepare the rigging. It would be only a matter of weeks before they set sail, so Ernestine began preparing for her sea voyage.

17

The Silver Gull, 1934

The *Silver Gull* wasn't a big boat, but it was one of the most beautifully furnished and carefully fitted-up vessels Ernestine had ever encountered. Now, as the yacht stood proudly at its Fremantle dock, its owners ready and anxious to set sail, she could not help but marvel. Stepping aboard the little ship that had taken almost two years to complete, she found it a revelation in seafaring splendour.

The *Silver Gull* was grandly fitted with electric lighting, a refrigerator, several bathrooms and a laboratory. It was as luxurious as a vessel could be, and Ernestine was thrilled to be invited on its maiden voyage.

There was little chance of uncomfortable camping for anyone. The crew's quarters, in the bow of the vessel, were built to a very high standard, including the bathroom. The dining room for the captain and his wife was situated centrally, on the main deck, and off that there was a living space with a library. Down below, Beatrice Grey had her bedroom; attached to this was an extra cabin for a passenger, which was to be Ernestine's private space for the trip. The captain's quarters were on deck, together with the deckhouse.

Captain Grey had originally intended to crew the ship

with Chinese sailors, but when he witnessed the excellent training of the Perth Sea Scouts he decided to recruit his crew from among these young boys and young men. He selected seven of them, aged between sixteen and 28.

Beatrice Grey was a dark-haired, slender and active woman. Before she married Jack Reginald Grey, she had been Beatrice Buckland Taylor and had left Queensland to complete her marine biology studies in England. At the end of the war she had met Grey, and they were married in Tahiti.

Beatrice had helped design the ship and been involved in its construction from the first blueprints. Once underway, she was to share the work and watches of the captain and crew. Since their meeting a few years earlier and their collaboration on their film script, Beatrice and Ernestine had become close friends. Now they were to become seafaring ladies together.

While Beatrice would use the trip to undertake her marine research, Ernestine planned to research life at sea for her book on Matthew Flinders. Of course, Ernestine realised that travelling on the *Silver Gull* would be utter magnificence compared to sailing on the *Investigator*, the ship Flinders had captained on his 1801 charting mission along the coast of New Holland. But they well knew that the opulence of the *Silver Gull* could not shield them from the hazardous and perilous seas they would inevitably encounter. Little did they expect, when they set sail on 3 February 1934, that they would sail into one of the worst periods for summer cyclones in recent years.

As the happy, excited scouts waved goodbye to family and friends, the ship slipped its moorings and settled upon the gentle ripple of the Fremantle waters. The Greys had no real itinerary, only to sail for Broome and visit different ports along the way. Ernestine planned to leave the ship at Broome, but the yacht and its crew were to sail on to Java. They expected to arrive at Broome in two or three weeks, after collecting sea snakes and corals along the way.

The first stage of the journey took them to Jurien Bay, a then uninhabited bight surrounded by sandhills and low shores 190 kilometres south of Geraldton. Overnight they encountered brisk southerly winds and fairly heavy seas, but at dawn they saw the unattended lighthouse of Escape Island and, making their way through reefs and smaller islands, they anchored around midday. The young men were great fishermen and set out to catch dinner with their rods. The meal that evening was a feast of seafood.

Tumbling through the seas the next day, they were blown about by stiff winds for another 200 kilometres as they headed for Pelsaert Island, which they reached a day later. They soon discovered that the charts were quite inaccurate. They had been drawn up by Commander John Wickham and Lieutenant John Stokes on the *Beagle* in 1840 and been revised in 1887, but sea and sand had shifted since then, and identification of submerged rocks was difficult, to say the least. Mangroves that Wickham and Stokes had marked as 4.5 metres high had now vanished, and the build-up of sand and the growth of coral had altered the geography considerably in the forty-seven years between the publication of the original map and its revised version.

The crew found the islands delightful and pretty, and they enjoyed sailing and mapping them. The scouts had the time of their lives, hunting wallaby and catching enough fish to fill hungry mouths for the evening dinners. One of the scouts turned out to be an excellent cook; Ernestine reported that one of his best dishes was steamed parrotfish with oyster sauce.

But the crew's peaceful life sailing the islands soon came to an end. The privileged little party, ignorant of the dangers ahead, sailed straight into perilous winds and monsoonal storms, which battered the little vessel and pushed and shoved it about the sea, leaving the crew fearing they all might perish.

After heading for the Montebello Islands, where they sheltered from the weather, they were trapped for a week. There was hardly any food there, no game or fish so, with provisions running low, Captain Grey decided to brave the storms once again, setting out for Cossack on the mainland in an attempt to replenish their supplies.

As the vessel came out of the lee of the islands they found themselves once again battling heavy seas, with the little boat tossed around like a cork. The next morning the weather conditions only seemed to get worse as a furious gale blew huge waves over the deck and deckhouse, and rain poured down all day. The poor scouts worked almost around the clock to keep the yacht on course, despite everyone being seasick and everything on the ship becoming drenched. Ernestine described the scouts as 'brave and wonderful, fighting the storm all night'.

Sailing into fierce winds, they hardly made any headway, no more than sixteen kilometres all morning. The captain now decided to take a chance, go about and run with the sea.

Everyone realised that turning like that could be a very dangerous operation, as the boat could easily topple over if she was caught broadside by the waves. Ernestine feared for her life, as did the others.

This trip had given her more than she had bargained for, but she knew that if she survived, she could write a very vivid first-hand account of enduring a storm on a small ship. For now, however, sitting sick and frightened in her cabin, she realised that this was the first time in all her travels that she had felt so miserable and afraid. Even her five days on Midgeree the camel could not compare to this ordeal.

As the captain started to turn the ship so it could run before the wind and the waves, he ordered the scouts to fetch as much oil from the engine room as they could carry and take it to the front deck. This was no easy feat with a constant gush of water running down the deck, but they managed to pour oil onto the sea as the captain began the manoeuvre. The oil stopped the sea from breaking too violently over the ship and they got about safely, but they were still in some danger of capsizing. The scouts now took out all the heavy ropes and, after attaching them to the fenders, threw them overboard in order to slow the ship down and keep it before the waves.

The scouts worked hard and long but after struggling for 28 hours in one stretch, with the boys pouring oil on the highest waves to prevent them from flooding the engine room, they were forced to abandon their course. The captain had no other choice than to make a dash for the shelter of Enderby Island in the Dampier Archipelago.

By now no one had eaten for two days. The poor boys were so tired that, when the anchor was finally dropped, they flopped on the deck like exhausted pigeons. Beatrice poured glasses of rum to revive the boys and one of them boiled a huge quantity of rice but Ernestine stayed in her cabin, too sick to move. The ravaged and damaged vessel was left as it was while they all crawled gratefully into bed. Rugs, mattresses, pillows, everything was soaked, but still they slept the sound sleep of the genuinely exhausted, and woke the next morning from the best sleep many of them had ever had.

They had no radio, so nobody in the outside world knew where the *Silver Gull* and its crew were; in fact, according to the newspaper headlines at home, they were feared dead. A day later they made several attempts to get to Cossack, but the weather was just too bad and to their dismay they had to return to within a couple of miles of their former anchorage.

It was not until 10 March that the *Silver Gull* finally reached Cossack and could send a message home that all was well. As they sailed north a couple of days later, a heavy swell brought an abnormally high tide of eleven metres to Broome. It flooded the Japanese quarter of the town as the *Silver Gull* and its crew found shelter in the port.

Although the little ship had proved itself a tough little vessel, able to brave the seas, everyone realised how badly things could have turned out. On disembarking Ernestine heard that the hurricanes they had endured had largely destroyed the town of Onslow to the south, wrecking its jetty and levelling most of its houses.

18

Adelaide

Ernestine returned to Perth early in May 1934. Her mother, Aunt Kit and Bob were waiting for her at the airport. They too had heard the news of Packer's death.

Over the years Robert Clyde Packer had become an Australian icon and his death made headlines all over the country. The news left Ernestine perplexed, her feelings veering from sadness to concern and everything in between. He had died on 12 April of a heart condition. The newspapers said he had been ill for some time and had travelled to England in the hope of a cure. Ernestine had never known him to leave Australia, so she thought he must have been very desperate.

He had been sailing just off the coast of Marseilles, on his way back to Australia, when he died. He was only 55 years old. It would take a while for his body to reach Australia and for a service to be held, and this would give her time to decide on the course of action she should take.

Her boy, now almost ten years old, would not grieve for the father he had never known; it was a cruel twist of fate that he had lost his father at almost the same age as she had lost hers. During her lifetime she never named Robert

Packer as the father of her son and Robert Hill only talked about his assumed paternity after her death.

Thinking back, she may have realised for the first time how young and naive she had been when she joined *Smith's* and how much, so many years later, she had matured. She was now a more confident woman, if still a tad self-conscious, but she had made a life for herself and her family. After that first time, she had never again let herself become so easily impressed by a man. In fact, after her son's birth she seemed to have abandoned altogether the idea of a man in her life. In retrospect, she might still have sympathised with the infatuated girl who had fallen in love with the handsome, cynical and impressive Packer.

R.C. Packer had been so strangely complex—always inspiring, always on a quest, always searching for exciting copy, always wanting to sell more newspapers and usually succeeding. He'd had a keen nose for the type of news the general public liked to read, and during his life had generated much envy and admiration and, in equal measure, much resentment. To Ernestine he would probably remain the most exciting man she had ever known, 'the love of her life'.

On that momentous day in 1924 when she realised that she was pregnant and things had gone horribly wrong, she learnt that the love she had thought was mutual was probably not so. But her articles always found space in the Packer newspapers and she remained his favourite journalist. Now, hearing the sad news of his death, she could not reveal her true feelings to her mother, who was adamantly negative about him. It would have hurt Madge to discover that her daughter felt so unnerved, sad and miserable.

No record remains today of the monthly payments

Ernestine received. She must have wondered what would happen now and if there was a codicil. She had no idea if she was mentioned in Packer's will, but his lawyers would no doubt contact her if she were.

Packer had been a wealthy man. He sold *Smith's* to Hugh Denison in 1930 and received some £175,000 for it—a huge sum, about $13 million in today's money. He also received 400,000 preference shares in Associated Newspapers when he sold two newspapers to them.

Now that he was dead, Ernestine had no idea if the *Sunday Sun* would still run her copy or if she would continue to be its feature writer. She saw no reason for it not to, but no one there would feel any obligation towards her. Certainly, Robert's legal son wouldn't; after all, it was Frank Packer who had sent out the team to investigate the Granites rush. She had no reason to trust him, he had no reason to like her and she wondered if she would want to keep writing for a newspaper run by him.

She did not have to wait long for the situation to become clear. No codicil had been found and the monthly payments stopped. She decided not to pursue it. She had earned enough to sustain her family over the past three years, and they would get by without the extra money.

Lloyd Dumas, managing editor of *The Advertiser* in Adelaide, had previously asked her to join his staff, letting her know that he would love to employ her as a feature writer. Until this point there had been no reason for her to move to Adelaide, but now she contemplated taking up the *Advertiser's* offer.

She had been travelling for almost four years, often taking her son with her but with only small interludes of rest. She feared that all this spasmodic travelling, disrupting Bob's life, might have a negative influence on him. Madge was now in her seventies and Bob was growing up fast. Ernestine began to think it might be time to establish a permanent home. She was also in need of an office where she could work on her notes for the two books she planned to write.

Two weeks later, on 17 May 1934, Ernestine, her mother, Aunt Kit and Bob boarded the *Karoola* to Adelaide. Dumas and Ernestine had come to an agreement; she had been appointed to the *Advertiser* staff as a feature writer and would remain there for the next four years.

Until she found a more permanent place to stay, their home for the time being would be the South Australian Hotel on North Terrace. The hotel was slightly in decline but the lease had recently been taken over by Louisa O'Brien, an ambitious and determined woman from a family of hoteliers. O'Brien immediately set about restoring the grand old place, and guests had already noticed her skilled feminine touch. It was clear that it wouldn't take her long to restore the old building to its former majestic self.

Robert Clyde Packer was buried on 21 May; Ernestine Hill did not attend the funeral. She could not. It was not only her new job that prevented her from going to Sydney, although she probably used that as an excuse to herself. For her to stand at his grave and bid farewell to his coffin would have embarrassed his wife and children, and her. So she let the day pass in contemplation of their mutual history while never regretting its consequences. Without realising it, he had given her the greatest possible gift—never a day passed by when she did not rejoice at her son's existence.

Just a week after she set to work for the Adelaide *Advertiser*, the East–West Express (the service from Alice Springs) brought with it an old friend. To Ernestine's great surprise, Daisy Bates had left her tent at Ooldea and come to Adelaide. She had been named a Commander of the Order of the British Empire (CBE) in the New Year's Honours in January and was now in town to attend the investiture ceremony. The lieutenant-governor, Sir George Murray, would be presenting her with the award in recognition of her lifetime's service to Indigenous people.

It was a just reward, Ernestine thought, for Daisy's hardship and work. A day later she accompanied her friend to Government House, where the medal was pinned to the lapel of Daisy's coat and she was congratulated for being among the first women in Australia to receive a CBE.

It also meant that Daisy would receive £1000, which would make life a little easier financially, but she would still be 'poor as wood' as she herself expressed it. She looked very proud and was doted on by officials, some of whom had to endure her sharp tongue but still refused to be put off by her manner. Having heard about this strange old lady for so long and been given the opportunity at last to meet her in person, they had no intention of letting the guest of honour spoil it for them. They engulfed her like hungry seagulls prancing around a bag of chips, making a fuss of her.

Ernestine concluded that Daisy loved every minute of it, but regrettably she couldn't tempt her to linger in the city. All too soon, Ernestine saw her off again, waving to the small figure sitting on the train that would take her back to her tent and 'her people'. Ernestine worried about her friend returning to that drought-ridden land.

Daisy was now old and frail. The United Aborigines Mission had recently opened a post at Ooldea Soak about four kilometres from Daisy's camp. In charge was Annie Lock, whom Daisy openly despised, but Ernestine hoped that Lock would perhaps take heart and keep an eye on her.

In July 1934 Ernestine gave a lecture about the wellbeing of the Central Australian Aboriginal people at a social event organised by the National Council of Women. Ernestine and Violet de Mole, the vice-president of the Adelaide Lyceum Club, discussed the valuable information that had been gathered by Daisy Bates. De Mole, who considered the matter one of federal importance, promised to send a letter to the Council for Scientific and Industrial Research (CSIR, the predecessor to the CSIRO), recommending that it make a proper record of Daisy Bates' knowledge.

Ernestine never heard what happened to this request, but she later sent another plea for the establishment of a safe location where all written knowledge about the Aboriginal people could be protected from the ants and the elements. Daisy's valuable records were being kept in a tin trunk and, in the event of a fire, would all inevitably be destroyed. Ernestine wondered how much archival material Daisy had carefully collected and accumulated out there, vulnerable to the elements and perhaps already lost forever.

During the rest of the year, Ernestine busied herself settling in Adelaide and writing copy for *The Advertiser* and the *Sydney Sun*, which continued to run her articles. Her stories were mainly about local people—the 'half-castes' living in the city, the glorious gardens and the romance of early tomatoes growing in glasshouses just beyond the city limits. She wrote about Lydia Longmore, a remarkable teacher at Goodwood Primary School, and about a school for the blind in the city centre; there were articles about Adelaide's tea and coffee, and the Adelaide parakeet and lorikeet. During that year she also worked hard at writing her books, running from bus stop to desk top, smoking her Craven A cigarettes, typing her copy, sorting her notes and memos, and gathering new ideas.

For months the city had been the centre of her roaming, but by the end of 1935 she was starting to yearn for open spaces again. She was beginning to find the subject matter available to her in the city slightly mundane and boring, but she willed herself to stay, knowing that her books had to be written and money had to be earned. She smoked, fretted and wrote her way through that year.

Feeling every day ever more stifled and cramped in the city, Ernestine one day entered Lloyd Dumas's office and boldly requested that she be given the chance to travel through Central Australia again. The stories she would be able to write would be far more interesting, she explained. She was also suffering from respiratory problems and was coughing a lot. She hoped the interior's drier air would help her feel better.

To her surprise, Dumas consented. She supposed he realised that keeping her in the city would only add to her rising stress, and he no doubt hoped she would deliver exciting feature articles for *The Advertiser* in the months to come.

So she headed back into the interior—to Alice Springs and beyond.

19

From Alice to Dumas

Once again, Ernestine Hill was spending her days in Central Australia, collecting notes for the book on the Australian interior that she planned to call *The Great Australian Loneliness*. First, she celebrated Christmas and New Year with her family in Alice Springs, the town that would be her base for the next three months.

Alice Brown, the doctor's wife, was a good friend and Ernestine always found it a pleasure see her. Alice could ride and shoot as capably as any man, and tell a good yarn too. She had moved from the Alice to Katherine with her husband the year before, but she came down to spend a few days with Ernestine during the Christmas holidays. The two met at the ice-cream parlour to catch up on the latest news about old friends and life in the city. So engrossed were they in their storytelling, they did not notice the parlour doors had closed and the proprietor had almost shut them in for the night. Making their way to the Stuart Arms, they slipped into their hotel rooms.

The next morning there was a rumour that two gold thieves had been arrested at Winnecke Depot, a goldmining site some 80 kilometres to the north-east. When Ernestine arrived there, she found the place nearly deserted except for three old prospectors, whose presence was a bleak reminder of the old gold rush days. They assured her they still found a few nuggets every now and then, but only ever enough to buy food and small necessities. The accused men had already been taken into town, so she left the depot a little disappointed that she had been unable to record their story.

The trial of the two gold thieves was held in Alice Springs in February 1935, in the newly created Supreme Court of the Northern Territory. Before then, all defendants had to be sent to Darwin to be tried, because the town did not have its own court. Ernestine found the courtroom crowded, with lots of excited people craning their necks to witness every aspect of an actual trial for the first time in their lives.

The courtroom at Alice was very small and not really adequate for accommodating so many people, primarily because the new jury box that had been sent from Adelaide took up most of the floor space. After the court officials, prisoners, witnesses and spectators had entered, Ernestine joked that there was hardly enough room for her to fold out her camera. She pitied the jurymen—they had been bunked up overnight in the local hall, in thirteen beds that lined the walls. But no one complained—Alice and its people were proud to finally have their very own courtroom.

Alice Springs was becoming quite a sprawling and well-populated city; the gold rushes had led to an influx of prospectors and others, many of whom had never left. Easy access by train and car had increased the popularity of the little town, but unfortunately there was still no proper hospital. The hostel created at Adelaide House by the

Presbyterian Church's Australian Inland Mission (AIM, which was founded by John Flynn, later of Flying Doctor fame) did a great job, but the small building had no isolation ward and could hardly be called adequate.

Ernestine felt compelled to write an article drawing attention to this situation. There was at the time no hospital between Port Augusta and Darwin equipped with an operating theatre. Increasing numbers of people suffering from tuberculosis sought refuge from the coastal cities in the dry, bracing air of Central Australia, but there was no sanatorium and the disease spread due to patients living in hotels and hostels. Without precautionary measures, community health was at risk. A doctor already flew to remote areas from Cloncurry—in a single-engine, fabric-covered biplane capable of carrying a pilot and four passengers—but there was also a need for a nationwide organisation that could send a doctor by plane to reach families in remote areas who otherwise had to travel vast distances to seek treatment. It was not uncommon for people to die, like the Reverend Carl Strehlow, on their way to a mission or town. In time, Flynn's AIM Aerial Medical Service received the backing it needed to become the Flying Doctor Service.

Ernestine also wrote a series of six articles for *The Advertiser* called 'No outback now' that were republished in *Walkabout*, a magazine published by the Australian National Travel Association. It combined cultural, geographic and scientific content with travel writing, and since its foundation the previous year, she had contributed regularly, and this had enhanced her popularity considerably. *Walkabout*'s editors were active promoters of Australian photojournalism, often publishing half- or full-page photographs. Until then, Ernestine had been frequently disappointed by how her photographs looked in print, the ink turning them into smudgy, dark, phantom-like images. The first publication of her photos in *Walkabout* excited her—the slightly shiny, thicker paper upon which the magazine was printed gave her photos a clearer, glossy appearance.

Her days in the Alice passed by all too soon, but Ernestine was keen to return to her desk and finish *The Great Australian Loneliness*. *The Advertiser* had also sent her a telegram indicating that a letter addressed to her from Daisy Bates was waiting for her. With so much pulling her back to Adelaide, she rode the railway tracks of *The Ghan* and the Trans-Australian south.

Daisy's letter was dated January 1935. 'The bush was alight, she wrote, the temperatures at Ooldea rose to 120 degrees Fahrenheit almost daily and the Indigenous locals had fled.' As should Daisy, Ernestine thought to herself as she folded the letter back into its envelope. This frail old woman should be brought to safety, but Ernestine knew how strong-willed and stubborn she could be, so she wrote back expressing her concerns but leaving a decision to Daisy.

Just a few weeks later, another letter came that compelled Ernestine to take action. Fires were now raging through Daisy's camp; she had buried her notes in the ground, hoping to save them from the all-consuming flames. Her eyesight was almost completely gone, she wrote. Someone had to save her. If no one else felt compelled to do so, then Ernestine would. Rising from her desk, she knocked on Lloyd Dumas's door.

Dumas was a large robust man. He was a Huguenot by ancestry, despite the speculation that he was descended from the great novelist Alexandre Dumas. Dumas came from a long line of newspapermen, his father having been the founding editor and sole proprietor of the Mount Barker *Courier*. A newspaperman in his heart and soul, Dumas had been hired as a cadet on *The Advertiser* at the age of fifteen.

If Ernestine could convince anyone that Daisy had a story to tell, it would be Dumas, she thought. She told him that, if she could manage to get Daisy into the *Advertiser* office to tell her stories first hand, they would sell lots of newspapers and might make further profit from syndicating her stories to other news media.

As she tried to convince him, Dumas eyed her through his glasses. He had met Daisy before and knew what he would be letting himself in for. His most polite description for the old woman was that she was 'a prickly bush', but Ernestine relied upon his instincts as an editor. He could spot a good story, even if its narrator was a strange, somewhat erratic old lady fighting flames hundreds of miles away.

After she finished, Dumas sat quietly, still looking at her from behind his glasses with intense eyes. Breaking the silence, Ernestine went on to explain how Daisy might reveal her life story in a series of articles and how they might be able to make a book out of them. 'The Advertiser could share the rights to publication,' she added optimistically.

Dumas answered with a doubtful look. 'The lady is almost blind and, from what I've read, her prose these days is hopelessly out of date and too obscure to publish.'

'I could ghostwrite her.' It was out of her mouth before she realised what such a task would entail.

Dumas smiled, tapped his pen on his oak desk and said, 'Go tell Mrs Bates that Lloyd Dumas would be proud to receive her in the *Advertiser*'s office and that all expenses, including transport, board and office space, will be paid for and arranged according to her wishes.'

Ernestine was at first stupefied and, just for a moment, almost lost all sense of decorum and hugged the man in her enthusiasm. But Dumas was already busy with the papers scattered across his desk and she managed to suppress her glee. With no more than a small and unobtrusive but sincerely felt 'Thank you', she made a dash for the door.

Just before she left his office, Dumas coughed. Without looking up from the paper he held in his hands, he said, 'Ernestine, I know you won't let me down.'

Ernestine scurried out of the building to the post office, to send an urgent telegram to Mrs Daisy Bates of Ooldea. She felt privileged to have been given this opportunity to rescue Daisy's valuable data, and relieved that the old woman would be safe in the city and far away from the dangers of her camp-site. Of course, she was also absolutely delighted by the prospect of being able to work with her.

Alas, just a fortnight later Daisy, in a very polite but candid manner, refused this generous offer. In her explanatory letter she wrote that rain had now fallen, that 'her people' were back and that the prime minister, the Right Honourable J.A. (Joe) Lyons, was soon to visit her at Ooldea. He would be travelling from Melbourne to Fremantle on the Trans-Australian, in order to board a boat to London. He had sent Daisy genuine letters of interest and she had requested a personal interview. Although she had received no answer, she was sure that the prime minister would want to meet her when his train stopped in Ooldea. She had been summoned at short notice the year before to advise the Lyons government on policy towards the Aboriginal people of northern Australia but, to her great disappointment, her offer at the time to act as a special commissioner had been turned down. She thought that perhaps now Lyons might be willing to appoint her.

Ernestine was deeply disappointed as she headed for Lloyd Dumas's office, holding this letter. Her frustration was evident as she told him of Daisy's rejection. But to her surprise he reacted with relief. 'Well, I suppose that's that,' he said as he stuffed the letter back into its envelope and returned it to her with a small but buoyant smile.

Noting her crestfallen state, he advised her not to take it to heart: Daisy had an appointment with eminence and she couldn't compete with that.

A few weeks later, another letter was delivered to Ernestine's desk. Daisy's urgent meeting with 'eminence' had turned into a humiliating disaster. The prime minister had been asleep when the train stopped at Ooldea. His secretary, Frank McKenna, wanting to protect the PM from the harsh heat of South Australia, had refused to wake him. Not fully understanding Daisy's reputation, he had waved her away as if she were a niggling magpie. But she had stood her ground and had waited in the heat, patiently holding the collection of Aboriginal artefacts she wanted to present as a gift, desperately hoping Joe Lyons would wake up.

Left Mary Gilmore, 1927.

Below J.F. Archibald, c. 1910.

Top Gool Mahomet and his grandson, Leon Todd, in Mulgaria, South Australia, 1949.
COURTESY OF THE MAHOMET/TODD FAMILY

Above Adrienne Mahomet outside their home on Afghan Hill in Farina, South Australia, with Payrosa, her youngest daughter standing in the doorway at left, c. 1935. COURTESY OF THE MAHOMET/TODD FAMILY

Left Daisy Bates, Adelaide, 1935.
NEWS LTD/NEWSPIX

Below Mary Durack with her husband Horrie Miller and their daughters (from left to right) Robin, Patsy, Marie Rose and Julie, 1952. NATIONAL LIBRARY OF AUSTRALIA [PIC 12288/66 LOC ALBUM 1130/2]

Left Eleanor Smith. COURTESY OF
SALLY HINKS

Below Ernestine Hill, 1949.
D. GLASS, NATIONAL ARCHIVES
OF AUSTRALIA [A1200, L12288]

A few of the local Aboriginal people had looked on with curious indifference and Daisy had felt her cheeks burn with shame behind her veil as time dragged on. In the end, as she watched the train slowly depart Ooldea, she had not even caught a glimpse of the prime minister, let alone talked to him. Embarrassed far beyond acceptable outback proprieties—and all of it in front of 'her people' and the sceptical eyes of the settlement's white community—the poor old lady had then hidden herself from sight in the station's lamp room until darkness.

On top of all of this, Daisy wrote, she was sick of having to play second fiddle to Annie Lock. She was losing control of what she felt was her private domain. She felt betrayed by the new mission's intervention and was most annoyed that the care for 'her Aboriginals' had been placed in the hands of 'this illiterate woman'. She believed that her work as the rescuer of the Indigenous people at Ooldea Soak had come to an end.

She was as ready to come now, she wrote, as she would ever be. For those of 'her people' who did not want the mission handouts, she had arranged for the policemen at Cook and Tarcoola to hand out rations. With her authority and self-esteem badly undermined, she was left with no reason to stay. Other places and other roles in the outside world beckoned to her, and for now she had decided to indulge herself somewhat in life's luxuries. She was leaving Ooldea for good, Ernestine sensed. 'I want only the best,' she wrote.

Two weeks later, in May 1935, Daisy Bates emerged from *The Ghan* in a black frock, lace blouse and white lace gloves, a mirage from the desert, as mystifying as ever. Ernestine had no conception then of the amount of work that was about to fall upon her, nor of the almost impossible conditions under which it would have to be done. She did know, however, about Daisy's distrust of collaboration.

In 1910 Daisy Bates had taken part in an otherwise all-male anthropological expedition under the leadership of Professor A.R. Radcliffe-Brown. She had been appointed a travelling protector tasked with inquiring into various Indigenous issues, such as employment on stations, guardianship and 'the morality of native and half-caste women in towns and mining camps'. Later she accused Radcliffe-Brown of publishing some of her findings as his own discoveries.

So Ernestine had downplayed her own intended role: 'It must be your book ... no other person must intrude,' she had written in her attempt to persuade Daisy to leave her tent. She also stressed that all expenses the move incurred would be paid for. 'I cannot live in a town on less money than 400 pounds a year,' Daisy had once written, and then she had added that she saw no middle ground between that kind of a life and the basic existence of tent life. It was perhaps understandable, therefore, that once in the city, the small demanding lady would begin to live a life of extravagance.

Adelaide was happy to pay her homage. Due to the articles Ernestine and other journalists had written about her, Daisy had become quite a celebrity, and every newspaper now found an excuse either to interview her or to write about her. Everyone seemed to want to be photographed with her or to ask her for her autograph. She had been regarded by some as a crank, but now she became a star, and she behaved and was treated accordingly. Her eccentric manner and appearance, once ridiculed, were now regarded as enchanting.

Daisy loved the attention. She had been in the desert for sixteen years, with so few visitors that she could call them 'joyous little interruptions from my own kind'. Having to live for years on no more than ten shillings a week had robbed her of the bare necessities of life.

Indulging in the luxury of the Adelaide Hotel, she took long soaking baths, attended every social event held in the city, and was hailed day and night by bellboys and hotel staff. She had flowers, letters and notes delivered to her room daily, and with the money that jingled in her purse she bought whatever she desired, although it was mostly presents for others.

Ernestine looked on with some surprise as her friend Daisy Bates turned from solemn to frivolous in a matter of days. Since *The Advertiser* was paying, Daisy ordered only the best for her guests. Meanwhile, the actual purpose of her stay in Adelaide—to write a series of articles—seemed to have slipped her mind completely.

With growing alarm, Ernestine remembered Dumas's statement that the whole project would be her responsibility. She tried to get Daisy back on track, but she also felt some compassion for her and did not have the heart to call a halt to her new and lavish lifestyle just yet.

During those first weeks the two of them had an enjoyable time, drinking tea with Ernestine's friends while Daisy told hair-raising or hilarious stories about her life in the desert. Daisy particularly loved to visit Alys Truman, one of Ernestine's friends, who wrote a weekly women's column in

The Chronicle under the by-line Beetee. When they visited, Daisy would insist on cream cakes; she had been deprived of cream for so many years, she would lament. Alys, in return, loved Daisy's presence and her genteel, cultured, old-world demeanour, so they spent many hours eating cream cakes and drinking tea at the *Chronicle*'s offices.

But there was work to be done and, when Ernestine cautiously began to remind Daisy about this obligation, the older woman just looked at her young friend with an air of surprise as if she had forgotten the reason for her move to Adelaide. 'Daisy found the manual labour of typing and editing too depressing . . . So method and manner of writing were left to Ernestine.' Ernestine returned to her desk and started to work through Daisy's notes, some of which were written on scraps of paper or pieces of cloth. There were diaries full of Aboriginal words, anecdotes and faded newspaper clippings of articles she had written, all in such a jumbled state that it was almost impossible to shape or structure them into a readable form. So Ernestine asked Daisy to join her at the *Advertiser*'s office in the mornings to tell her tale in her own words so she could begin to un-jumble the chaotic state of the notes.

To Ernestine's surprise, in a matter of days Daisy managed, with little effort, to set aside her frivolous life during the mornings. She would arrive at the office every day at exactly half past nine, using the stairs instead of the lift, alert and ready to read Ernestine's copy. They were crammed into a tiny office space, but Daisy never complained.

Ernestine regretted that her own literary aspirations would have to be set aside for the time being. Her ideas and notes now made way for the tales of the iconic figure who entered her office every morning.

The first of a series of twenty-one articles resulting from Ernestine's collaboration with Daisy Bates started to appear in *The Advertiser* on 4 January 1936 under the title 'My Natives and I'. The articles were syndicated to the Melbourne *Herald*, Sydney *Sun*, Brisbane's *Courier-Mail* and Perth's *West Australian*, and so were read throughout Australia. Daisy Bates became a household name. As had been agreed, none of the published articles carried Ernestine's name.

20

Writing books

In January 1936, Ernestine's agent, Curtis Brown, informed her that they had found an English publisher for *The Great Australian Loneliness* and urged her to finish it. The London-based publishing house Jarrolds wanted to publish the book for that Christmas.

Jarrolds' most noted book, published in 1877, was about a horse and became one of the most famous children's titles of all time—Anna Sewell's *Black Beauty*. Ernestine was thrilled by the prospect of being published overseas.

British readers were fascinated by stories about their overseas colonies. They wanted to know what living in such remote areas was like and were eager to read the adventurous stories emerging from those faraway corners of the Empire. Ernestine felt sure that her stories about the little known areas of Australia, and its endearing and strange inhabitants, would capture the British imagination. 'For me this might mean a springboard for the future,' she confided to one journalist. People in Australia were by now very familiar with her articles and, although she had not quite become a household name, she was well known to the reading public. Being published overseas might bring international fame.

The book would largely be a collection of the articles she had written for the Sydney *Sunday Sun*, but she knew these would need extensive editing, sorting and some additional chapters to transform them into a publishable book, not to mention the photographs that would illustrate it.

It became a race against time. She always worked best at night, with her notes scattered across the table and her typewriter at hand. As she laboured for hours, smoking obsessively and only stopping when she could no longer type, her book started to take shape. Each night she would go on for as long as she could, first transforming her shorthand notes into English sentences with a pencil. She would often work until dawn and then, with her ashtrays full and her nails bitten to the quick, she would stumble into bed as the town awoke. Ernestine would later complain that the book had many imperfections: 'It was all pushed (much too quickly) onto a small canvas and helter skelter from there on.'

It was May 1936 before she could send the manuscript to the publisher. The final typesetting took longer than expected, and Jarrolds later informed her that it would not be finished in time for Christmas. Publication would now occur in February 1937. It was a pity, but she had given it her best shot.

Of the 2250 copies of *The Great Australian Loneliness* printed, around 600 were shipped to Australia. The book was out of print in Australia by October 1937 but, although there was a lot of demand, Jarrolds kept postponing the second printing, arguing that more than 1000 copies remained unsold in Britain.

Ernestine was also disappointed at the price of her book in Australia. A reader had to pay 21 shillings, much more than for the typical local edition of an Australian book, which usually cost around nine shillings. She complained to Jarrolds, saying that, although she was proud of her book, she thought the Australian public was paying too much. They explained that there were substantial shipping costs involved and that the many photographs made printing the book expensive.

After she had sent the manuscript to England back in May, Ernestine had returned to the book she had promised to edit for Daisy Bates. Although the series of articles in the Adelaide *Advertiser* had been published under the title 'My Natives and I', Dumas suggested to Daisy that she call her book 'Kabbarli', the name 'her natives' had given her. There was debate in the office as to which would be the more appropriate; although Daisy had a preference for 'Kabbarli', Ernestine retained 'My Natives and I' as a working title.

Time and work dragged on; the months changed their names and the trees that lined the streets of Adelaide started to bloom with the onset of spring. In mid-September, Ernestine met one of Australia's most distinguished photographers, Frank Hurley, who was in town to take pictures for Adelaide's centenary commemorations. Ernestine, as an enthusiastic photographer, couldn't believe her luck.

Hurley's artistry had already produced many memorable images from all over the globe—from jungle to polar ice. Ernestine was a great fan and was delighted to be able to interview him for the *West Australian*. He explained the importance of waiting for one's chance then taking the photo—at any cost. 'To make unusual pictures you must get into unusual places,' he said. She observed that he took all his photos with a short-focus lens, working with only a small camera. He explained how to take better pictures with her little fold-out Zeiss Ica, and wait patiently for the right moment.

Hurley took great risks to secure his thrilling photos; others who tried to copy them had even paid with their lives. At Rosa Gully near Wollongong in New South Wales, above a death trap of sweeping spray, three friends set out to copy one of Hurley's pictures and two of them drowned.

Both Hurley and Ernestine were asked to contribute to *The Centenary Chronicle*, the centenary issue of *The Chronicle* published on 5 October 1936. It was the most elaborate newspaper production ever attempted in South Australia. The cover design depicted 'Light's Vision', showing Adelaide's planner, Colonel William Light, making his survey and envisaging the great city of the future. Ernestine's contribution was a short history of the state, illustrated with historic pictures from the *Chronicle*'s archives department.

At the end of October, Ernestine received a letter from the Australian Dried Fruits Association saying it would like to commission her to write a book about the development and establishment of irrigation districts along the Murray River, to commemorate the jubilee celebrations of the Murray Valley irrigation settlements.

Daisy's book was almost finished. It would need final editing and retyping but it was almost ready to be sent to a publisher. Ernestine loved Australia's big rivers, so the prospect of travelling along the silver ribbon of the Murray was tempting enough to persuade her to leave Daisy and her book to others. Max Lamshed, one of the literary editors on the *Advertiser* staff, would take over and act as both editor and agent. Ernestine set off to roam the Murray, certain that she had left her friend and her book in capable hands.

When Daisy's book appeared in England in 1938, it contained no reference at all to Ernestine Hill, and to Ernestine's surprise the publishing house, John Murray, had changed the title to *The Passing of the Aborigines* and expunged the passages she had written about Daisy's own life so that only the stories of Aboriginal life remained.

The Passing of the Aborigines caused some controversy, as the public's views on certain Aboriginal matters had moved on from Daisy's over the years. On the whole, however, it received very good reviews in both Australia and England. At the time, Ernestine said nothing publicly about her involvement, but in later years she felt the need to make her contribution known.

21

The silver river

In December 1936 Ernestine left Adelaide in search of the story of the Chaffey brothers, who had tracked the Murray from its source at Cowombat Flat in the Australian Alps, Victoria, to the point at which it flows into the Southern Ocean at Goolwa in South Australia. The summer heat followed Ernestine along the flat shores of the big river, where straight lines of fruit trees and vines grew in a display of fertility. The development of irrigation—the productive use of land by means of dams—was an epic story. As she travelled along the great river with her son Bob, writing notes and collecting copy as she went, Ernestine uncovered the story of two brothers who had embraced a vision that transformed dry unfarmed areas into orchards and fields of waving grain.

The Chaffeys, William and George, originally from Canada, were engineers and irrigation planners. Alfred Deakin, who in the mid-1880s was the Victorian minister for Public Works, had met the illustrious brothers while visiting the irrigation areas of California in 1885. Deakin listened closely as George Chaffey explained how he had solved water-management problems in America, then urged the black-bearded man to cross the ocean and share his insights with Australia.

George visited Victoria the next year. He got so carried away with the prospect of developing an irrigation system along the shores of the Murray that he sent a telegram to his brother, urging him to sell their interests in California and join him in Australia. William followed George's instructions, but the rushed sale of their business in the USA cost them quite a lot of money.

They had thought they would immediately receive permission to start work, but debate in the Victorian parliament about their ambitious plans, which encountered significant suspicion, held them up considerably. Just as today, there was no common agreement that irrigation would be in everyone's best interests. Delay, debates and months of haggling disheartened the two Canadians, who hailed from a continent where the 'encouragement of innovation was paramount'. In the meantime, the premier of South Australia, John Downer, made the Chaffeys an offer and the brothers travelled across the border, where they soon went to work in Renmark. When agreement was reached in Victoria, they were instrumental in the establishment of Mildura.

To enthuse farmers to buy plots of irrigated land, the Chaffeys produced a book called *The Australian Irrigation Colonies*, written by the journalist J.E. Matthew Vincent. 'The Red Book', as it was known because of its blazing crimson cover, portrayed a grand vision of a new life at Mildura. In their enthusiasm, however, the Chaffeys had overlooked the fact that Australia is not California, nor like anywhere else on earth. The brothers faced many challenges they had not anticipated, and when their Australian projects finally went bankrupt, it was a sad end to eight years of hard work and brought disappointment to many investors. George, disheartened, returned to the United States, but William stayed and established the Mildura Winery. He also became a leading member of the Mildura and Australian Dried Fruits associations.

Ernestine was a great enthusiast for the Murray irrigation systems, and a year later she gave her book the title *Water into Gold*. Towards the end of January 1937 she returned to Adelaide with her many notes and numerous photographs—a voluminous treasure packed in her suitcase. She was soon hard at work again, because the book was scheduled for publication in August that year.

By then *The Great Australian Loneliness* had been on sale for a month and in March the first reviews appeared. There was overall praise from critics and Ernestine saw this as reward for all her hard work. *The Advertiser* called it 'a manual for the unknown interior of the country'. The reviews in most Australian newspapers reflected the view that the book was 'graphically written and extremely well illustrated'. When the English press followed suit, she was thrilled. It gave her the energy to sit for long and stressful hours once again, a slave to the typewriter, writing *Water into Gold*.

The book on the Chaffeys was to be published by Robertson & Mullens in Melbourne. Working feverishly for three solid months, Ernestine finished the first draft by the end of April 1937. She spent another three weeks in Melbourne busying herself with corrections and additions, and both she and the publisher were very pleased with the final result. Fifty autographed advance copies of *Water into Gold* were released in August 1937 and handed to such people as W.F. Dunn, chairman of the Water Conservation and Irrigation Commission at the time, who had done much to promote water conservation and irrigation.

In retrospect, Ernestine's views on Murray irrigation were much too optimistic. Until this time, no one had taken into account that the river had specific cultural relevance to the Aboriginal people and that the disruption of the river's natural flow would cause them concern and so create disputes. There were also ecological issues—even during the early days there were signs that irrigation would increase salinity. But Ernestine was confident that in time the benefits would far outweigh any shortcomings.

At the end of 1937, Ernestine decided it was time to return to Sydney. Both the *Sydney Morning Herald* and the Melbourne *Argus* had asked her to become a feature writer but it was time, as a mature woman and an acclaimed writer, to go back and face her past. She was still a little haunted by old ghosts, but she believed she had nothing to be ashamed of, so before Christmas she moved with Bob and Madge to Point Piper in the Eastern Suburbs where Kitty would occasionally come down from Brisbane for a visit.

Her son, now a teenager, found Sydney irresistible. 'He is completely suburban,' she wrote to Coy. Bob loved the city, with its Harbour Bridge, beaches and bustling life. Ernestine now had enough money to live relatively comfortably, and the two of them, sometimes accompanied by Madge and Kitty, indulged in life's pleasures. During the day, if Ernestine wasn't working, they would spend many hours on the beach, which she had always loved—many of her childhood poems had been inspired by sand and sea.

One day, running along the beach at Point Piper, Bob found a charred and rusted plane rudder. At thirteen he had a keen interest in anything technical and was over the moon with this find. The rudder appeared to have been in the water for months and had probably floated for a considerable distance before being washed up. Bob knew a lot about planes; indeed, according to his mother, his only loyalty thus far had been to the inside of aeroplanes. Bob thought the rudder must have come from a Moth, but there was no record of such a plane having been lost in the harbour. Later the mystery was solved by the discovery of a seaplane that had sunk at Rose Bay seven years earlier and was never recovered. The plane had been sitting on the harbour bed rusting to pieces ever since. The rudder had probably drifted onto the beach after rusting away from the rest of the plane.

For a while life seemed to be going wonderfully, but Ernestine was constantly worried about her first book. Well into the next year, she was still awaiting a reprint, but had by now given up hope. 'The English people have pretty well killed the *Loneliness*,' she complained to Henrietta Drake-Brockman. 'It has all been nothing but woe.'

In 1939, Robertson & Mullens offered to take action and made an offer to Jarrolds for the copyright. On Ernestine's behalf, the Melbourne publisher requested termination of the contract due to neglect on Jarrolds' part and announced a plan to print 3000 copies in August. Jarrolds offered Ernestine £30 for the complete copyright of *The Great*

Australian Loneliness. Ernestine was appalled and flatly refused, considering the offer highly unreasonable.

By now war was looming again in Europe. Robertson & Mullens let Jarrolds know that they were sympathetic to their situation and offered to pay an advance of £25 on the first 2000 copies if they would agree to do the printing. But Jarrolds refused and its solicitors threatened to take action should Robertson & Mullens go ahead with publication in August. Ernestine knew that the English publication rights would revert to her by the end of the year anyway so, after discussions with her Melbourne publisher, decided to wait.

On 22 December, Ernestine was at last free of 'the English affair', and an Australian edition of *The Great Australian Loneliness* was published in March 1940. Both Bob and Ernestine were very proud of the 'new' edition. 'It was time it shed its grisly jacket and reappeared in new garb,' she said. The Australian version had been cut by 30 pages due to printing costs, but the buyer would now have to pay only nine shillings for a copy.

22

Radio star

Ernestine wrote a short radio play for the ABC, her first attempt at a drama, and it aired at Christmas 1938. *Santa Claus of Christmas Creek* proved so popular that it was aired every Christmas thereafter for several years. The story is about Joe Hacket and his wife Janet, who live on an isolated station in the far north of Australia. Janet is the only white woman for hundreds of miles. The Hackets are hoping for a good Christmas, but everything depends on their orders arriving on time. On Christmas Eve, a prospector called Lorimer, whose wife has died and left him with an infant to care for, knocks at their door. He is followed a little later by old Dolly Pot Mick. As it is a Christmas story, the packages everyone is waiting for arrive just in time and all ends well. It was an entertaining play and it was obvious that Ernestine had picked up ideas for the characters on her travels.

The people at the ABC were so pleased with the play, they asked her to write a weekly page for women in their national magazine, the *ABC Weekly*. Madge was now unwell, so Ernestine asked Aunt Kit to come to help her with her mother and Bob.

Bob had grown into a gangling teenager, with stick-like limbs and a great sense of humour. At this stage in his life Ernestine described her son as 'a gay exhibitionist but a deliberate one with a smile'. He had painted his bicycle white and scooted about on it 'like a skeleton in the dark'.

Despite his childlike antics, Ernestine realised her son would be eligible for military service in just two years' time. The threat of war in Europe was by now very real. When Paris fell in June 1940, Ernestine felt panic-stricken, certain she could not and would not let her son become a soldier. He had never killed a living thing in his life. She had always been a pacifist, and the thought of Bob being slaughtered on some unknown battlefield filled her with horror. She became fretful as her mother deteriorated and the war crept across Europe. She could do nothing but hope that it would all go away.

For years now the story of Matthew Flinders had been hiding in her thoughts like a pearl in a clam. She had always wanted to write it for her mother; now that Madge was ill, she decided it was time to take the story seriously in hand. She applied for and received a grant of £100 from the Commonwealth Literary Fund to write the book, steeled herself and set to work.

Although she had been very pleased with the way Robertson & Mullens had handled 'the English affair', she sent her Flinders manuscript to Angus & Robertson (A&R) in Sydney. Henrietta Drake-Brockman, who regarded A&R's editor, Beatrice Davis, as a genius, forged the connection. After Henrietta published her book *Sheba Lane* with A&R in 1936, she and Beatrice had become good friends.

When Ernestine sent A&R the first draft, she was slightly apprehensive. Being a novelised biography and a story of the sea, it was a complete departure for her. The people at A&R were well aware of this, but she did wonder how they would react to her inclusion of Welsh dialect in the dialogue. To her relief, Beatrice Davis told her she thought it was the best Australian novel she had read in years.

Ernestine's working title had long been 'He Named Australia', but as A&R's managing director, Walter Cousins, pointed out, this was a more appropriate title for a history book for schoolchildren. Bob had devised a jacket design, using a parchment map as a background and a wave on the flaps, with faint numbered latitude lines and compass. He was almost seventeen and Ernestine thought he was becoming a fine artist, so she saw no reason why his design could not be used. To her dismay, Cousins was having none of it. He instead commissioned a jacket design from Geoffrey Ingleton, a former sailor and a naval illustrator. He also asked Ingleton for title suggestions, one of which was *My Love Must Wait*. Ernestine sent quite a few furious telegrams to the A&R office, but Cousins called her bluff, telling her she must accept publication on his terms or the deal was off.

When Madge died of a stroke on 15 June 1941, Ernestine was, of course, heartbroken. Her mother had always been her best critic and a huge inspiration. Now she would never see *My Love Must Wait* in print. The book appeared in November that year and did well straight away. When a reprint had to be ordered before Christmas, Ernestine sent Ingleton a gracious letter of thanks.

The ABC saved Ernestine from a protracted state of grief. Its Adelaide office approached her about presenting a radio program on her journeys and she gratefully accepted. Sydney no longer made her happy. It was too busy, with too many people pushing and plodding their way down its streets. 'I have ochlophobia [a morbid fear of crowds],' she wrote to Henrietta Drake-Brockman, 'Five of my own kind can frighten the life out of me.' She got on quite well with the sky, she went on, but with people she always ended up grieving. She was happy to return to 'the quieter Adelaide'.

On 8 December 1941 a shock rocked the country. The day before, the Japanese had bombed Pearl Harbor in Hawaii and the war, which to that point had seemed so far away, announced itself ruthlessly as a daunting reality to 'remote' Australia. For Ernestine, a feeling of deep fear took hold as she realised she might lose her son so soon after losing her mother. Bob would be eighteen and eligible for the Citizens Military Force in only ten months' time.

Ernestine was already well known for her books and articles, but the staff at ABC Radio in Adelaide had never seen what she looked like. They were perhaps a little disappointed and surprised when a small, thin, large-eyed lady stepped into the office. From her reputation they might have expected an Annie Oakley—someone who could shoot and ride and handle herself out in the wilds. Ernestine was very much the opposite and did not have the demeanour of a calm, collected pioneering woman. How this self-conscious and somewhat tense person managed to write and produce radio talks, let alone go tramping around the outback, was a mystery.

Always arriving with a lit cigarette and leaving with a lit cigarette, Ernestine would fidget around with her papers before she settled into working mode. It was only when her show started that it all came together and she could speak calmly into the microphone in her smoke-affected voice. Her program about her travels was called *This Place Australia*; later she presented another called *Talk on Australia*, in much the same vein. She usually took the outback or the strange Australian places in the north as her topics, and her programs became very popular, both in the cities and far outside them.

Ernestine realised, possibly better than anyone, how important radio could be to those remote outback women who were deprived of news and entertainment. She told her colleagues that when she had begun travelling around Australia some ten years earlier, many of the outback homes had no radio and the quietness had often saddened and depressed her. The lack of music and talk on the homesteads, where women had nothing to listen to but the sound of their children's voices, sometimes made for bleak and hollow lives. Some women were so isolated that the weekly visit from the postman was their only means of hearing news from the outside world. In those homes there was usually no musical instrument or gramophone, nothing to break the monotony of the silent evenings filled with sewing and reading.

But once the wireless reached the outback, it brought liveliness, music, talk and worldly matters. 'Imagine what it would mean for a woman to have a radio!' she wrote. 'The music coming from it, the stories and plays to be heard and the news. So now, when the postman comes in, he's the one who asks the lady of the house about the latest gossip and news.'

Ernestine had very patriotic ideas, but she was also a mass of contradictions. She hated the Australian accent, for example—she was quoted as saying, rather surprisingly, that the Australian drawl disappeared as soon as one distanced oneself from the city. 'The further outback you travel, the less you hear the Australian accent. Though it's spreading like wild-fire in the cities, the faraway escapes contact and people still remember the vowels of the King's English.' It is surprising that on the one hand she would embrace Australia, telling people to take more notice of their heritage and to teach their children about their wonderful land but on the other would scoff at the accent.

During this period, while more and more men were leaving their homes and jobs to join the army, the ABC's management questioned whether they should still cater for women as a separate audience. Women were leaving their homes to take up war work beside the men, leaving an ever-diminishing number of increasingly busy women at home in the mornings to listen to the radio. In Sydney the ABC appointed its first female announcer, Rae Millar, to replace the male announcers now on war duty.

Ernestine had always been a working girl so, for her, working outside the house was a part of everyday living. But she never seemed to have much sympathy for women's issues. She was certainly no feminist; she wasn't even political, she would say. She had her own beliefs.

When the Japanese attacked Darwin on 19 February 1942, everyone was horrified. The general Australian public had had no idea that the enemy had already based itself in Timor. The Japanese flew to Australia using drop tanks, an extra fuel tank placed under the aeroplane. Ernestine had always argued that the inland and coasts should be more densely populated, and suddenly popular opinion agreed with her. People felt that the sparsely populated country was very vulnerable. If the Japanese landed in the north, they reasoned, no one would know they were in the country until they reached Sydney. It was a chilling thought, even if the difficulties for anyone making it from the north to Sydney without assistance would be almost insurmountable.

News came from Broome that the Japanese pearl divers who had lived there for years were being interned. Ernestine had previously written of the hospitality of the Japanese there and how courteous they had been to her during her visits to Broome. She found it difficult to believe that these polite and respectful men had become the 'enemy' overnight.

At this time Japanese, German and Italian migrants living in Australia, and their descendants, were approached with a certain wariness. Even on the streets of Adelaide, they seemed to be treated with increasing suspicion. Ernestine and Bob's landlady was Elena Rubero, an Italian migrant who ran a guesthouse at 32 Lefevre Terrace in North Adelaide. Elena and her mother had previously made a living by importing Italian goods, but this had become impossible since the outbreak of war. The two women, trying to maintain a low profile, managed to earn some kind of income by renting out rooms in their two-storey house.

In 1938, during a visit to Italy, Elena Rubero had been invited, as a respected member of the local Italian community, to visit the warship *Raimondo Montecuccoli* and meet Admiral Alberto Da Zara. Rubero believed that this meeting was causing concern among Australian officials, now that Italy had joined forces with the Germans. She even thought she was being spied on.

Bob spent much of his time at the house typing his mother's notes. Ernestine claimed that he had helped her enormously in writing her new book, *The Territory*, which would document the first 100 years of white exploration, pioneering and settlement in Australia's tropical north. 'He has a great sense of drama,' she wrote to Henrietta Drake-Brockman, 'and an even better sense of phrase.' She believed he would ultimately become a writer himself.

In June 1942, Ernestine Hill was the first creative writer to be appointed to the ABC board. Apparently, Prime Minister John Curtin had nominated her himself. He thought a woman with such a love for her country might offer something new. She needed to travel to Canberra to join the board, and she set off with the intention of taking up her new responsibilities very energetically, even though she was apprehensive about the other board members' expectations. Stopping over in Sydney on her way to Canberra, she gave an interview and was quoted as saying: 'I hope there are no politics to be exploited, for I know nothing whatever of them ... My only ambition is to continue my work for all Australia and I look upon my appointment to the ABC as a truly great opportunity for this.'

She had been so inspired by her appointment that in her introductory speech she immediately began urging the men in charge of programming to explore all aspects of Australian life as actively as possible. There was a strange contradiction in her nature that allowed her to suffer from a great deal of anxiety and shyness but at the same time be confident enough to talk to a large group of men in a tone that inspired and motivated them. John Curtin was very impressed with her speech.

Like those of many public figures, Ernestine's words were weighed and judged and sometimes misunderstood. One interview published in several Melbourne newspapers quoted her saying that she had 'received word of the ABC appointment whilst droving cattle across the country'. Readers and journalists wondered how she could possibly have been typing away in the saddle in the middle of a droving trip. She had to explain that her words had been a figure of speech: 'I was droving a mob of cattle overland on the typewriter, of course, not in actual fact in the saddle. I was writing about the great cattle migrations to and from the North of Australia.' She had been speaking metaphorically, she said, 'the stockwhips cracking only in her imagination'.

During the war years, life for Ernestine became increasingly strained, problematic and challenging. There were optimistic times, but her life became ever more turbulent. Articles detailed how obsessively she was trying to keep her son out of the army and the extremes to which she went to have him exempted. The prospect of losing Bob would take her to the verge of a nervous breakdown.

23

Exemption

Dr Leon Opit met Ernestine Hill in October 1943 during her battle to have her son exempted from military service. Bob had previously been granted six months' exemption; when this expired, Ernestine and her lawyer, Jim Brazel of Alderman, Reid and Brazel, had applied for a further extension due to her mental state. Opit had been asked to assess her state of mind for the court.

Having examined her the day before the court hearing, Opit concluded that she was one of the 'most neurotic women he had ever encountered.' She was in such an unstable state that he was unable to make a thorough examination—she appeared to think that he had been hired by the military in a conspiracy to deprive her of her son. No matter how Opit tried, he couldn't convince her that he was an impartial witness answerable only to the court.

Opit believed there were extenuating circumstances to be taken into consideration. Ernestine had suffered a great deal of stress during the last two years. Her mother, her confidante and a great stabilising factor in her life, had died in 1941, and her aunt had died in May 1943. After suffering a stroke, Aunt Kitty had been taken to hospital but never regained consciousness. Ernestine felt that both she and Bob had lost two mothers. She claimed that Bob was her only living relative and that taking him from her would have a disastrous effect on her health.

Opit agreed that the loss of her son's company might possibly make her mental state more disturbed. She had told the doctor that her husband died when her son was eight. Bob claimed to be a student, but he did not attend any educational institution; he had not even passed the Intermediate Certificate. He had, however, been assisting his mother with her work.

Ernestine claimed that Bob was the only person she could rely on to type up her notes and assist properly with her research. He had helped her in this way for a few years, she said, and no one else could read her shorthand (which over the years had deviated so far from standard Pitman as to be almost indecipherable). At the time of the court hearing, she was working on *The Territory*, which would run to 200,000 words and was, she claimed, due to the publishers in January 1944. Mother and son had been working on the book from 10 a.m. until midnight each day for months, and she could not continue this work without his assistance.

Bob also accompanied her on her trips interstate and looked after everything for her. She said her income had been drastically cut due to the war, as paper shortages had resulted in her books often being out of print. Without the assistance of her son, she would have no income, which would ultimately result in her having to leave her current address. During the past year she had earned about £900 in royalties from various books and about £350 from working as a commissioner for the ABC. In a letter to the prime minister Ernestine claimed her income was grossly overstated by the papers. She received only £500 in two years for her books and the income from the ABC.

The magistrate, Reg Coombe, granted Bob another two months' exemption, to enable him to assist his mother with her book, but he would be expected to report to the Adelaide suburb of Wayville for military service on 6 December 1943.

In the meantime, Ernestine tried to involve Prime Minister John Curtin. Since Curtin had personally proposed her nomination to the ABC, she hoped he might use his authority and influence in her son's case and asked him for at least two years' exemption. In her letters to the prime minister she claimed that Bob's help was of no less than national importance.

The prime minister replied, curtly and somewhat sarcastically, that 'although he appreciated the importance of her work, the enemy was at the gates and was not particularly concerned about literature, unless it contained instructions for the armed forces in the art of waging war'. He also made it clear that he did not want to interfere in army matters involving individual people, and advised her to take whatever legal steps were open to her.

Out of compassion and courtesy, Curtin invited Ernestine to his office for a personal talk one afternoon, during which he suggested enlisting her son in the merchant navy. Although she greatly appreciated this suggestion, she remained adamant that her son could join the merchant navy only after he had finished assisting her.

Curtin also suggested that Bob might find employment in work of national importance, such as cattle droving or building aerodromes in the north, but he made it clear to her that giving advice on this matter was all he was prepared to do—'The decision must be left to the authorities,' he told her. Bob's case was just one among thousands, and only a few exemptions were ever granted.

When Robert Hill failed to report at Wayville on 6 December 1943, the area provost sergeant was sent to his home at Lefevre Terrace. There Mrs Rubero informed him that Ernestine and Bob had left on 6 November and she had no idea where they had gone. The deputy director of Manpower, Leslie Hunkin, rang Ernestine's lawyer, Jim Brazel, but he too said he knew nothing about their disappearance. He said he would do his best to contact them and advise them against their course of action but that he was 'in no way a party to the events taking place'. The staff at the ABC and A&R were also questioned about her whereabouts. All denied any knowledge.

Before Ernestine went bush, she had sent another letter to the prime minister, this time threatening to resign from the ABC. She was adamant that the court hearing had not done justice to the case, complaining that she had heard about Opit's visit only the afternoon before. She had been upset that a doctor had been engaged to assess her against her wishes and she claimed that he had made no attempt to properly examine her. She had found his evidence 'most harmful and untrue', and she claimed that misstatements made during the trial had 'caused her harm'. Because of all the publicity, she had been forced out of her home and, being homeless, she was now incapable of continuing her work. She feared that in time her son would be seized by the military and sent to prison 'although the boy has done nothing wrong'.

Ernestine had fled with Bob to a place she had always felt safe, attracted by the possibilities it offered for her to become anonymous and disappear—the outback. They were at Cordillo Downs, to be exact, a lonely cattle station tucked up in the north-eastern corner of South Australia and less than 160 kilometres from Birdsville, over the border in Queensland. The rains had come down in such torrents there that it became conveniently impossible for the two fugitives to return to civilisation, at least for the moment.

During their stay at Cordillo Downs, Bob seemed to flourish. 'Bob was happy at Cordillo', Ernestine wrote, 'with six thousand square miles of stones, its curious red sand hills and much fierce and obscure beauty'. He even loved the 'dust storms that left the world in a thick white mist with just the pale white sun for company'. Bob's new aim in life was to become a stockman.

When Robert David Hill was finally tracked down, both mother and son claimed to have had no idea that the army authorities were searching for them and that they were listed as fugitives. Bob was made to appear at a police court at Broken Hill on 25 April 1944. He was represented by William C. Beerworth; Leslie Hunkin appeared for the military. The hearing, however, was adjourned until 11 May, when the application for exemption was surprisingly withdrawn. No reason was given, except that Mr Beerworth claimed to have received instructions to withdraw it; he did not state from whom. Perhaps both parties had come to an understanding, or perhaps Ernestine at last gave in. By the end of May, she returned to Adelaide.

On 18 July 1944, she sent a letter to John Curtin, telling him that Bob was in the army and her mental state was such that she must resign from the ABC board. She could not bring a 'clear and confident mind to such a responsible position', she wrote. The prime minister did not directly accept her resignation, but thanked her for her services anyway (she in fact had to resign three times before the board finally let her go). Her efforts to keep her son out of the army had lasted eighteen months and must have had an enormous impact on her mental health. Later she explained that her decision to resign was not only due to her son's predicament but also because 'I thought I could help in the appointment and creative sphere but it was all purely administrative. I was a very small voice in a big departmental wilderness.'

Before becoming an official member of the Citizens Military Force, Bob was stationed for two months at the prisoner-of-war camp in Cowra, 300 kilometres west of Sydney. During this period Ernestine wrote again to Curtin, providing a summary of the nine books she claimed to have in progress and informing him of her erratic state of mind. She asked him again to have her son exempted from the forces and pleaded with him to allow Bob to be stationed at Cordillo Downs as a cattle hand. Curtin promised to present the letter to the minister for the army for his consideration.

On 4 September 1944, a letter to her from the minister of the army shattered all her hopes: the request for a discharge on compassionate grounds could not be granted. Robert

David Hill finally joined the Citizens Military Force at Wayville.

He was relieved of his duties, however, just a few months later. No one knows why, but Bob was suddenly released from the army on psychological grounds and returned to his mother at Cordillo Downs to fulfil his dream of becoming a stockman. It could well have been under the orders of the prime minister himself, but both mother and son always refused to discuss the matter. Ernestine wrote to Mary Durack that 'God must have sent the intervention of a perfect stranger'. There was a certain stigma attached to not having served in some capacity, and in later years Bob seemed remorseful and apologetic about having been discharged.

Although Ernestine had already resigned, her resignation had not been made official and she was scheduled to attend an ABC board meeting in Sydney. The rains had been atrocious that year, however, and she was marooned at Cordillo Downs. She decided to make an urgent call to the Flying Doctor Service. It happened that one of the doctors, John Grieve Woods, and his pilot, a Mr Bowden, were flying from Tibooburra, in the Corner Country of New South Wales, to Innamincka in South Australia, where some patients needed attention. There they would be just 160 kilometres south of Cordillo Downs. They very kindly agreed to refuel at Innamincka and from there proceed to Cordillo, where they would pick her up and treat anyone who needed medical attention. She hoped they would fly her to Broken Hill and she could fly from there to Sydney to attend the meeting. Unfortunately, by the time Dr Woods arrived, she had discovered there was no flight from Broken Hill to Sydney that week. Reasoning that it would be impossible to arrive at the meeting on time, she decided to stay put at Cordillo with Bob.

Although the initial purpose of Dr Woods' trip was no longer necessary, it was not in vain. It had been quite some time since a medical man had visited the district, and patients had been queuing up all afternoon. As soon as he stepped from the plane, the poor man found himself besieged by ailing patients, black and white. While witnessing first hand what it meant for people in these remote areas to have a doctor visit, Ernestine started to contemplate writing a book about the Flying Doctor Service.

Meanwhile, Doubleday, Doran & Company had published *The Great Australian Loneliness* in the United States as the *Australian Frontier*. Ernestine was thrilled at the prospect of being published in America during the war. 'It's a grand thing to be known in America,' she said in an interview, 'to rush my best and most arresting articles about this country on to America to make them conscious of what a loss we'd be. Britain has never realised that.' Ernestine found the large, handsome American edition wonderfully well presented, and was gratified when the *New York Times* and the *Herald Tribune* published flattering reviews. She later forwarded a copy of *Australian Frontier* to the Australian prime minister.

The Americans thought the book would be a great asset for their troops in Australia. It was informative and entertaining, and it would give them an idea of the country and its inhabitants. So American soldiers stationed in Sydney and in other large Australian cities often found a compact version of

Ernestine's book tucked into their kitbag. The armed services edition was a small and handy 21 by 13 centimetre book consisting only of Part One, 'Ports of Sunset', of the original three-part volume.

Despite all the worries she endured during the war years, Ernestine managed to write a rather patriotic book called *Australia: Land of Contrasts*, edited by Sydney Ure Smith and published in 1943 by John Sands in Sydney. The 28-page booklet had 27 colour plates of paintings by notable Australian artists, but it did not sell well.

Leaving Bob at Cordillo Downs, Ernestine returned to the east coast to spend Christmas 1944 with friends and family. 'I am writing a book about the Flying Doctors,' she wrote to Coy in 1945, 'just a very quick one.' Once more she set herself to sorting out the notes and ideas she had gathered, selling them as articles before they became a book.

In March 1945, Bob returned to his mother, disillusioned with the hard work on the cattle station. He had given up on becoming a stockman, he said, finding life in the saddle too harsh and the benefits too unrewarding. Ernestine, by then, had written most of the Flying Doctors story.

She was still working on *The Territory* and now decided that she would need to return to the wide open country to gather more notes. She planned to travel independently this time—she'd had enough of waiting for trains, mailmen and trucks. It was time for Bob and her to take travelling into their own hands.

24

Travels with Bob

While they were living in Adelaide, Ernestine tried to structure Bob's days. Because he was attending neither school nor university, his days were quite empty apart from typing out Ernestine's notes. To her dismay, Bob sometimes disappeared during the day and did not return until the early hours of the morning. She would lie in bed in the darkness, watching the shadows made by passing cars on the ceiling, until she heard his keys jingling in the front door. Her perhaps peculiar solution was to get Bob some driving lessons. It would give him something to do and, as she did not drive herself, she thought it might come in handy for her later on.

In May 1945, the two of them set out for Mount Isa in the Gulf Country of northern Queensland. They intended to buy a vehicle there and then head into the Territory with Bob driving. Mount Isa was at the time a little mining town in an arid landscape. After Darwin was bombed in 1942, Mount Isa's air-raid shelter had been converted into an underground military hospital. This had been a precautionary measure, in case the enemy tried to bomb the area, but as a result a lot of abandoned army equipment was now scattered about the town.

They found a forlorn-looking flat-nosed army truck in the yard of a small car dealer. As soon as Ernestine saw it, she must have understood what the truck would mean—freedom! At last she would not have to sit inside nameless post offices or out on deserted roads for days waiting for a mail truck, train or camel. They would have their own wheels and be able to choose their own itinerary. It was undoubtably a new and wonderful feeling, and they both fell hopelessly in love with the old green rattletrap.

The dealer described it as a great and reliable truck—'an antique, made especially for our troops; you won't find better quality'. But then he was a used-car salesman. Bob tried to give the impression that he knew what was what, looking under the hood and kicking at the tyres to check if they were flat. He did know quite a lot about the insides of cars, planes and ships, but Ernestine still regarded him with wonder as he pranced around the truck.

After Bob had finished his little performance, they came to an agreement. The salesman would double-check the vehicle the same afternoon—inspecting its engine for any defects, topping up its oil and filling its tank with diesel—then they could pick it up and take it for a drive the next day. If they liked it and paid cash, it was theirs. For the first time in all her travels, a feeling of calm crept over Ernestine. She would no longer have to make reservations and plans; they could simply pick up their belongings, throw them into the truck and leave. Both Bob and Ernestine were very pleased with themselves as they left the car yard.

It always surprised Ernestine that people expressed envy of her way of life, thinking that travelling around, free as a bird, must be fantastic. But despite her incurable wanderlust, her life had been anything but free and easy, and she often hated all the travelling. The stress of not knowing where she would sleep at night, wondering if she would be able to find a place to eat, never having a quiet and peaceful spot or a home to come back to—these had had serious consequences for her state of mind and her health over the years. The contradiction in her life was that, every time she tried to settle down, her compulsive need to move on would soon gnaw at her and she would be off again. 'I never seem to have time to settle or belong to anything,' she wrote to Henrietta Drake-Brockman. She looked forward to owning the truck; if the dire need arose, it could even provide a roof over their heads.

The next day it became evident that Bob was anything but a competent driver. Watching him back the truck out of the gates and onto the street during his trial run clearly horrified and terrified the car salesman, who closed his eyes. Manhandled by Bob, the truck appeared to be in great pain, gasping and moaning in agony as it hiccupped its way down the town's main street, turning quite a few heads as it passed. Ernestine must have silently wondered where the money had gone for all those driving lessons and probably concluded that either he'd had an inexperienced teacher or he was an appalling student. It was certainly clear that, in all the weeks he had been taking lessons, he had acquired no great knowledge of driving. After he made a U-turn at the end of the street, his driving did improve a little. When he drew up beside the footpath, he got out of the truck looking quite smug. Ernestine paid the salesman and the vehicle was theirs.

A few hours later, when they had settled on the verandah of a local cafe, sipping coffee and proudly keeping an eye on the truck, a woman approached them. She had overheard them saying they would be heading for the Rankine River and wondered if they would be willing to take a passenger.

Florence Mofflin, who lived in Rankine River with her husband, the local police constable, was in Mount Isa because her son was being treated in the hospital. The little boy, just a little over a year old, had stumbled into the ashes of a fire and seriously burnt his feet. During her son's treatment, Florence had stayed in town to be with him, but now she wanted to get back to Rankine and give her husband a detailed account of the boy's condition. Ernestine agreed to take her, and their passenger boarded the truck with no reservations, even though she had witnessed Bob's driving in the main street.

The truck still didn't run smoothly. It crept along at what seemed to be about sixteen kilometres an hour, but Ernestine didn't know whether this was down to Bob's inexperience. She urged him to go faster, but he turned and shouted furiously, 'All right, Mother!'

Flo, as Mrs Mofflin insisted on being called, remained silent and watched as they arrived at a junction in the road. They were not sure which direction to take. Although Ernestine asked Bob to stop the car, to give them time to decide which way to go, he was deaf to any such suggestion and just chugged off in the direction he preferred.

After a while, a house came into view with quite a few animals in the yard where a woman was pegging out clothes. Bob immediately turned the car into her driveway and headed towards the woman, probably intending to ask her for directions. But it all went horribly wrong when he apparently forgot how to use the brakes.

The poor woman, seeing the car approach, dropped her basket and fled, accompanied by dogs and chooks running every which way. There was a lot of yelling and her husband dashed out of the house screaming at them to stop the car. Bob banged his head as he stuck it out the window, trying to explain to the man and his wife that the car was uncontrollable and to get out of the way.

Bob and the car finally found the driveway again and, without stopping, headed out onto the road, leaving a bewildered couple and some terrified animals behind. Flo and Ernestine went into hysterics, but poor Bob was embarrassed and furious at being laughed at.

At Rankine River, Flo's husband had been informed by radio that they were coming, but it took Bob so long to drive there that, fearing they were lost or there may have been an accident, the constable had sent out a search party. The party found them crawling down the road just a few miles from the house. Bob and Ernestine delivered Mrs Mofflin safely to her worried husband and for their troubles were invited to stay the night. They left the next day.

The Borroloola mailman, whom they met at Avon Downs, finally fixed their truck. He was a whiz with an engine and, together with Bob, ensured it was fit to travel the outback roads. Bob and Ernestine were on the road for a little over six months, travelling across the Barkly Tableland to the Gulf of Carpentaria. They broke down near Nicholson Station one day and had to be rescued by the station hands, but otherwise the truck held up remarkably well.

Travelling over the famous overland road, they were among the first returning pilgrims to visit poor and sorry old Darwin after the war. The town had been scarred and the gaps where houses once stood were painful mementos, especially for those who had known the town before the attack.

Leaving Darwin they made a dash into Arnhem Land. They were camping on Jack McKay's cattle run on the Mainoru River one night when Ernestine awoke to a clicking sound, like a tongue against the roof of a mouth. Bob was in his own tent nearby, so she called out and asked if he had heard anything. He had not and said he wished she hadn't told him. 'Go back to sleep, Mother,' came his irritated reply when she became more insistent.

She was trying to do what he asked when she was suddenly surprised by the sound of three rifle shots cracking through the night. It was too dark to see anything, so she stayed where she was, considering it the safest option to avoid being shot by mistake. The next morning, Jack McKay told them there had been visitors during the night. 'Some blacks roamed around the camp,' he said. 'They meant no harm but I fired my gun, thinking I would let them know I had it, just in case anyone got any ideas.'

Later that day, some of the same Aboriginal people came up to their camp, making the same clicking sounds as they had during the night. They were very friendly, and one of the station hands traded some plugs of tobacco for a spear, which he handed to Ernestine as a souvenir from Arnhem Land. She felt both sorrow and admiration for these people.

They returned via the Murranji Track and Wave Hill Station into Western Australia, then travelled south through the Hamersley Range, taking the old gold road into Cue. It had been a wonderful journey, and Ernestine was certain that the trip through the goldmining centres then on to the coast, along Eighty Mile Beach, would make one of the most magnificent tourist routes in the world.

They had done more camping out than she had ever experienced and she was 'powerful tired', but her notes had been made and the books she planned could now be finished.

25

Henrietta Drake-Brockman

Henrietta Drake-Brockman was by now one of Ernestine Hill's best friends on the west coast. Most of Ernestine's family lived in the eastern states, but her dearest friends lived in Perth or elsewhere in Western Australia. Nearly all of them were writers or artists.

Henrietta and Ernestine were both writers who had spent considerable time in the outback. Henrietta's husband, Geoffrey, was a civil engineer who worked in remote areas of the country, having been appointed commissioner of the newly formed Department of the North West. Both women were particularly interested in history, especially Australian history. Their books and characters were Australia-based, and by the 1940s they shared a publisher, A&R, and were friends of Beatrice Davis, the editor there.

Ernestine was often fazed by Henrietta's stamina. Her friend not only wrote novels and novellas, biographies, children's books and radio scripts but also edited anthologies, raising two children in the process. 'Henrietta is a brick,' she wrote to Beatrice Davis; to Coy she wrote: 'Henrietta is one of the most endearing and dashing people in Australia.'

Ernestine clearly loved this big boisterous woman. She had

only known her complain once. When her children had become ill, Henrietta wrote, 'I am suffering from one of the trials of the outback, [sic] no maid, a husband in the outback and a family with mumps.'

The friendship did seem to outsiders an unlikely one, because their personalities and physical appearances were so very different. Henrietta, a tall, elegant woman with a sense of authority and a penchant for wide-brimmed hats, was in no way similar to the physically petite and unassuming Ernestine. Ernestine was often overwhelmed by a room full of people, whereas Henrietta seemed to thrive on having an audience or being called upon to play a leading role. Although Ernestine possessed an inner toughness, her demeanour was reserved and she always appeared fragile. By the 1940s she was uncomfortable talking to a large audience and she often paid a terrible price for her public speaking, with her nerves unsettled for days before and after.

Henrietta's days were filled with writing; over the years she contributed almost continuously to magazines and newspapers. Writing had always come easily to Ernestine and she could finish a quite complex book in three months, but these days she seemed to be stumbling from one bout of frantic writing to another, smoking almost ceaselessly in the process. Henrietta, as one of the founders of the Fellowship of Australian Writers Western Australia (FAW) and a member of almost every state literary committee, was forever running from one meeting to another.

One afternoon in August 1946, when Ernestine was due to speak to the FAW that evening, Henrietta picked up Bob from Darjeeling, the guesthouse at Roleystone in the outer suburbs of Perth where he and Ernestine were staying at the time. Bob and Henrietta were due to visit the Museum and Art Gallery in the city for an unofficial preview of Elizabeth Durack's new exhibition called 'Time and Tide'. The subject of Durack's watercolours was Broome: her paintings depicted the graceful Aboriginal children and violet-black wet-season thunder clouds, so typical of the pearling town. Her sister, Mary Durack, had written stories that supplemented this artwork.

Ernestine should have been there too, but was feeling unwell and had stayed home and taken a few aspirins at Henrietta's express instruction. Henrietta assumed that a major contributor to Ernestine's illness was being due to speak as the FAW's guest of honour at that evening's 'Corroboree', as they called this annual event.

Bob was turning into a pleasant young man. 'Breezing about in his utility and with many schemes buzzing around in his head,' it was clear he would never be a successful businessman, Henrietta thought. He just wanted to earn enough money to be able to paint. He had a good sense of humour, a keen eye for art and was eloquently charming to women, but over the years Henrietta had observed with concern his relationship with Ernestine becoming fraught and at times even obsessive. Henrietta was the confidante of both Bob and Ernestine, listening patiently as each complained about the other.

The problems with Ernestine's anxiety attacks appeared to be increasing. Henrietta now wondered if her friend would be able to cope with the speech at all. From the start it was a difficult evening, with people constantly walking in and out and talking loudly. Ernestine had dragged herself onto the stage and seemed edgy when it was her turn to perform. She could hardly concentrate on her speech, which was about inspiring and encouraging young writers to explore their country and write about it.

Halfway through her address, she suddenly stopped and became totally dumb. It was horrific and it must have been humiliating. Speaking in public had become a physical and mental ordeal with which she could no longer cope. Mary Durack and Henrietta took over and excused their guest, telling everyone she had been ill all afternoon and thanking her for braving her illness to come and talk to the members. Ernestine excused herself and hurried home.

Bob called Henrietta the next morning, apologising for his mother 'going bush', as he described her disappearance. He said she had been mortified by the whole affair. Ernestine later wrote Henrietta a letter apologising for her part in an evening she described as difficult. 'I realise that the complication was to some extent due to me...but speaking is a physical and mental ordeal that, in a big gathering, I cannot face.'

Along with her mental problems, Ernestine was also suffering from financial worries, so she now left Darjeeling and moved in with her good friends the Smiths. Gordon Smith ran a shirt-manufacturing business with his brother Ronald; he had served on the minesweeper HMAS *Mercedes* out of Darwin during the Second World War and was a good golfer and a keen sailor. He owned a motor cruiser called *Nokomis* and would often sail to Rottnest Island, where the Smiths owned a summer cottage; Ernestine was a guest at times. Eleanor Smith would soon be leaving for Sydney, to try to find a publisher for a children's book she had written. She invited Ernestine to stay at her Perth house for as long as she needed, so she could write her book about the Flying Doctor Service.

Although *My Love Must Wait* had been a tremendous success, Ernestine still suffered from financial problems. By 1948 almost 100,000 copies had been sold; it been adapted for radio and published in both America and Britain. (In 1958, it was published in Germany and it was even suggested there would be a Dutch edition, although this never came about.) Ernestine had always been somewhat surprised by the novel's popularity. More than once she had heard readers describe it as 'too solid'.

It was rumoured that the British publisher Victor Gollancz wanted to acquire the film rights to *My Love Must Wait*, but the celebrated Australian filmmaker Charles Chauvel, accompanied by his wife Elsa, visited Ernestine while she was vacationing in Goulburn, New South Wales, to attempt to make a deal. In May 1946 newspapers reported that Chauvel had paid her an enormous sum—rumoured to be four figures—for the film rights to *My Love Must Wait*. That sort of fee was unheard of in Australia at the time.

Chauvel later had the idea of offering Sir Laurence Olivier the role of Matthew Flinders and was willing to surrender the screen rights if the actor agreed to come on board. Ernestine was very pleased with the choice of Olivier as Flinders: 'Most important,' she said, 'is the association of Australian history with a great English actor like Sir Laurence ... It gives me pleasure to know that responsible people are bringing

Australian history to the notice of an actor like Sir Laurence who plays historical characters with such an admirable approach.'

Chauvel paid her a first instalment of £600 within the first year and another £600 a year later. After that she had no news from either Olivier or Chauvel for four years; then, in 1950, Chauvel let Ernestine know that he was 'no longer interested in the matter'. Without explanation the rights reverted to her on 7 May 1950. She was very disappointed and said she would willingly have agreed to any reasonable proposition by Chauvel so he could recoup the £1200 he had paid her. Her novel never, however, made it to celluloid.

A four-figure sum in 1946 represented a fortune, and her colleagues were all pleased for her, if slightly envious. But regrettably, money never lasted long in Ernestine's world; Henrietta wrote to Beatrice Davis that she was often shocked at how quickly 'mother and son could let any amount of money disappear'. Some of it may have gone in supporting Bob, Henrietta thought. As soon as he became involved in any new art project, he would need money to buy all sorts of expensive materials to aid the production of his masterpieces. More than once Henrietta told him that her typewriter was old and some of the keys were almost completely worn, but nonetheless she managed to write novels on the battered contraption.

It took Ernestine three months of continuous writing to finish her book on John Flynn and his remarkable medical air service, *Flying Doctor Calling*. In this epic, the human aspect predominated—patients, doctors, nurses and wireless operators; she was a master at portraying living people. They were the ones who made the drama and, when Henrietta read the manuscript, she was surprised how vividly her friend had been able to capture the magnificent spirit of the medical staff.

Before Christmas 1946, Ernestine sent the manuscript to Beatrice Davis, but because of rising costs and a shortage of workers, she had to wait almost a year to see *Flying Doctor Calling* in print. The delay may also have had something to do with squabbles that arose between Beatrice and Ernestine over the final editing. Beatrice in the past had often only made minor corrections to Ernestine's work, but in this case she had made quite a few alterations. Ernestine believed she reduced the colour of her prose by insisting on grammatical purity.

Ernestine had stayed in one place for a little more than three months, but she soon announced to Henrietta that she was about to leave for Adelaide and Melbourne, travelling across the Nullarbor Plain. Henrietta had witnessed Ernestine becoming ever more despondent over the previous months and had feared for her mental health. 'I love the work and will never stop,' Ernestine assured Henrietta. 'Living is the strain.' One moment Ernestine would sound in splendid spirits, only to sink again the next.

Longing to return to the wide open spaces herself and secretly jealous of Ernestine's nomadic lifestyle, Henrietta suggested taking Bob's place as the driver for the trip, meeting up with them at Norseman. Bob would then leave them and make his way to Melbourne, where he planned to take a course at the National Gallery of Victoria Art School. Ernestine was delighted by this proposal and so was Bob. It appeared that both mother and son were in dire need of time away from each other.

In April 1947, Henrietta joined Ernestine at Norseman and set out travelling along the new Eyre Highway across the Nullarbor in the flat-nosed army truck. Katharine Susannah Prichard, who joined them at Coolgardie, later wrote that Ernestine 'seems to take...flies and red-backed spiders galore...in her stride. She's a strange otherwhereish creature with big beautiful eyes, a hoarse voice and curious incapacity to argue logically about anything.'

The friends retained endearing memories of their trip. They had fun and laughs, they cried and fretted, they disagreed and agreed, they quarrelled and made up. In the evenings the women would watch in awe as the soft purple Australian twilight disappeared into a star-scattered black night. Henrietta returned to Perth only reluctantly, by plane from Adelaide on 1 May 1947.

26

A dog and a caravan, 1947-48

After her literary road trip, Ernestine set up house for a time in Melbourne, where she and Bob bought a caravan and a dog. Her first dog, Jarrah, had been hit by a car on the Nullarbor a few years earlier, and now Bob had found a very similar dog, a little black-and-white Sealyham terrier, an enthusiastic, jumpy little thing they christened Bill. Ernestine thought it would be nice to have a dog around as company because she was spending long periods alone. Bill did stay with her during Bob's absences, but essentially he became Bob's dog.

Over the past year, she had received some letters from Daisy Bates, who was now staying with the Thompson family at Streaky Bay, on the eastern side of the Great Australian Bight. Daisy was contemplating writing a book of Aboriginal legends especially for children, but she couldn't find a ghost-writer; she asked, in a roundabout way, if Ernestine would be up for the job.

Ernestine had to disappoint her old friend because she was knee-deep in the history of the Territory, with a publisher waiting impatiently. Her mass of notes was slowly turning into a monumental manuscript, and she needed to devote most of her time to this project. To finish it was now her first priority, because it was becoming a burden. She had long carted most of her notes around in a big tin trunk, to keep them safe from ants. All her interviews, newspaper cuttings, draft chapters and everything else that mattered found a place in the trunk; mostly it contained bits and pieces about the Territory.

Daisy was greatly disappointed when Ernestine declined her request, but replied that she would love to see her anyway and suggested they might be able to travel together along the old outback tracks of her past. Ernestine decided that a caravan would be useful for such a trip. Daisy was old and, if she were to travel with her and Bob, she could not sleep in a tent. The caravan would make a comfortable alternative.

Ernestine found postwar conditions in Melbourne terrible, with people queuing up for food and the power failing at random. Every day new boatloads of immigrants would arrive and spill out onto the streets, but with nowhere to go and no work on offer, they became destitute nomads. Often, when Ernestine stayed in one of the larger Australian towns or cities, where the tragedy of everyday life was so openly on display on the streets, she and Bob were more than happy to head for the hills once more. In their old army truck, with the caravan swaying along behind, they rattled over the Princes Highway to Adelaide and beyond.

When Ernestine finally reached Streaky Bay, she was rather taken aback by how old and frail Daisy appeared. She now needed constant care and her short-term memory was failing badly. After talking it over with Bob, Ernestine decided it would not be a good idea to take their old friend along on their journey. They were told that Daisy's welfare was now in the hands of the Department of the Interior and that a relative was living close by. Fearing that such a trip, even with the caravan for overnight accommodation, would be too much of an ordeal for her, they abandoned their plans. Ernestine sent Coy a letter asking her if she could buy some silk for blouses and underwear for her friend: 'She [Daisy] has always been such a queerly difficult woman but wildly and promiscuously generous. The poor dear's clothes are an epic of tatters.' Later Ernestine also arranged for Daisy's allowance from the Commonwealth to be increased to £5 5s a week.

They spent a week with Daisy before they left; each evening Ernestine would sit on Daisy's bed as she talked about her life. Although her short-term memory was failing, the old lady seemed to experience no difficulty in recollecting the past in great and vivid detail. Before Ernestine left, Daisy handed her four manila folders of her notes, plus some of her own versions of the legends from Broome, Bibbulmun, Eucla and Ooldea. Ernestine promised to look at them and try to convert them into a book at some stage. A few days later, they bade her farewell, expecting to catch up with her again soon.

In the meantime, *Flying Doctor Calling* had finally been published in November 1947, having taken almost a year to appear. It sold well from the start, selling out by Christmas, and the reviews were excellent. In her newspaper review, Henrietta Drake-Brockman described the book as an 'epic of the air' and went on to tell how Ernestine Hill in her 'inimitable brilliantly sympathetic manner tells the story of these heroes of the air'.

Some were surprised by its popularity, given its less romanticised depiction of the people involved. Some of the characters she portrayed were downright wretched, caught as they were in a life-or-death struggle on remote properties, hoping the air service would arrive in time to save a baby or a mother or a station hand. A decade after the Depression and a couple of years after the war, readers were apparently ready to recognise the misfortunes and hard work of others.

From Streaky Bay, Bob and Ernestine travelled across the Nullarbor back to Perth. After two years of experiencing the wild and sometimes wide open spaces, she was seriously contemplating settling down in Western Australia. 'I'm now looking for that fable "the right place",' she wrote to Mary Durack then, as an afterthought, 'but a [whole] house is too much for me.' Perth had been her home for years and, after visiting Daisy, she must have realised that she too was getting older and that travelling around the country most of the year might one day become too exhausting.

In May 1948, Ernestine set out for Key Farm, a country guesthouse in Toodyay, Western Australia. She planned to stay there for three or four months, hoping to finish *The Territory*, which was due to A&R before the end of the year.

Having taken Daisy's notes with her to Key Farm, she realised that, because of the state of Daisy's health, it had become more urgent to write that book for her friend. Daisy was declining; if she were to have any chance of seeing her book in print before she passed away, Ernestine would have to make haste. So she started to work simultaneously on both books.

But when she had almost finished her first draft of Daisy's book, a strange note arrived from her friend requesting her to forward all the manuscripts and notes to Daisy's bookseller friend in Adelaide. After spending so much time selecting and rewriting the legends, Ernestine was annoyed, shocked and frustrated that Daisy now insisted on the return of her material. It felt like a slap in the face.

After pleading with Daisy to allow her another few weeks to finish the job, she received a telegram demanding the immediate return of the manila folders she had given her at Streaky Bay. So Ernestine sent them to Adelaide but did not send her own typescript versions. She had worked hard on *The Passing of the Aborigines* and had never received any acknowledgement; she was determined not to let that happen again.

She heard no more about the notes or about the publication of any book but was later informed that the bookseller in Adelaide had been unable to translate Daisy's notes into a book of any kind, finding them too muddled and disorderly.

Bob stayed with Ernestine at Toodyay for a while and she wrote to Mary Durack that 'he totters about all day playing tennis and cricket, running little engines and then starting to paint a car and then he chalks the caravan and baths the dog and goes into town for this and that and gets out all the doings for a water colour and then grieves for so little done'. She complained that her son was easily distracted, restless and had trouble keeping on track. In a letter to Mary Durack's mother, Bess, Ernestine said 'she [herself] is [also] busy all day but I don't know what I do. Mostly I'm confused.'

After some weeks Bob returned to Melbourne, to study at Max Meldrum's art school. Born in Scotland, Meldrum was the founder of an art movement called Australian Tonalism, a representational style of painting, and was also highly praised for his portrait work. Ernestine was not a great lover of his paintings, however, as she always found them somewhat 'misty'. When she confessed this to Bob, he sighed, 'Yes, Mother, but *that*'s the point.'

While Bob was a passionate follower of Meldrum and a dedicated believer in his ideas about art, Ernestine found Meldrum's views prejudiced at times (he had criticised Nora Heysen's 1938 Archibald win, claiming that women could not be expected to paint as well as men), but she was pleased that Bob was pursuing his talent.

Meanwhile *The Territory* was proving a difficult assignment. In time her words formed themselves into chapters, but the book's overall structure constantly shifted about, as though she was trying to build a mountain out of grains of sand. She had never been so insecure about her writing. Fretting that she might be making things too hard for her readers, she posted a few chapters to Beatrice Davis to see what she thought.

The letters that came back from Beatrice could not have been more encouraging. She assured her that what she had written was brilliant and compelling. While she did complain that the chapters were rather randomly organised and she had no idea where they were supposed to go, she said she genuinely enjoyed reading them. Her much-needed praise drove Ernestine on, and every day she sat drafting and redrafting chapters until way past midnight.

The book was by no means finished when, a few weeks before Christmas, Ernestine received a letter from an old friend. Iris Reid, who had worked with her on the Launceston *Examiner*, invited her to spend New Year at her summer cottage in Tasmania. It was some twenty years since Ernestine had last seen Iris and visited Tasmania.

Iris Reid had a cottage at Deviot, in the Tamar Valley; her husband had died the year before and she had invited several friends to the cottage for the holidays as it was her first Christmas without him and she thought she might need company. So Ernestine left for Tasmania near the end of December 1948, looking forward to meeting up with a few old friends.

After having roamed the mainland for some twenty years, she found it delightful to set foot on the little green heart-shaped island again. Launceston, she found, had not changed a great deal, although the population had doubled since 1930 and 'up in the foothills weatherboard houses now peeked through the trees and new suburbs were springing up'. Compared to the mainland, Tasmania appeared fresh and smart. The incredibly white sheep, the lines of fruit trees and the shimmering lakes refreshed her wonderful memories of the past. The island was too small for her to stay long, but for a few weeks she savoured its beauty.

27

The Territory

While Ernestine was on the east coast in 1949, Bob was busy pedalling his way along the south-western coast of Australia. His bicycle had a small trailer attached to it, in which he carried his art supplies and Bill, the dog. This must have pleased the little Sealyham no end, Ernestine wrote to Mary Durack, as she was sure that 'Bill thought himself a magnificent dog and always had a smug smile beaming from his snout. Being pedalled around the coast by his human servant, Bill must have considered himself ruler of doggie kingdom.' She jokingly hoped he would not become too arrogant by the time he returned to her.

In Sydney, Ernestine received a postcard from Bob in Pemberton in Western Australia, telling her that he was planning to hold an exhibition in Perth and was having a wonderful time. Keeping the dust and flies off his canvases was a pain, he wrote, but he was very pleased with the oils and watercolours he had done of the timber country. She missed him, even missed their little squabbles, but she was thankful that he was finally developing his own talent. He did not intend to join her in Sydney, as he was aiming to meander his way along the coast.

Along with the postcard, he sent a clipping of a small article that had appeared in the *Albany Advertiser*. In it, Bob Hill was portrayed as an interesting, quiet and unassuming visitor who impressed all who met him. Ernestine was delighted that her son was so well received. The article was accompanied by a photograph of Bob on his bicycle with Bill 'smiling' behind him in the trailer. There were words about the little dog in the article as well, of course. Bill had come in for his fair share of attention.

Beatrice Davis at A&R had now edited her manuscript for *The Territory* but was concerned about its length: she thought it would need to sell for twice the average book price if she did not cut it down. It was a monster, no doubt, and Ernestine promised to shorten it to an acceptable length. Beatrice invited her to her house at Folly Point, Cammeray, so they could identify cuts together, but despite being elated to have been asked, Ernestine never did get there.

She had never been happy in Sydney and now it was wearing her down; she found it ever more difficult to cope with city life. At that time Sydney was a city where coal strikes turned into blackouts, where the weather had been horrible and gas shortages left hotels and houses cold and dismal. The daily postwar noise and tumult—of buildings being torn down and rebuilt, of streets being tarred—became too much for her to bear. She also thought that Sydney was being rapidly Americanised. After a cold and miserable July, she wrote to Beatrice that: 'Sydney had become a horror and I couldn't stay.'

After some more royalties came in from A&R, Ernestine set off first for Narrabeen and then to Mornington, on the eastern side of Port Phillip Bay. There she thought she would be able to finish the necessary corrections for *The Territory*. As soon as she was on the move, her nerves appeared to settle. It was as if travelling took her mind off any daily inconveniences; although it tired her almost as much as staying in the city.

At Mornington, Ernestine worked hard and put in long hours but was still unable to finish the book. It had become ever more difficult for her to organise her thoughts and her notes. Her writing wasn't flowing as it had in the past. She now wrote only in fits and starts, and felt distracted and disheartened. With Christmas approaching, she contemplated touring the north-west again, but the heat was just too oppressive.

A lighter moment came when word reached her that the most horrific of trains ever to set its carriages on a track, the appalling Leaping Lena, was on its last wheels. The end of one of Australia's most notorious trains was imminent, but Ernestine did not feel saddened by its demise. The ageing Lena, now 73 years old, had become an icon and institution over the years. For all that time, her timetable and whistle had served as calendar and clock for the locals. Never would Ernestine forget the atrocious jolting and jumping downhill runs and snail-like upward rides. The passengers said that as soon as Lena smelled beer, she would automatically pick up speed. 'She was regarded as a social lass—always willing to pause to pick up a bushman and sometimes stopping to let passengers boil a billy or take a swim on a hot day.' She had her vices and her virtues, and although she would no doubt be missed by some, Ernestine would not be among them. She was pleased to see the old rattletrap go.

Almost a year later, in September 1950, Ernestine received news that Michael Patrick Durack had died at the age of 85. It was twenty years since she had met him in the distant border country of the Kimberley. As a result of this meeting, she had become a frequent visitor to the Duracks' Perth flat overlooking the Swan River, enjoying the company of MPD's wife, Bess, and becoming good friends with their daughters—not only Mary but also Elizabeth, who was a gifted artist and had been approached by A&R to do the drawings for *The Territory*.

Ernestine thought of MPD as a pioneer who had conquered and colonised a large part of the country. To the Aboriginal people he probably brought destruction to their land, but Ernestine may have thought he brought 'civilisation'. Ernestine seemed to have compassion and understanding for the plight of Indigenous people—describing an Aboriginal girl, she once wrote: 'Civilisation has clothed her in shameful rags that hide her swift and slender grace'—but she also embraced the romantic notion of the pioneering pastoralist.

Durack was the last of his kind, Ernestine wrote. She had known him as a keen historian and a lover of nature, but he had been a reluctant station owner and, to his family's dismay, just before his death had sold off most of his properties. His sons and daughters now had only their memories of the stations and gorges, from the Leopold Ranges to the desert, and from the Ord to the Victoria River. His daughters especially had developed a deep love of the country and had been shocked by the sale of the land they thought they were to inherit and that had inspired their books and paintings. Of course, by now the glory of the waterhole was fading and the great droving days were disappearing. It was 1950 and times were changing rapidly; Kimberley beef was now being transported by air for the first time in history.

For most of the rest of that year, Ernestine fussed and worried about writing and money, and could not concentrate fully on putting anything to paper. Bob, after living for a time in the Melbourne suburb of Brighton, had recently moved back to Perth, where he found a pleasant little house—'two stone rooms and very picturesque'—near the Swan River. Both Ernestine and Bob became regular visitors at Mary Durack's home.

Mary was married, but her husband was rarely home and she always welcomed company. She had first met Horace (Horrie) Clive Miller in 1934, while she was working at Ivanhoe Station. 'He dropped in from the sky,' she would later say. Horrie was Mary's senior by twenty years; he had been married before and already had a child. Her friends and family by no means considered him a suitable husband, and MPD was seriously opposed to their marriage. Somewhat against her seemingly easygoing nature, Mary made up her mind; in 1938 she left Perth and, with no family present, married Horrie in Melbourne.

Miller had been trained as a fighter pilot and fought in France during the First World War. In 1928 he founded MacRobertson Miller Airlines and became its managing director, establishing commercial air services in Western Australia and also supporting the Flying Doctor Service. Financially, Mary was well cared for; when the couple returned to Perth, they had a large house built.

Although a very outgoing woman with many friends, Mary often felt lonely in Perth. With Horrie away in Broome for most of the year, she was left alone in a huge house. She often entertained, but once everyone had gone the house felt deserted. She wanted children and soon filled the emptiness with five of them. It became apparent, however, that Horrie was not a dedicated father. He was often away, tending to his business in Broome, and as a loner did not understand or sympathise with Mary's need for company.

Ernestine would often be seen going 'down for a little party with Mary's bunnies', as she referred to the Miller children. She greatly admired Mary, of whom she wrote to her mother, Bess Durack: 'She manages five babies, a beautiful home and being a genius all in one.'

New ideas for books kept bubbling up, but so far only in Ernestine's mind. Finally, in the mid-1950s, she let A&R know that a new novel, a love story, was taking shape. Her new hero would in no way resemble Matthew Flinders, the stout and courageous sea captain. The leading character in the new book would be an albino Aboriginal man. It was no more than a rough thought at that moment—a pencil outline and still very vague—but the idea excited and enthused her. Sometimes the magnitude of the work she wanted to finish before her death would alarm and unsettle her for days. For the first time in her life, she wrote to Beatrice, she realised 'that time was running out'.

Her notes needed sorting. Her trunk was beginning to look very much like Daisy Bates' jumble of random papers. Files and folders were packed with disorderly notes and ideas; her notebook scribblings had become a chaotic heap. No one else—well, maybe only Bob—would be able to arrange and organise the treasure trove of writings in her trunk. Nearly all of it had been jotted down in her own version of Pitman shorthand, and she realised it would be quite a task for anyone to turn it into anything readable once she was gone.

By October 1950 she had almost finished *The Territory*, with just two chapters to complete and some revising to do. She was in Broome again, where the streets smelt of frangipani, exotic herbs and shellfish. Her home was the Continental, then considered one of the finest bungalow hotels in the tropics.

One thing about living in hotels is it rids you of housework—no ironing, no dishwashing and no making the beds. So for the moment Ernestine indulged in this luxury, hoping her strength and inspiration would rush back—and they did. Initially intending just a short stay, she kept postponing her departure and did not return to Perth for a couple of months.

The little pearling town had been attacked during the war but had recovered wonderfully. Roaming around Broome, you would hardly have known that the Japanese had raided it. The Japanese strikes had clearly focused on the Allied planes sitting on the airstrip and the flying boats in the bay rather than the town itself, which had survived the war remarkably unscathed. At low tide in Roebuck Bay, however, you could see the many sunken flying boats that had been destroyed during the Japanese raid of March 1942. At such times they would come to the surface like eerie carcasses. Parts of the aeroplanes destroyed on the airport runway had been salvaged by Broome residents and in some instances been given an unusual new life as garden ornaments.

Ernestine would watch as luggers came in at high tide and their crews tied them to the jetty. She found it fascinating to see how, as the tide receded, the boats became marooned. The luggers made an extraordinary sight as they sat on the sand like helpless beached whales, waiting for the tide to return hours later to save them. As the tide rushed back into the bay, the stranded luggers seemed to rise with effortless ease until they were once again bobbing happily on those amazing peacock blue tropical waters.

Writing suddenly became easy again and, taking advantage of the unexpected inspiration, Ernestine started to send revised chapter after chapter to Beatrice Davis in Sydney. The book was still of mammoth size, which caused concern, even for Ernestine, but when A&R said it was too big and asked her to consider publishing it in two volumes, she stood her ground. She had always envisaged the book as one whole story, and she refused outright to compromise her original concept. After all, as she argued rather grandiosely, one would never think of asking Michelangelo to cut his *David* in half because of its size. She found the suggestion ludicrous and her answer was, and remained, no.

Bob at this time was living in Perth doing odd jobs for Mary Durack, building cabins in her garden and doing repairs around the house. He had also been hired by the council to sound the midday gun, which involved aiming a cannon across the city and lighting a wick every day at one o'clock.

He complained in a letter to his mother about recurrent headaches. Ernestine missed her son, but she was pleased he was seeing Mary regularly. Both of them lived pretty much alone; with Horrie living in Broome and Bob not involved with anyone, it was a nice thought that they had each other to talk to and confide in.

It was no secret that Ernestine thought highly of Mary, but she was slightly apprehensive that Bob might be imposing himself too much on her. 'I hope you are not being a trouble to Mary,' she wrote, reminding him that Mary also had a writing career and five small children to look after. Mary often had to write at night while her children were asleep, and Ernestine knew her friend well enough to know that she was much too nice to ask Bob to leave if she was busy or he were intruding in any way.

In April 1951, Ernestine was still in Broome 'working like a woodpecker at her typewriter', as she put it to Beatrice Davis. To her relief, and to some extent her sorrow—finishing a book always felt a little like saying goodbye to a dear friend—she sent the final chapters of *The Territory* to Beatrice during the first week of May.

The Territory was finally published in November 1951, the problem with its length partially solved by reducing the type size. Ernestine let A&R know that she was very pleased with the final result: 'Betty's [Elizabeth Durack's] bright and interesting pics have brightened up *The Territory* enormously.'

All her doubts and struggles—her fretting about its readability, her grinding away for endless years and the battle she had fought to have it published the way she envisaged—were worth it in the end. From the start, the book garnered rave reviews, and the English edition, which appeared almost simultaneously, was received with equally flattering praise. Partly due to Elizabeth Durack's wonderful artwork, the book looked magnificent.

Reviewers and readers alike believed the story would go on to become a classic, and the first 15,000 copies sold swiftly. Ernestine had now written five books, two of them best-sellers, and her brain was brimming with new ideas. She openly wondered why so very few new young writers aspired to write bush narratives these days. Some critics believed that outback writing had become unfashionable, but the success of *The Territory* showed that descriptive, historical landscape writing could still reach a significant readership even in the 1950s.

With her notes stowed away in her trunk—a small fortune in words waiting to be turned into books—Ernestine believed that the future held the promise of many more books to come. Despite her recent struggles, she had no doubt what-soever that she would write them.

28

Eleanor Smith, 1952

Ernestine and Eleanor Smith had been friends for a few years, and Ernestine had encouraged Eleanor to take up writing. In the 1940s Eleanor self-published a book of poetry called *Carinya* and in 1953 she wrote *Isle of Girls*, a history of Rottnest Island. In it Eleanor wrote: 'grateful thanks and acknowledgments are due to Mrs Ernestine Hill, who encouraged me to write it'.

In May 1952 Bob, Ernestine and Eleanor set out on a trip through the goldmining area of Western Australia. Ernestine wanted to collect notes for new books and Eleanor loved the idea of travelling around. Eleanor owned a small black-and-white Holden at the time, which came in handy because Bob and Ernestine no longer had transport. So the three of them embarked on a trip that would take them through Geraldton, Northampton, Yalgoo, Mount Magnet and Meekatharra.

Ernestine always appeared very busy during her trips, jotting down notes in endless notebooks. Now she was collecting material about the rise and decline of the WA goldfields. Eleanor had been slightly apprehensive about accommodation, expecting to have to sleep in a 'lean-to', but Ernestine had bought some little Gair-brand tents she saw advertised in *Walkabout* magazine. They used them when nothing else was available.

Although Ernestine had been known during her earlier years of travelling to have roughed it, during this trip they stayed in comfortable hotels when they were available. Bob was now a confirmed vegan, eating only cereals, salads and fruits, so dining out became a bit of a problem.

Ernestine's money came primarily from her royalties, and Eleanor had the idea that most of it disappeared as fast as it came in. She also had the idea that the amounts of money being forwarded to Ernestine were relatively small and she suspected that her friend had constant financial worries. Ernestine had asked A&R for an advance to fund the trip just before she left.

The goldfields they were visiting were vanishing rapidly. Many towns that had once flourished were now no more than collapsed brick and stone along a railway line. Broad highways led to nothing and ended in narrow bald patches in the mulga. Rows of rusty constructions, reminiscent of the Eiffel Tower, poked up from the many derelict mines; in the once-bustling settlements, dogs now slept undisturbed in the middle of the streets, roused only by the few people who stoutly persevered.

Now that the towns were vanishing, their elderly residents themselves were being forced to move but, having nowhere to go, they lingered in the settlements where no shops, no post offices and no other people remained. There was still gold to be found, they told the travellers, but no people left to dig for it.

During their visit to the goldfields they met many elderly prospectors trying to live on a small pension, often crippled with arthritis, almost blind or suffering from lung and heart disease. They needed medical care but refused help for fear it would mean an institutionalised life in Perth. They were even afraid to cash in their gold finds, as this would rob them of the only reliable income they had, their government pension. Some of them died uncared for on the fields they had once worked.

Ernestine pleaded for a home for these pioneers—not in an institution in Perth, but in a safe haven on the land they had once excavated. She proposed an old RAAF building at Boulder, near Kalgoorlie, that had once been used to house migrants but now stood empty. The article she wrote for the *West Australian* was a passionate plea to take note.

When the party stopped at Lawlers, now a ghost town near Leinster, two startled emus fled from its streets. No one was left in the small mining town except a Mr and Mrs Hahn, who tended their six empty hotels. The doors and windows of the remaining houses in the town stood wide open, as if everyone had only just left.

They pushed westwards and arrived at Sandstone, where the population consisted of 75 men, women, children and kangaroo dogs (it has since rocketed to a population of 105). The people there told them the last man in Lennonville had died a year before. At Wiluna they passed through a 'dead' town that had once boasted 8000 people. Their trip through the gold country made them reluctant witnesses to the end of an era.

Ernestine always carried her little fold-up Zeiss Ica with her, but she was becoming ever more interested in colour photography, so she bought a new camera in Perth before they left—an Exakta Varex. With so many years' experience she had become quite adept in the art of taking a photo and was thrilled whenever she found a shop that could develop a roll of colour film. If the result was good, she would take out the batch of photos to admire them again and again, always aware of imperfections and always eager to learn. She bought photography magazines whenever she could. The shiny Kodak prints did not impress her; she preferred Agfa: 'Matt prints and nicer sizes.' She could talk endlessly about cameras and photography. 'It's the only real recreation I have, a fascinating little recreation for my old age.'

One afternoon Eleanor brought up the subject of Ernestine's old friend Daisy Bates, who had died the previous year. When Eleanor read the obituaries in the press at the time, she noted that none of them were accompanied by Ernestine's by-line. Nor had Ernestine attended the funeral held in Adelaide. Ernestine explained that she had not been invited and had been busy writing the last chapters of *The Territory* when Daisy passed away, so she had only heard the news of her death months later. Eleanor thought that an anonymous article, published in the Adelaide *Advertiser* on 20 April 1951, could have been by Ernestine, as its style was similar to her writing, but Ernestine remained adamant that she had not written an obituary. Eleanor wondered whether Ernestine still felt betrayed by her friend, who had so abruptly ordered her to return her notes and folders, but Ernestine did not want to discuss the matter further.

After the trip, Eleanor returned to her Perth home and Ernestine to Darjeeling, where she set to work, writing about the goldfields as well as more articles for the *West Australian*.

During the 1950s, a new generation of writers was starting to look towards European and American authors as a source of inspiration. Ernestine, always a keen supporter of young writers, encouraged them to find publishing opportunities, especially now that there were ten or twelve new Australian book publishers and periodicals. This new generation, she emphasised in interviews, should conceive and build their own traditions for Australian writing. She had succeeded without setting a foot abroad; there was no reason why they shouldn't.

In an article for the *West Australian*, she asked young Australian authors to step forward and write about their country, to fight, as she had done, for the cause of homegrown literature. Where are they, she wondered aloud. Were they afraid to try?

Mary Durack, commenting on this article, assured Ernestine that there were so many people trying to get published that a 'statistician might even be able to prove that the rejected manuscripts of aspiring Australian writers, placed end to end, would equal the length of the Transcontinental railway'. The problem, Mary believed, had more to do with craft than subject matter. Only writers who had exceptional luck or were gifted with extraordinary talent could succeed in getting a book published these days.

Unlike Ernestine, Mary believed that more writers would spring from the universities, from journalism and literary groups than from the wide and wholesome bush; most writers would live in the cities, because Australians, by and large, are an urban people. Ernestine disagreed, holding tenaciously to the notion that writers who truly loved their country had an obligation to travel through it and write about it. If she could do it, they could do it. Ernestine's call to young writers created a great deal of discussion, in literary circles and beyond, about writing in Australia. Critics either called her naive and unrealistic or lauded her as a truly patriotic author.

Admirably and gallantly, Bob came to her rescue. Writing to the *West Australian*, he attempted to explain what his mother had meant: 'My mother, in urging young writers to write, did not exhort either hard labour or success, but, for them, joy in the use of those resources of which they are conscious ... True creation is a labour that does not fatigue. Beyond duties to State, family and self, the writer tenders a gift to thought and beauty. With a full heart he has made his "gesture before eternity".'

It was a strangely written piece that confused everyone who read it. Although Bob was generally outgoing and an entertaining talker, he did not have his mother's great literary talent. He was known to write occasionally, and had written two poems for the *Winthrop Review*, a student magazine, in 1954—one called 'Thoroughfare' and the other 'Sonnet on a Flying Saucer'—but Bob never pursued a writing career.

A year later, Ernestine sent a letter to Eleanor from Mackay. She had left for the east coast a few months earlier, hoping to find enough peace of mind and tranquillity to write. To her dismay, she could not return to Darjeeling because it was for sale and its owners were moving out. The weatherboard cottage had once been a home for servicemen injured in the First World War and had later served as a home for stolen children. Eva (who was known to one and all as Wirlie) and Bill Moore had bought the house in 1945 and turned it into a guesthouse. They had both become Ernestine's friends over the years.

Bob was still living in his little house on the Swan River near Mary Durack's, Ernestine told Eleanor. He was still painting and taking up odd jobs here and there. Her letter made no mention of her goldfields book, which Ernestine had seemed so passionate about during their trip, taking photographs and scribbling in her notebooks. She claimed to be gathering material for a new novel, and she let Eleanor know she was also seeking information for overseas publications.

Eleanor later read a newspaper interview in which Ernestine said she was now thinking of writing a book about Queensland, a state she believed would play a big part in her future work. As it turned out, the letter she received from Mackay was one of the last Ernestine sent her.

29

Art and age

By 1954, Ernestine was back in Western Australia, living in Cottesloe near Henrietta Drake-Brockman, in an apartment on Broome Street looking out to the sea. Her health wasn't good—as a result of her incessant smoking over the years, she had developed emphysema—but she hoped Perth's sea air and its fiery and glamorous sunsets would do her good, although she predictably continued to smoke. Bob insisted that she change her diet—some days she would eat only biscuits and drink tea—but she couldn't be bothered. She would always have fresh fruit on the table, just in case he decided to drop by.

Bob came from his house on the Swan to visit her almost every day. To Ernestine he seemed to have three homes: his own, hers and Mary's. Bob was still constantly visiting Mary, and Ernestine was pleased they got on so well.

Although very busy with all her own goings-on, Henrietta visited Ernestine every now and then. One day she came by to tell her that William Dobell was considering painting a portrait of Dame Mary Gilmore. Gilmore, a well-known writer and left-wing activist, had known Ernestine since she was very young and had always looked upon her as 'a special child'. According to Henrietta, Mary thought it would be a good idea for Dobell to paint Ernestine's portrait as well and was thinking of asking him. She had heard that Bob had been in Dobell's art classes some years earlier.

Henrietta already knew the answer she would get. As someone who didn't even like to have her photo taken, Ernestine had no desire to sit for a portrait. In 1943, when Dobell's controversial painting of his fellow artist Joshua Smith had won the Archibald Prize, Ernestine was appalled. 'That year I thought art had gone truly mad,' she said. 'I could not believe that the caricature he had created had won the prize.' Aside from Ernestine's opinion of Dobell's art she was still highly self-conscious: 'I am skinny and sinister and resemble a scarecrow. I have no desire to see it come to life in paint. Heaven forbid.'

Henrietta laughed her big booming laugh as she went to leave, telling Ernestine she should smoke less and eat more. Ernestine bid her goodbye with a flourish of her cigarette and let her friend shut the door behind her with her usual bang.

A few days later an up-and-coming female reporter knocked on Ernestine's door. She was asking older celebrities what they would do today if they were 21 again. Ernestine told her she would roll up her swag and travel Australia. The young woman looked a little disappointed and said she would have liked a more surprising answer. When Ernestine suggested that she should go out and discover the country and write about her experiences, the reporter, who was on her way out, wrinkled her nose in distaste. Ernestine felt disheartened by her lack of appreciation for her own country and wondered what on earth could be more inspiring than telling stories about it.

When she got to the street, the young woman looked back towards the older and waved enthusiastically. From the window of her flat, Ernestine watched her step into her car. She mused that if this girl went travelling the outback, she would never have to wait for a ride for five days, as she herself had done. A trace of melancholy shadowed this thought. Not for the first time in her life, she felt old and lit another cigarette.

The 1954 annual meeting of the Western Australian FAW was held at the organisation's headquarters, Tom Collins House, in Swanbourne. Ernestine attended somewhat reluctantly, as even when she wasn't speaking she found these events a strain, but in the end it was a very pleasurable evening. Henrietta was there, of course, as a founder, as were Keith Ewers, Paul Hasluck, and Elizabeth and Mary Durack. Hasluck, who had been an MP since 1949, made a speech in which he toasted the FAW and emphasised Australia's need for sociological writers—people who could write about Australia's origins and development, and the structure of its society. He also hoped that a great Australian play would one day be written.

Mary, Betty, Henrietta and Ernestine shared a few drinks and laughs as usual. Bob was spending more and more time at Mary's house, and Mary talked about Bob with much admiration and affection. Ernestine hoped her son was helping out in some way.

Although almost 30, Bob had not settled into any occupation. His paintings did not earn him any money, and

Ernestine often worried about him and his future. She was pleased when, a few weeks earlier, Bob announced that he had found a job at the Perth Observatory. According to Ernestine it was 'right up his particular little street'. He was a clerical offsider to astronomer Hyman Spigl and appeared to be extremely happy with the position—so much so that he had taken out a three-year lease on his house, planning to stay in Perth for quite some time. Ernestine hoped he had finally found peace of mind.

Later that year, Ernestine's health improved a little and she took the train to Adelaide and then Melbourne to visit Coy, moving on to Sydney to discuss an advance for her new book. When the train stopped at Cook, in the middle of the Nullarbor Plain, a railway official told her that a memorial cairn to Daisy Bates was being unveiled at Ooldea that very day. The train would not arrive in time for Ernestine to attend the official unveiling, but she hoped to see the monument when the train stopped at Ooldea around midnight. The train drew into the station at 12.30 a.m.; Ernestine inspected the cairn, illuminated by a brilliant moon.

A straggling young journalist who had reported on the unveiling was waiting at the station and couldn't believe her luck when she stumbled upon Ernestine Hill, who agreed to do a little interview. Ernestine told the reporter how she had met Daisy in 1932 and that she herself was still an incorrigible wanderer. She was now on a journey gathering material for her next book.

When the young woman asked if a new book might come out soon, Ernestine told her that a book on the Birdsville Track was nearly completed, one on the history of Broome was finished, and she was preparing something on great Australian women, which would include material on Daisy Bates.

The truth was that although Ernestine had been writing she had been unable to finish anything. Whenever she tried to go through her notes, she kept losing track of the story she was supposed to be working on. There were so many stories waiting to be told, and whenever a particular subject became momentarily perplexing, she would simply jump to another one. Throughout 1954, due to ill health and anxiety, she had been unable to finish anything, not even an article—mainly because she was never satisfied with the result. If she did manage to finish anything, she would discard it after re-reading. 'I am working away,' she wrote to Bob, 'but I'm always disgusted with what I write.' She was now heading for Melbourne, hoping to find at Coy's place the serenity she needed to write what she considered could become her greatest work.

Her story about the albino Aboriginal man called Johnnie Wise-Cap was still no more than an outline, but she had decided to discuss the idea with A&R. Money problems forced her to ask her publisher for an advance on the story, so she hoped to convince them that she could write it in three months. All it needed was some serious writing time, she claimed—it was all there in her head, just waiting to surface.

A&R did sympathise and came through with an advance, so she stayed in Sydney, intending to do nothing but write for the next three months. In fact, A&R was confident enough to print a flyer announcing a new Ernestine Hill novel for September 1955, describing it as: 'The story of an aboriginal, named Johnnie Wise-Cap, that begins in Broome in the '80s with the recruiting of aborigines for pearl diving and the discovery of a native so pale that he might be a white man. The story is dramatic and swiftly moving, telling the tale of the impact of civilisation on this native, who is taken to Melbourne, where a German scientist undertakes his training in white men's ways.' Ernestine had convinced herself that she would produce the story by her own deadline and was confident she wouldn't disappoint her publishers.

30

Mary Durack

Mary Durack was M.P. Durack's eldest daughter. Argyle Downs Station had been her home during the first years of her life but as soon as Elizabeth was born, the family had moved to Perth.

Like Ernestine, Mary started writing poems at an early age, and by the time she was ten her poems were appearing in the *Western Mail*. The family was well known in Perth's elite circles, and events in their lives often produced newspaper copy. At sixteen the young Mary decided to leave school and take up her father's offer to live up north for a while. She stayed for a year, returned to Perth, then in 1934 left Perth again, this time accompanied by Elizabeth. The girls helped in the kitchen at Argyle Downs.

Both Mary and Elizabeth loved life on the station, and Elizabeth in particular had a great affection for the Aboriginal children. The two sisters often took time to spoil and fuss over the girls, plaiting their hair and clothing them in dresses they made themselves.

But it was at Ivanhoe Station that the two found independence. When the station was in dire need of a cook, they didn't think twice and decided to move there. As the station had no manager at the time, they stayed and ran it independently for eighteen months. In later years, whenever they looked back on their months at Ivanhoe, they regarded it as the happiest time of their lives. It was there that Mary started writing seriously and Elizabeth took up art in a committed way.

From early childhood, becoming a writer had been Mary's great ambition, and even with five small children running around and a huge circle of friends, she managed to produce newspaper articles and to write books. Her first children's book, *Chunuma*, was published in 1936; it was followed by *Son of Djaro* and *The Way of the Whirlwind*. All three were illustrated by her sister. From 1937 Mary was on the staff of the *West Australian*, writing specifically for country women and children under the by-line 'Virgilia'. Her experience in the north led her to voice her sentiments in her newspaper articles on the treatment of Indigenous Australians by whites. She pointed out that, if nothing else, Western Australians had 'certain obligations to their land's original inhabitants'.

Ernestine and Mary became very good friends, not least because they lived in the same city. Perth at that time was still small enough that people could meet everyone they knew simply by strolling down the street. Ernestine and Mary shared a love of the north and of writing; they admired each other. Bob was fourteen when Mary married Horrie Miller and, according to Ernestine, her son had thought that her marrying an aviator was the best thing that could have happened. 'Now you will always be able to fly for free,' he had said to Mary.

By 1954 Mary and Horrie were living separate lives. Horrie had a permanent house in Broome and Mary had the house in Perth. Mary visited her husband during the school holidays but when Horrie visited the family in Perth, he largely wanted to be left alone and did not involve himself much in family matters.

Like his mother, Bob adored Mary, and it pained him to see her unhappy. His company seemed to cheer her up and their daily rendezvous were the highlight of his days. Bob loved the kids and they seemed to like him. Mary's eldest daughter, Patsy, recalled how Bob once had suggested stealing a bus. She could not remember why 'but Bob was always dreaming up schemes. He was handsome and a lot of fun'.

During 1954, Mary had been in the process of writing a book called *Keep Him My Country*, a novel about a white man's love for a black girl, but at the beginning of January 1955 it became evident that she was pregnant again. The pregnancy was difficult and, as the months passed, she felt ever more ill. Having heard about Mary's difficult time, Ernestine wrote a sympathetic letter from Pomeroy, near Goulburn, New South Wales, telling her 'not to worry about anything'. She advised Mary to read poetry or to take a good book in hand, to help her take her mind off things, and think of the time ahead after the baby was born: 'Children are such wonders.'

The birth of John Christopher Miller in May 1955 left Mary exhausted, both physically and emotionally. Her knowledge that the baby was not Horrie's might have had something to do with the stress of the past months. John was Robert Hill's child.

Bob, in an attempt to save Mary from a lonely life without a husband and eager to take up the role of father to her children, asked her to elope with him. But the pragmatic Mary decided that eloping with her six children into the arms of a man of little means would not be a good idea. She decided the child would be raised as a Miller, as one of the fold, and Bob would have to get out of her life. It is uncertain what precisely the deal was but Ernestine and Bob kept their distance from that point on.

In August that year Mary's book *Keep Him My Country* was published to mixed reviews. Some were very flattering, but some classified the book as more traveller's guide than novel. According to one critic, it was too neatly structured and depicted characters so real that they became boring. That Mary had been able to write the book at all could be considered a small miracle.

When Ernestine learnt what had happened in Perth, she found it extremely difficult to concentrate on her writing. She was stupefied by the unfolding events. After all that had happened it was impossible to return to Perth. She was living in Sydney's Potts Point, near Kings Cross, an area very familiar to her, having lived in the Eastern Suburbs when Bob was a teenager. She could still recall, when he found the plane rudder on the beach at Point Piper, what a proud and excited schoolboy he had been.

Until then, 1955 had been a reasonably good year for Ernestine. 'Things are looking up from the point of view of copy,' she wrote to Bob. 'I made the [*Sydney Morning*] *Herald* leader page, five pounds for five hundred words. They have also accepted work for the Saturday pages.' Relieved that some money was coming in, she wrote, 'After paying next week's board I wouldn't have had any money left.'

A&R was now pressing her for chapters of 'Johnnie Wise-Cap' but, after the news of Mary and Bob's son, Ernestine was in no state of mind to deliver. Beatrice Davis and A&R, who of course had no knowledge of recent events, let Ernestine know that they were displeased she had not kept up her end of the bargain. In an attempt to find a solution, Ernestine suggested to Beatrice that she write her story in 1000-word sections, as she had been used to doing when she wrote radio drama. She hoped she might find this less daunting. Her letter to Beatrice revealed that she was becoming ever more depressed and confused. Her accommodation was also becoming too expensive: 'I am leaving for the north due to money problems. I cannot afford to stay where I am now living,' she wrote.

Ernestine insisted that A&R send her more money, telling them the *Sydney Morning Herald* had offered her £2000 for a novel. She also furnished a long list of books she was working on, but it was all a ruse. To Bob she revealed that, although she was working hard, she made little progress. 'I work, work and work but don't get any further,' she wrote.

The need to move was always there. 'Why stay in a room when the map is so grand?' The story of Johnnie Wise-Cap wandered off to a forlorn corner of her mind, where it stayed for a long, long time. 'I can see it clear in my mind but then I bog down.'

Every now and then she would dust it down and work on it again, but the story never fully materialised.

31

Bob

Bob was in a mess. He had fled Perth in a state of depression and sorrow. He had no money and neither did his mother, but, most pressingly of all, he had nowhere to go. Not wanting to stay in Perth, he had cancelled the lease on his house after resigning from his job at the observatory. Eventually doing what he and his mother had always done, he rolled up his swag and left. He roamed about for a while and finally returned to the east coast, ending up in Mackay, where he took a job as a postman.

His state of mind was by now so turbulent that the letters he had been hired to deliver ended up in the wrong mailboxes and he was sacked soon after. Desperate for money, he took a job as a porter at Mackay railway station. His seventeen-year-old predecessor had resigned after being attacked by youths while on the job.

Because of the attack, the police were especially alert and a few weeks later took in an astonished Bob as a suspect. According to the police, 'He looked really wild and we thought he might have had something to do with the molestation.' Once they realised that the man they had picked up was, in fact, the new station porter, and had had nothing to do with violence of any kind, they let him go. The station-master, however, thought the bristly and rough-looking Bob would not fare well with the travellers he was supposed to be helping, so he was sacked again.

The turning point came when Bob found a job near Cairns with the Queensland Water Resources Department. He was required to camp in a national park, and the work was very light. Even better, it was all expenses paid. The tranquillity of the environment had a relaxing effect on him; on his travels with his mother he had become accustomed to the quiet life of the outback, so he calmed down for a while.

Ernestine's letters to him were full of her anxiety and concern. She assured him that she loved him, and told him to look after himself and keep her informed about how he was getting on. Bob's replies reveal his irritation with his mother. In the solitude of the park he had time to reflect, and in one letter he blamed her for what he called 'this madness'. 'It was she who preached [the] "romance" of the Australian Outback to me when a prudent influence would have been objective.' Although he visited her in Cooktown on her 61st birthday, he described the visit in a letter as 'a nightmare'.

Still feeling very unstable and realising he needed some kind of professional help, he visited the psychiatrist at Townsville Hospital. The doctor, finding little wrong with him, assured Bob he was certainly not mad and prescribed Ritalin (the drug now used to treat hyperactivity in children) to calm him. This seemed to put Bob in a much better frame of mind. He convinced himself that his mental problems came from having led such a sheltered and spoilt life, and not being taught to cope with the realities of life. All that travelling around had made life seem unreal, like a dream, he thought.

Bob later described the letters he and Ernestine wrote to each other during these years as 'an alternating wail'. But despite their strained relationship, he did not abandon his mother and, whenever he could, would send her a few pounds. Ernestine would always write a letter of thanks back to him, but he stayed away for two years.

A&R by now had given up hope of Ernestine ever producing another book, but she herself still very much aimed to write the book she had promised them. All she needed, she believed, were peace, quiet and a suitable location where she would not feel panic-stricken and pressured. Beatrice Davis sent her encouraging letters, but it became ever more difficult for Ernestine to settle into any kind of productive working mode. She wrote a miserable letter to her editor saying: 'my life is getting out of hand in a chronic grief and guilt induced inability to manage things...' But she would also write an occasional optimistic letter, saying, 'I have been working away at the typewriter.' At A&R they assumed that all this frenetic typing might have become a way for Ernestine to cope with her mental instability. The sound of the typewriter had always been part of her life, and the noise of the keys rhythmically striking the ribbon probably had a soothing effect on her now.

She may have had nothing to show for all her diligence because she was simply retyping notes that had already been typed out, then retyping them again. She seldom went out anymore and was obviously becoming lonely. While staying in Mosman, on Sydney Harbour, she described New Year's Eve 1958 as: 'quiet. All dressed up and nowhere to go.'

In February 1958 she was granted a Commonwealth Literary Fund pension of £7 a week for life. It was just a pound a day to survive on, but it was better than nothing. Remembering her efforts ten years earlier, when she had requested an increase in Daisy Bates' government pension, she now realised how meagre Daisy's income had been. The poor thing had survived on next to nothing and Ernestine really could not imagine how she had ever made ends meet. No wonder she had so easily returned to her life in a tent after that brief taste of opulence during her stay in Adelaide. As soon as her finances dried up, she had once again lived on almost nothing. Now that her own working life was fading and her money problems were becoming ever more acute, Ernestine wondered how the old lady had coped.

After she had been granted the pension, Ernestine received word from A&R that the German contract for the publishing rights to *My Love Must Wait* had come through. Just a week later an amount of £75 was forwarded to her bank account. It would pay the rent for the coming months and she would at least be able to buy food and cigarettes as well. Over the years she continually asked A&R for money and they would often send advances on her royalties; although the sums were small she managed to keep herself afloat.

Bob, in the meantime, had a new lady in his life: Jacqueline (Jacky) Scrivener, a pretty, shy 25-year-old, with blue eyes and a gentle voice, dressed in blue jeans. Ernestine, pleased that Bob had found a serious girlfriend, described Jacky as 'a good and earnest little girl'. Shortly after they met, Bob and Jacky bought a vintage car, a 1929 DeSoto;

they were both fond of sketching and travelling, so they drove around the Burdekin shire, painting the landscape and making vague plans for the future. Bob was in his thirties; although he was still restless, he did have thoughts of settling down.

Ernestine moved to Thursday Island. She had always loved the island and its inhabitants, and felt ever more estranged from the country Australia was becoming: 'Australia has changed before our eyes. Neon lights and swimming pools everywhere.' On the island she often missed what she called 'that gracious life of sweet sophistications', but when she heard 'the drunks singing down stairs', she reminisced later, 'I wouldn't have missed it though for the world.'

Ernestine sometimes had trouble remembering where she left things, for which she blamed 'the drooks'. 'My mother's people were Irish and she knew all the Irish fairy tales and she always blamed the "drooks", mischievous little people who skip off with things,' she wrote to Wirlie Moore.

On Thursday Island Ernestine suffered a serious accident that might have been due to her forgetfulness. Her arm was badly burnt, and she was admitted to the hospital confused and malnourished. Bob rushed up to see his mother; by the time he arrived, she was looking very frail.

The hospital staff had given Ernestine her own room. They told Bob she insisted on having her typewriter with her and she had been typing away, burnt arm and all, and the constant noise of her fingers hammering on the keys had disturbed the other patients. Bob, wondering what he would do with his mother after she was discharged from the hospital, turned to Beatrice Davis for advice.

His mother was in hospital, very confused, very thin and very ill, he wrote; he wondered if, after she was discharged, he should find a place for her in Sydney and if Beatrice could help in any way. Beatrice was surprised that Bob asked her for help; although she did sympathise, she had no intention of looking for a house for Ernestine. She also advised against letting Ernestine return to Sydney: 'Living in Sydney has never made her happy.'

Ernestine was still on Thursday Island when, in April 1961, Australian Consolidated Press, owned by Frank Packer, bought *The Bulletin*. She declared that 'Archibald would moan in his grave'.

Things got worse for her when Frank Packer sent an open letter to A&R's shareholders, presenting himself as a nominee for the board of directors. Australian Consolidated Press was prepared to buy 50 per cent or more of A&R's shares at more than market value so the company might have a substantial representation on the board. Ernestine was appalled: 'I don't want to be connected to the new management in any way,' she wrote to Bob, 'and the only thing I can see is to press for outright sale of all book publication rights.'

Ernestine moved back to Townsville and decided to offer A&R all her copyrights, hoping this would give her enough money to buy a house and at the same time rid her of any connection to the Packers. A&R refused and wrote a concerned letter stressing that this would leave her without any income at all, apart from her Commonwealth Literary Fund pension, in the future. Beatrice Davis, having no knowledge of Ernestine's strained relationship with the Packers, took the opportunity to inquire how her 'Johnnie Wise-Cap' book was progressing, subtly letting her know that by now everyone at A&R doubted it would ever be completed.

Ernestine was furious that her offer had been refused. Wondering how to deal with the Packer takeover, she seriously considered simply leaving A&R. Things took a turn for the better when Packer's attempted takeover was stymied by a share-splitting deal arranged by Colin Roderick, who had been nominated to the board of A&R by those opposed to Australian Consolidated Press. Facing such substantial opposition, Packer backed off, but he still owned a significant proportion of the shares. He was in the United States and threatened to sell the shares to an American company; he gave A&R the first opportunity to buy them, but at a very high cost.

A&R's managing director, George Ferguson (a grandson of its co-founder George Robertson), sought help from the British. In order to keep the Americans from invading what they saw as their turf, a group of British publishers decided to buy the Packer shares. They paid well and Frank made a handsome profit. The British promised to sell their shares back to someone friendly to the A&R board sometime in the future. Many, including Ernestine, let out a sigh of relief. In 1962 she wrote to Bill and Wirlie Moore: 'I have had some trouble with my publisher A&R but of course I won't leave them.'

Amid all this drama, however, she was dealt another profound blow.

32

Disasters and grandchildren

Coy Bateson passed away in 1962 at the age of only 59. Ernestine's grief was long and heartfelt; for a time it caused her pen to dry up almost completely. Although the two cousins had had their fallings-out in the past—'Most family arguments were very Irish,' Ernestine wrote to Henrietta Drake-Brockman, 'with explosive and harsh and hard truths'—the two women had been very close. After Ernestine's stepsister Ray left and apparently was never heard of again, Coy became the closest thing Ernestine had to a sister.

Her mental state and money problems, along with her emphysema, were by now causing fear and concern, not only to herself but also to those who cared about her. The general public thought she had retired, because the name Ernestine Hill had not been on a new book cover or any newspaper articles for years.

But by 1963 Ernestine had managed to overcome her grief and was feeling much better than she had done for some time. She wrote to Wirlie Moore: 'I really feel as if I am having my second wind.' Writing came easily, she wrote, and at last she seemed to be able to cope again. If it had not been for all the other worries—her turbulent relationship with her publisher, her money problems and ill health—she was sure she would, in time, have been able to write many books. Over the years, Ernestine never doubted her own capacity to produce another book.

For her friends and her publisher, the details of Ernestine's life had by now become increasingly vague, and her constant moving about and incapacity to produce another book were sometimes subjects for gossip. She was also becoming ever more defensive about her lack of productivity and could react vehemently to anything she saw as an act of betrayal. After visiting Sydney that year, she heard rumours about a letter allegedly written by Beatrice Davis to Henrietta Drake-Brockman saying that Ernestine 'had visited Sydney incognito', and wondering if she 'was still drinking'. Ernestine reacted to this 'betrayal' with a furious letter to Beatrice, in which she wrote that she had never travelled 'incognito' and that she was hurt by the very mention of the word. On the use of alcohol she wrote: 'There is no question of alcohol neurosis in my case, for often I do not have a drink for many months.'

She went back to Townsville in a state of fretful depression, but returned to Sydney to live when a reprint of *Flying Doctor Calling* provided her with a little supplementary income. As was always the case, however, Sydney did not fulfil any of her needs. The city was changing and Ernestine had trouble adjusting to the new times: 'It's amazing for me to find city people staring away at their TV screens—idle minded people watching their lives away in the New Space Age with so much wonder of their own about them.'

By 1962, Bob and Jacky had married and were living in Adelaide, where Jacky's family lived. When they ran out of money they would pick grapes in Mildura or do odd jobs here and there, although Bob eventually managed to find a job as an art teacher at the South Australian School of Art. Bob's life with Jacky appeared to have provided him with some stability, and even Ernestine recognised the improvement, writing to Wirlie Moore of the couple, 'They are busy with bright doings in a small way, with a little car for the beaches.'

Although he had not really kept in touch with Mary Durack, Bob did write to her once in a while. His letters were mostly accounts of what he was doing and his plans for the future with Jacky, but some letters were passionate outpourings of his beliefs. In his letters he would casually ask how 'Johnnie' was doing. He had certainly not forgotten about his son, but he kept his distance, possibly according to their agreement. As a result, father and son did not meet until after Mary had died.

In 1965 Bob rang his mother to tell her she would soon be a grandmother. This time, for Ernestine, there was reason to rejoice when in January 1966 Bob and Jacky's son Luke was born—they called him Lui. From the outside all seemed well, but Bob and Jacky's marriage slowly disintegrated. What problems they had is not clear, although Jacky seems to have been involved in some kind of religious movement and Bob appears to have gone along with it for a while, acting as a devout Christian: 'He wears a cross and makes sure I can see it,' Ernestine told Coy as early as 1961.

In 1967 Jacky left Bob, taking Lui with her. Ernestine, upset by the news, packed her bags and left for Adelaide. She had sent word ahead but Bob, upset and miserable, mixed up the date and left his mother standing at the station for hours. Ernestine eventually hailed a taxi. She decided to stay in Adelaide. Her health was deteriorating and it would be easier for both mother and son to cope with the situation together.

Jacky unexpectedly appeared on their doorstep just a few months later. When she had left, she was already pregnant with her second child; now she decided to give it another go. With Jacky back and another baby on the way, Ernestine moved out and went to live at Toorak Gardens, close to the centre of Adelaide.

Thinking of ways to enhance his income, Bob came across a little printing press and bought it. Ernestine was very enthusiastic, and saw numerous business possibilities. Her book *Australia: Land of Contrasts* had been printed by John Sands, one of the first companies in Australia to print Christmas and New Year cards. Ernestine imagined a little artistic studio where her photographs could be turned into postcards and then printed. 'The photos could earn us hundreds a year,' she told Bob, 'if only we were a bit business-like about it.'

To get the business underway, Ernestine sat down seriously and began to type out a story that had been at the bottom of one of her tin trunks for more than thirty years. *Paul Johns' Statement about Lasseter, as Told to Ernestine Hill* was published in 1968 in a limited edition of 100 copies. Bob named his little publishing company Scrivener Press, after his wife, Jacqueline Scrivener, and she provided the artwork for the booklet.

Although the 'book' 'was only fourteen pages long, Ernestine had finally proved to herself that she could still write. The fire was still there. Not wanting to lose the momentum, she wrote to Beatrice Davis, telling her she intended to write a biography of Daisy Bates and asking if A&R would be interested. Although the publisher had just contracted Elizabeth Salter to write a biography of Bates, they let Ernestine know they were interested anyway. After the Johnnie Wise-Cap debacle they probably doubted Ernestine would be able to produce. They might also have thought that, if she did, Ernestine would be able to write the better book, having been one of Daisy Bates' close friends.

Bob and Jacky's second child, Celeste, was born in 1968. Ernestine loved her grandchildren and wrote about them fondly in her letters. To Bill Moore she wrote: 'Celeste is a big child, much like Bob, with big pop-eyes for a wonderful new world.'

By now the couple's home was becoming too small to accommodate their growing family, but their financial means were still slim and the printing business wasn't really going anywhere. Bob came up with a scheme of having his mother move in with them and combining their incomes in order to rent a bigger house for his family. Jacky half-heartedly agreed and the family moved to a nice roomy house in Elizabeth South with a garden for the children.

It was Ernestine who almost immediately started to grumble about the set-up. She complained about not having enough room to sort out her notes and work without being disturbed by two little children. Bob was dismayed, because in his mind the two incomes had created the possibility of a fairly happy and comfortable existence. Ernestine, however, remained adamant.

She was coughing continually and became exceedingly cranky, quarrelling with Bob about food, smoking and the children. Given his own inability to do anything about the situation, he turned to A&R in 1969, asking them outright if they would consider lending him $2000 as a deposit on a larger house that could accommodate the whole family, to be bought in the publishing company's name if they did not accept his guarantee to repay the loan quickly. A&R refused; Beatrice Davis did not think that purchasing a house for one of its writers was the company's responsibility. So Bob did not press the matter further.

In their quest for more space, the family eventually found a much larger house in the outer suburb of Crafers, where Ernestine would have more room, but they only lived there for a short while. Shortly after they moved in, the landlord decided to reoccupy the building and so they were forced to move again.

By now Bob had lost not only the roof over his head but also his job. The South Australian School of Art was cutting costs and had dismissed him. Not knowing what to do and fed up with his accommodation problems, he bought a Bedford truck, packed up the family and headed for Maroochydore on Queensland's Sunshine Coast, actually ending up in nearby Buderim. Ernestine came along; she told the Moores that she found living in Adelaide too cold anyway.

A picturesque little town perched on the Buderim Mountains, overlooking the coast and the ocean beyond, Buderim was the home of Jacky's aunt, Stella Herbert. She lived there alone in a comfortable little house and told Bob and Jacky that Ernestine was welcome to stay with her if she liked. The house was just an eight-minute drive from the beach and was set in beautiful surroundings. Red cedars, eucalypts and silky oaks reached for the sky, as if competing with each other in height and splendour. The air there had a magnificent smell of native pollen from rainforest and bushland. Bob was more than pleased to leave his mother with Stella, while Ernestine hoped that living in a quiet house with the fresh mountain air to breathe would help her feel better. By now her emphysema was so bad that she was practically living on bottled oxygen.

The peaceful surroundings and the tranquillity of the small town made it possible for Ernestine to start writing again. She knew she did not have much longer to live, and she felt the need to finally explain just how much she had been involved in writing Daisy Bates' book *The Passing of the Aborigines*, making it clear that, although Daisy had delivered the material, she, Ernestine, had written the copy. But first and foremost Ernestine wanted her biography to be a memoir of and a tribute to her old friend. Having already written some 7000 words when she had contacted A&R about the book, she now took what she had already written in hand and settled down to peck away at the keys of her typewriter once again.

From the start, writing the book was no easy task. During most of the writing, Ernestine was in and out of hospital and was constantly battling ill health. She fretted about her notes and the manuscript, and what would become of them once she was gone. It was quite surprising, therefore, that when an unexpected visitor appeared on her doorstep one afternoon, she felt well enough to talk to him and invite him in.

The caller was one of Buderim's residents, Sam Sydney Fullbrook, an acclaimed artist. Visiting Brisbane one day, he had stopped at the bookshop of Louise Campbell, Coy and Charles Bateson's daughter, and she told him that her mother's cousin, Ernestine Hill, was living in Buderim and he should look her up.

Fullbrook, often described as the last of the 'bushman painters', was a big-framed man, and his down-to-earth language contrasted completely with his delicate and poetic work. After an inner-city Sydney childhood, he had left home at fourteen and worked in forestry and farming. He volunteered for the army when he was eighteen and served in the Middle East and New Guinea. When he returned to Australia, he studied at Victoria's National Gallery School of Art as part of the returned servicemen's education scheme. He knew he liked to draw, but to that point he had never learnt anything about painting. The very talented student soon became a renowned artist. Between 1948 and 1971 he exhibited everywhere, from Melbourne's Australian Galleries to the Raymond Burr Galleries in California.

Sam showed up at Ernestine's house uninvited that morning but he had that rough outback feel about him and she felt comfortable in his presence. They chatted about the west, where Ernestine had spent so much of her time, and she told him she was working hard on a book about Daisy Bates and had almost finished the first draft. Sam, thinking that Ernestine would be a marvellous subject if she would agree to sit for him, asked her to his studio for afternoon tea.

The self-conscious Ernestine never regarded herself as picture-worthy. Given she had refused to sit for any artist before, it is somewhat of a mystery that she agreed to do so now for this rugged, somewhat crabby man, but sit she did. With some encouragement from Bob, she decided to throw off her inhibitions and finally let someone immortalise her in oils.

The portrait Sam Fullbrook produced of the elderly Ernestine Hill became very popular. He entered it in the 1970 Archibald Prize but did not win. Some critics found this extraordinary, because they thought his portrait by far the best of that year's entries. The ever self-conscious Ernestine, however, hated the portrait. Her hair was too black, her face too pale, her eyes crossed and her lips a raging red spiky smear. 'It's horrible,' she moaned to Bob. 'It's like a rag doll out in the rain or an old harpy actress putting on make-up in the dark.' Sam remained unfazed by her words.

It was not the first time, nor the last, that one of his subjects was disappointed with his work. Many years later, his portrait of the former governor-general Sir John Kerr was rejected by the committee that had commissioned it to hang in Parliament House because they considered it a caricature. Sam Fullbrook was an artist who painted his own version of the truth, and his portrait of Ernestine Hill as a graceful elderly woman, though lauded by many, apparently hit a tender spot with its subject.

By now word had spread that Ernestine was writing again, and that her new book would be about Daisy Bates' life. During the early months of 1971, Robert Helpmann, the world-renowned dancer and choreographer, approached her to inquire about the rights to the Bates story. He wanted a film project for his friend Katharine Hepburn and had envisaged her in the role of Daisy.

Meanwhile, Jacky had left Bob again, this time for good, it seemed. Had all this not been going on and had her health not been so terrible, Ernestine would have been very pleased with Helpmann's offer, but as things stood she was feeling ever more frail and poorly. Felled by emphysema, heart problems and family difficulties, she now struggled to finish her book.

Achieving almost the impossible, she sent the completed manuscript to A&R at the beginning of 1972. Its title was *Kabbarli: A personal memoir of Daisy Bates.* She must have known it would be the last book she would ever write.

The lady in the blue dress

As the girl turned the corner, she saw an old lady sitting on a bench at the bus stop. It was quite peculiar to see someone sitting on that bench, because the bus route had been cancelled the previous year. There was also something strange about the old lady, the girl thought, but she couldn't put her finger on it. It might have been the incredibly bright blue dress she was wearing, dotted with yellow, or maybe it was the strange dash of ruby-red lipstick that marked her mouth. Something was definitely off.

The girl noticed that the lady kept peering down the road every now and then, and wondered if she was waiting for the bus. As she approached the sharp-featured figure, the girl said: 'It's not coming.'

One eyebrow raised itself into a question mark as the lady's eyes turned to her, peering from beneath a straight black fringe. She had that old weather-beaten, wrinkled look of someone who had been out in the sun for most of her life; her dark hair, with a hint of grey peeking from the scalp, was razor-cut just below her ears.

'The bus isn't coming,' the girl repeated, with the impatient sigh of the young talking to the old. The lady looked down the street again, as if she expected the bus to show up any minute and prove the haughty girl wrong. The lady tapped her nails on the lid of a huge tin trunk standing on the footpath next to her, then draped her arm over it protectively, as though it were a pet.

'The route was cancelled a year ago, you know,' the girl pressed. 'So it won't come.'

The lady looked at the girl as if she had only just now noticed her. 'Oh, it will come,' she said in a strange raspy voice that was almost a whisper. 'It will come in the end. It always does.'

The girl's ponytail twitched in a jerky dance as she shook her head. 'It won't.'

'Patience,' the lady said. 'It's a matter of patience.'

This was one stubborn old lady, the girl thought. 'It's been *cancelled*,' she insisted.

Her derogatory tone went unnoticed as the lady replied, 'They do that sometimes—cancel a route. But if you have patience, transport will show up sooner or later. I know, because I have waited for buses, trains, mailmen and camels for so many years of my life. Sometimes you have to wait a day, sometimes a week, and in one instance I had to wait almost a month for a boat to come and get me off an island.'

The girl laid one hand flat on top of her head and pulled down the corners of her mouth with the other in a gesture of resignation. She made a long appraisal of the lady, thinking how strangely thin she looked and wondering how this frail, aged woman could have carried the large trunk standing by her side.

'Look, I could call you a taxi,' she suggested.

'I was a writer, you know,' the lady said, changing the subject as she opened her purse and took out a cigarette and a lighter. Lighting up, she inhaled and then sent the smoke circling back from her lungs into the air in misty curls. 'My name is Ernestine Hill.' The lady looked up into the girl's eyes, searching for a sign of recognition.

The girl shrugged her shoulders and looked down the street.

'I used to be very famous back in the thirties and forties,' she said, her eyes becoming distant. 'But then you wouldn't know, would you? Being so young.'

As she dragged on her cigarette, a sharp cough suddenly exploded from her lungs together with the smoke. When the coughing continued, the girl feared that the ancient lady might die right there on the bench.

'Are you all right?' The girl's concern was sincere.

'Well, I've undoubtedly been better. Where was I? A writer,' she repeated, knuckling the tin trunk with the back of her fist.

'What did you write about?'

The lady circled the air with the hand in which she held her cigarette. 'The outback. This country, Australia.'

'Did you make it up?'

'No, I didn't make it up. All the stories were out there waiting to be found. One day I rolled up my swag and left the city to discover my country.'

'Did your husband go too?'

The answer came as a cough or a laugh, it was hard to tell. 'Goodness, no. I didn't have a husband. Went out on my own and had the most wonderful time and met the most thrilling people. I wrote about it all for the newspapers. No one knew much about Australia back then.'

The girl's interest and attention started to wane as she gazed down the street, not hearing what the lady said but wondering what course of action she should take. The old lady wasn't her responsibility, she decided; she looked at her watch and started to say something when the lady promptly resumed her story.

'Some people say I was a romantic, good at portraying a rosy version of the truth.' The lady looked sadly down at the trunk. 'I guess I did forget to put the drunks in.'

The girl's sudden burst of laughter cut through the street's silence like a train whistle through the outback desert. 'I bet there were plenty of those out there,' she chortled.

'Yes. I didn't mention them. My articles were mostly about the good, wholehearted people. Looking back, it was the romantic version of what was out there. And I always wrote about others, never about myself. An artist's legacy should be his or her work, not her life. So I rubbed myself out, I'm afraid.'

The girl sighed again and tried to look as if she had to be somewhere else sometime soon.

The lady stroked the lid of the trunk. 'This holds my notes,' she said, looking up at the girl. 'My stories, all of them.' Looking into the distance, she added, 'A country's history is stored in this trunk, my life's work.'

The girl's eyes expanded as she realised the significance of this statement. 'That's why you need such a big trunk—because you have to store your life in it. I wouldn't need such a big one, not just yet. Maybe later, when I've lived a lot.' She thought about this for a moment and then asked, 'Why is it metal and not leather? Wouldn't that make it less heavy to carry around?'

'The ants, dear. They eat everything, especially the big white ones. At Borroloola marauding ants ate a whole library once. There were thousands of books there, and now they are all gone. Such a pity how indifferent we have been with regard to our history. Don't worry—I learnt how to keep my notes safe. Daisy Bates taught me— she kept her notes in tin trunks.'

The girl's eyes lit up as she recognised this name. 'I know her. That's the lady who lived in a tent. My mum always says she'll "pull a Daisy Bates" on us when we annoy her. She threatens to leave us to go live in a tent. Reckons the peace and quiet would be wonderful.'

'Yes, the peace and quiet. I might just roll up my swag and head out into the country,' the lady said.

She looked so terribly worn and thin that the girl thought she wouldn't even be able to walk to the end of the street. 'The bus won't come . . . ever,' she reminded the strange lady as she watched her light another cigarette.

'No, the bus won't come. But the train will. I've sent them a telegram. They know I'm here.'

The girl looked up in disbelief, suspecting the poor old thing must be suffering from some form of dementia. 'They terminated the route last year and there hasn't been a bus since then. And there has certainly never been a train line passing down this street.'

The lady smiled a distant smile and looked away.

'I have to go,' the girl said, realising the hopelessness of trying to convince the old lady. She was as stubborn as they come and there was nothing she could do for her.

So the girl said goodbye and walked off down the street. As she neared the corner she turned to look back at the old lady one more time. The heat of the day shimmered as it engulfed the woman in the blue dress. The girl saw how the smudge of blood-red lipstick formed a smile as the aged woman raised a paper-thin hand to wave. In the heat she appeared to be floating just above the bench; the yellowy orange dots, strewn across the blue dress like daisies, danced in the vibrating air.

The girl wiped her eyes to give her clearer vision. And when she looked back again this time, she saw what appeared to be a train stopping in front of the bus stop. It was all very hazy though, because smoke rose from its giant pistons and blurred the picture. As its doors swung open and then shut, Ernestine Hill, the trunk and the train suddenly vanished.

Once again the Trans-Australian was taking Ernestine out of town and along the tens of thousands of miles of sand between Kalgoorlie and Port Augusta, taking her further and further into the harsh country she had learnt to love. To the place where no one knew who you were and no one cared, where you could reinvent yourself if need be. She travelled once again through dust storms; she became bogged in salt lakes. She travelled on until she finally stumbled into the tropical north, where from November until April the wet reigned and where old rumours of gold dust, pearls and gems were whispered down every street. She was travelling once again to the north-west, where 'women are as rare as roses and old men sit in the firelight never noticing that something is missing'.

It was way out beyond Bamboo Creek where she finally lay down to rest. Just under a tree.

Epilogue

Ernestine Hill died in St Andrew's Hospital, Brisbane, on 21 August 1972 and was buried at Mount Gravatt Cemetery, 'Just under a tree', as was her wish. Her belongings at the time of her death amounted to no more than her Olivetti typewriter and a camera, along with ordinary household goods worth about $100.

Her executor, Charles Bateson, found no substantial new material among her documents and papers. Although there were multiple copies of the existing chapters, the long-awaited Johnnie Wise-Cap story consisted of only six completed chapters. Over the years, Ernestine had written endless notes on Aboriginal folklore, the characters in the story and the structure of the book, along with a synopsis of the characters and the typed draft chapters, but most of the material was written in her own version of shorthand.

The Fryer Library at the University of Queensland holds some 3000 photographs taken by Ernestine Hill.

After his mother's death and the break-up of his marriage, Robert Hill went to live with his second cousin, Louise Campbell, who was Coy and Charles Bateson's daughter. Robert Clyde Packer never acknowledged him as his son.

Robert Hill had three children: his eldest, John Miller, from his relationship with writer and historian Mary Durack; and Luke and Celeste from his marriage to Jacqueline Scrivener. John Miller is a well-known designer and jeweller and lives in Western Australia. He found out about 'the great secret' later in life after his mother died in 1994. Father and son first got together when John was already in his forties. Miller describes his biological father as 'a very talented but not very business-minded artist, with a bit of a gambling problem'.

In later years Bob Hill became 'obsessive about the considerable Packer legacy and sent DNA in the form of hair and fingernails to Kerry Packer on several occasions'. No answer or acknowledgement ever came from the Packer family. According to John Miller, 'Bob would waste all his earnings at the Crown Casino that was owned by Kerry Packer . . . Bob was always putting himself down and apologising for his lack of success in life. But he was a generally charming, intelligent and well-read man with many good quotations and a great sense of humour.'

Robert Hill died of cancer in 2003.

Louise Campbell describes Ernestine Hill as 'quite a fretful person, frequently highly possessive of what she regarded as her "province" of writing. She was well-read and highly responsive to literature but held academics in despise [*sic*] and failed terribly to see the world to come.'

Ernestine Hill did not live to see her final work, *Kabbarli: A personal memoir of Daisy Bates*, in print. She died before its publication in 1973.

Author's note

About 25 years after Ernestine Hill visited Alice Springs in 1933, my father bought her celebrated book *The Great Australian Loneliness*. He had come to Australia from the Netherlands during the early 1950s, hoping to escape the miserable aftermath of the Second World War and the scars it had left all over Europe. Like most immigrants he hoped his children would have a better and more promising future than postwar Europe could offer.

My father's hopes were simple: he wanted nothing more than to fit in and to raise his children as Australians. Eventually, like so many other migrants, he found a job, but he soon discovered that his poor English stood in the way of bettering himself. Hoping to jack up his language skills, he bought *The Great Australian Loneliness* at Griffiths Book Store in Geelong. His reasons for choosing this particular book were simple: 'It had Australia in its title and there were pictures in it.'

For a while the book just sat on our dining room table. Sometimes I would come in after school and find my father, who was a shift worker, studying the photographs inside. There were photos of Aboriginal people, strange-looking trees, and a graveyard with tombstones inscribed with what looked like Chinese or Japanese characters. The photos looked nothing like the Australia we were living in. They looked like they had been taken in another world.

Our small suburb of Norlane, sitting on the fringes of Geelong, harboured no Aboriginal people, baobab trees or crocodiles. The country where we lived was mostly flat and featureless. The most exciting thing about Norlane was the You Yangs, a small group of hills rising abruptly from the plain of dry, rock-strewn pastures. I had no idea at the time that it was Matthew Flinders who had first charted the You Yangs, nor that Ernestine Hill had written her only novel about him.

A month or so after *The Great Australian Loneliness* showed up on our dining room table, my father unexpectedly started reading it . . . aloud. Every evening he would read a few pages to me as a bedtime story. I was about seven years old at the time and attended Norlane State School, where my native Dutch was gradually being replaced by a fluent and unmistakable Australian drawl. My father was so impressed by the way I communicated with my Australian friends that he appointed me to correct his pronunciation, a task I undertook with vigour and a high sense of responsibility.

For a long time we had no understanding of the book and its contents. The stories in it were just words that needed to be pronounced correctly. On the cover it said that the tales provided the reader with 'a picturesque account of the outback', but I had no idea what an 'outback' was and neither did my father. When buying the book he had thought it was about gardens, because our Australian next-door neighbour said our own very Dutch flower garden was 'out back'.

One strange thing about the book was that its cover showed a man sitting on a camel. We wondered about this because we associated camels with Middle Eastern countries and not with Australia. The book had first been published in the 1930s, so we assumed Australia must have looked very different then compared to the 1960s we were living in. As you can see, we actually knew very little about our new homeland.

We often debated correct Australian pronunciations— whether 'harbour' should be pronounced 'harbah', or whether to say 'goodonya' rather than 'good on you'. Once in a while my father's newly acquired vocabulary, drawn from the pages of *The Great Australian Loneliness*, would turn heads or produce strange looks. After a violent downpour, my father told our next-door neighbour that 'those knock-'em-down rains' had ruined his strawberries. After taking a Heinz can down from a shelf at the grocery store one day, he proudly asked me to read the 'jam tin yabber' on the wrapper, looking around to see if there was an audience nodding their heads in approval of these typical Australianisms.

After a time, my father received his long-awaited promotion and Ernestine Hill's book gradually resumed its place on the dining room table, where it would sometimes be picked up. The reading aloud had stopped and, since I could read quite well by then, my attention had turned from *Loneliness* to *The Wind in the Willows*.

In later years, *The Great Australian Loneliness* became one of those nomads that found safe refuge in my book cabinet.

I had always been intrigued by the photo of Ernestine Hill on the back jacket flap of my edition. I often wondered who this woman could be, but most people knew very little about her.

This account of her life has come from many sources, including her own newspaper articles, letters to friends and family and two very rare interviews she gave to a young and upcoming journalist called Joan Pilgrim about her travels through Australia. I have tried to imagine what her life was like by following her paper trail.

Some parts of my narrative are romanticised versions of the truth, because there is no one left to provide an actual account. They are my own version of what could have happened. Most of the text, however, is based on the known facts.

Notes

To avoid repetition, Ernestine Hill has been abbreviated to EH throughout.

Prologue: Alice Springs, 1933

The prologue is my own imagined account, based on John Antill Pockley's Journal: *Flight of Ducks*, an online documentary developed by Simon Pockley in 1995. It revolves around the 1933 journal of Simon's father, John Antill Pockley: www.duckdigital. net/FOD/

xi   '...ascertain [how they] were able...': 'Doctors to study Aborigines', *The Advertiser* (Adelaide, SA), 4 January 1933, p. 8.

xi   'paint the "dead heart"': Ria Murch, *Arthur Murch: An artist's life 1902–1989*, Ruskin Rowe Press, Avalon Beach, 1997, chapter 5.

xii   'she had already passed judgement': Ibid.

1   The Foster-Lynams

4   'Remember the music': 'Blind Tom', *The Queenslander* (Brisbane, Qld), 17 July 1897, p. 125.

4   'eternal fitness of things': Ibid.

7   'She was happy in Townsville': EH, Letter to Wirlie
    Moore, 1964, Papers of Mrs W. Moore, John Oxley Library,
    State Library of Queensland, M296.

2   Child genius

12 'the nuns "had tried to take the credit" ': EH, Letter to
    Coy Bateson, 1941, undated, Fryer Library, University of
    Queensland Library, UQFL18.

12 'he would have been in gaol': T.P. Boland, *James Duhig*,
    University of Queensland Press, St Lucia (Qld),
    1987.

13 'permit ankles being seen': 'Genius unspoilt', *Sunday Times*
    (Sydney, NSW), 3 February 1918, p. 13.

14 'shy as a Wonga pigeon': Ibid.

14 'claim of genius': 'New star hailed: Queensland's girl poet',
    Weekly Times (Melbourne, Vic), 2 February 1918.

14 'overfond and proud mother': 'Genius unspoilt'.

14 'crush her ambition': 'New star hailed'.

3   J.F. Archibald and *Smith's Weekly*

15 'Stott & Hoare's . . . where Ernestine wanted to study':
    'Training brings a job', *The Argus* (Melbourne, Vic),
    7 January 1935, p. 5.

16 'deadly monotonous affair': 'New star hailed: Queensland's
    girl poet', *Weekly Times* (Melbourne, Vic), 2 February
    1918.

16 'just the thing': Author interview with Louise Campbell,
    March 2015.

17 'These are stirring times': Letter, EH to Timothy Keleher,
    April 1918, Papers of Timothy Keleher, State Library of
    Queensland, OM 73-73.

17   'chase a career in writing': Letter, Timothy Keleher to EH, 1918, Papers of Timothy Keleher, State Library of Queensland, OM 73-73.

22   'soler and heeler of paragraphs': Claude McKay, 'A living legend', *The Sunday Herald* (Sydney, NSW), [date unknown] 1919, p. 12.

22   'chuckle at the world': Ibid.

22   'If I must die': Josie Vine, *Australian Journalism Monographs*, vol. 12, 2010, p. 14.

4   **Robert Clyde Packer**

23   'love of her life': Email, Louise Campbell to author, 10 October 2005.

27   'This charming, unspoilt, gifted daughter': 'Genius unspoilt', *Sunday Times* (Sydney, NSW), 3 February 1918, p. 13.

30   'skinny and sinister': Sharne Wolff, 'Sam Fullbrook: Delicate Beauty review', *The Guardian* (Australia edition), 9 April 2014.

5   **Tasmania**

35   'Fancy, Mum, the lights in the city': Joan Pilgrim, 'Around Australia with Ernestine Hill', *The Land* (Sydney, NSW), 24 October 1947.

36   'the lights of a city on the hillside': Ibid.

36   'one of the worst floods': Phil & Matt Stephens, *The Flood of 1929*, Launceston Historical Society. http://launcestonhistory.org.au/history-of-launceston/notable-events-in-launceston/the-flood-of-1929/

6   **On the road, 1930**

40   'sharpened pencils': EH, *The Great Australian Loneliness*, Jarrolds, London, 1937, p. 17.

41   'This week's best tale': 'This week's best tale: The background', *Western Mail* (Perth, WA), 6 February 1930, p. 8.

43   'like a tapestry': *The Great Australian Loneliness*, p. 18.

43   'laughably like a clipped poodle': Ibid.

43   'fragment of a rainbow': Ibid.

44   'a broken-down store': Ibid., p. 27.

45   'Some sources say that the death rate': 'Australia's Pearling Industry'. http://www.australia.gov.au/about-australia/australian-story/australias-pearling-industry

7   **M.P. Durack**

50   'I'm heading for Auvergne': EH, *The Great Australian Loneliness*, Jarrolds, London, 1937, p. 123.

51   'The Victoria River Depot Races': Ibid.

52   'a baby crocodile, a pony or a galah': Brenda Niall, *True North: The story of Mary and Elizabeth Durack*, Text Publishing, Melbourne, 2012, p. 9.

54   'Reg "was rabidly communist" ': Letter, EH to Mary Durack, August 1944, J S Battye Library of West Australian History, Private Archives, MN 0071 Acc 7273A.

55   'an agricultural adviser': *The Great Australian Loneliness*, p. 124.

55   'he would need to stay for some time': Letter, Jack Lovegro to Robert Easton, 8 March 1932, J S Battye Library of West Australian History, Private Archives, MN 1826 Acc 5408A.

55   'you'll have to take the train': *The Great Australian Loneliness*, p. 124.

55   'It takes a great measure of courage': Notes from Michael Patrick Durack (MPD) diary, J S Battye Library of West Australian History, Private Archives, MN 0071 Acc 7273A.

56 'those fascinating big rivers': Letter, EH to Elizabeth Durack, 2 February 1939, J S Battye Library of West Australian History, Private Archives, MN 0071 Acc 7273A.

8 Victoria Downs and Darwin

58 'ingenuity displayed': Kevin Kenneally, *Exploration and Botany: The W.R. Easton 1921 Expedition*, talk given to the Kimberley Society, Broome, 4 December 2013. http://www.kimberleysociety.org/images/kimbsoc---eeniawadoo.pdf

58 'It is primitive to travel': Ibid.

58 'very well-spoken and charming': EH, letter to MPD, JS Battye Library of West Australian History, Private Archives, MN 0071 Acc 7273A.

58 'an old dingo hunter': EH, *The Great Australian Loneliness*, Jarrolds, London, 1937, p. 125.

59 'He'll be the bloke shouting the odds': Ibid., p. 127.

61 'Darwin is hell and heaven': Ibid., p. 196.

62 'Everyone holding a ticket': Tess Lea, *Darwin*, New South Books, Sydney, 2014, p. 20.

62 'yellow people': EH, 'The tragedy of Henry Lee', *Sunday Times* (Perth, WA), 4 January 1931, p. 7.

63 'Darwin is not a good place': *The Great Australian Loneliness*, p. 197.

63 'getting her copy to the post office': Ibid., p. 189.

63 'philologist from Philadelphia University': Ibid., p. 199.

63 'Gerhardt Laves, as it turned out, had been a student': Gerhardt Laves Collection: www.anu.edu.au/linguistics/nash/aust/laves/index.html

64   'It was a place where the roads': *The Great Australian Loneliness*, p. 199.

9   Land, sea and 'Blue Moon'

68   'fighting over a bite of *Smith's Weekly*': W.J. Carey, 'Letter to the editor', *The West Australian* (Perth, WA), 3 September 1931, p. 11.

68   'Up north, he wrote': EH, 'A disgrace to Australia', *West Australian* (Perth, WA), 30 September 1933, p. 4.

68   'Numerous other remarkable happenings have occurred': Ibid.

69   ' "patriotic and truer" Kendall': EH, 'Gordon and Kendall', *The West Australian* (Perth, WA), 7 October 1931, p. 4.

69   'spasmodic travelling': Letter, EH to Henrietta Drake-Brockman, 1949, Papers of Henrietta Drake-Brockman, National Library of Australia, MS 1634.

71   'film script . . . "Blue Moon" ': Registrar of Copyrights Commonwealth of Australia, 30 April 1932.

10   Adrienne Lesire

74   'balloon pantaloons': EH, *The Great Australian Loneliness*, Jarrolds, London, 1937, p. 276.

76   'This was the story Ernestine wrote': EH, 'Where Australians bow to Allah', *Northern Standard* (Darwin, NT), 7 October 1932, p. 11.

78   'a test case': 'The marriage ceremony', *Kalgoorlie Western Argus* (Kalgoorlie, WA), 11 June 1907, p. 36.

78   'Gool paid the defendant's fine': Ibid.

78   'beautiful, green-eyed': 'Where Australians bow to Allah'.

79   'the most hair-raising thriller': *The Great Australian Loneliness*, p. 274.

79   'I have so much respect': Letter, EH to Coy Bateson, 1945, Fryer Library, University of Queensland Library, UQFL18.

11   Daisy Bates

82   'Daisy had no money': EH, *Kabbarli: A personal memoir of Daisy Bates*, Angus & Robertson, Sydney, 1973, p. 108.

83   'veil attached to keep out the flies': Ibid., p. 96.

86   'photograph of a toddler with ringlets': Ibid., p. 27.

86   'mother who, he felt, had abandoned him': Ibid.

87   'had become an impediment': Ibid.

87   'marriage must have seemed': Ibid.

88   'Daisy had made such claims': Bob Reece, *Daisy Bates: Grand dame of the desert*, National Library of Australia, Canberra, 2007, p. 8.

88   'Theodor Strehlow, who accused her': Ibid., p. 87.

88   'some sensational copy': EH, *The Great Australian Loneliness*, Jarrolds, London, 1937, p. 254.

12   Jake and Minnie

89   'Minnie Berrington': Sue Britt, 'Coober Pedy street and road names: Santing Drive', *Coober Pedy Regional Times* (Coober Pedy, Qld), 20 December 2012, p. 4.

89   'women could go down holes': Minnie Berrington, *Stones of Fire*, Robertson & Mullens, Melbourne, 1958, p. 10.

89   'Jacob (Jake) Santing's': 'Coober Pedy Street and road names: Santing Drive'.

90   'She didn't really know if he could read English': Ibid., p. 30.

91   'considered one of the blokes': EH, *The Great Australian Loneliness*, Jarrolds, London, 1937, p. 261.

94   'described by other journalists as shy': 'Genius unspoilt', *Sunday Times* (Sydney, NSW), 3 February 1918, p. 13.

95 'Take your pick—about 500 miles': Andrew Denton, interview with Ted Egan on *Enough Rope*, ABC TV, 2 August 2004.

96 'There's nothing here': EH, 'Human moles of Cooper Pedy', *The Advertiser* (Adelaide, SA), 16 December 1933, p. 9.

97 'I ride with whatever comes along': *The Great Australian Loneliness*, p. 7.

13 Gold fever

98 'It was a one-man town': EH, *The Great Australian Loneliness*, Jarrolds, London, 1937, p. 301.

98 'she felt a little like the Queen of Sheba': Ibid., p. 303.

99 'loudly ungracious "bah" ': Ibid., p. 308.

100 'Heinrich had become very attached': EH, 'Man with the green umbrella', *The Mail* (Adelaide, SA), 22 October 1932, p. 2.

100 'After counting "one, two" ': Ibid.

102 'Joe Kilgariff . . . showed her his fist full of gold': *The Great Australian Loneliness*, p. 309.

102 'dig for hidden treasure': Mark Twain, *The Adventures of Tom Sawyer*, Penguin, London, 2002, p. 132.

103 'The Advertiser had already run a headline': 'Gold boom: Granites field trading at fever pitch', *Recorder* (Port Pirie, SA), 4 October 1932, p. 1.

104 'official record of the Granites gold rush': David Laws Logbook, in F.E. Baume, *Tragedy Track: The story of the Granites*, Frank C. Johnson, Sydney, 1933, p. 40.

104 'Ernestine's first article about the rush': EH, 'Granites is gold city in embryo', *The Mail* (Adelaide, SA), 15 October 1932, p. 3.

104 'a police station, post office': EH, 'New township', *The Advertiser* (Adelaide, SA), 4 February 1933, p. 16.

14   Eric Baume

106   **'Some brokers on the Melbourne Stock Exchange':**
'Speculation in the Granites: Melbourne brokers view it
with disfavour', *The Advertiser* (Adelaide, SA), 17 September
1932, p. 16.

106   **'F.B. Stephens':** 'The Granites boom', *Barrier Miner*
(Broken Hill, NSW), 19 September 1932, p. 2.

106   **'indications that it was a gold area':** Ibid.

107   **'Her stories had a punch':** F.E. Baume, *Tragedy Track:
The story of the Granites*, Frank C. Johnson, Sydney, 1933, p. 8.

107   **'it wasn't for her to question':** Ibid.

108   **'devoted servant':** Arthur Manning, *Larger Than Life: The
story of Eric Baume*, A.H. & A.W. Reed, Sydney, 1967, p. 56.

109   **'a party consisting of Mr Baume':** 'Madigan Party', *Barrier
Miner* (Broken Hill, NSW), 2 November 1932, p. 2.

110   **'In short . . . Alice Springs.':** *Tragedy Track*, p. 2.

110   **'The party was excellently funded':** 'Desert gold or Granites
mirage', *The Daily Telegraph* (Sydney, NSW), 12 October
1932, p. 1.

110   **'They [the *Sunday Sun*] must be desperate':** *Tragedy Track*,
p. 8.

111   **'They showed no sign of violence':** Ibid., p. 29.

111   **'every ounce of gold':** Eric Baume, 'Loneliest goldfield',
The Daily News (Perth, WA), 19 November 1932, p. 11.

111   **'People could find a handful of gold':** 'The Madigan
Report', *Sunday Sun* (Sydney NSW), 4 December 1932.

112   **'There was no gold in quantity':** *Tragedy Track*, p. 2.

113   **'little Mrs Hill':** Ibid., p. 8.

113   **'Turning gold fever into headlines':** EH, *The Great
Australian Loneliness*, Jarrolds, London, 1937, p. 312.

15 Borroloola

115 'a cat and her four kittens': Letter, EH to Mary Durack, 1952, J S Battye Library of West Australian History, Private Archives, MN 0071 Acc 7273A.

118 'sworn he would never take a woman': EH, *The Great Australian Loneliness*, Jarrolds, London, 1937, p. 208.

118 'all my innocence': Ibid.

118 'hung with cobwebs': Ibid., p. 213.

118 'Ernestine stood marvelling': Ibid., p. 215.

16 Perth

121 'He was sentenced to three months' imprisonment': 'Defrauded persons who befriended him: How Frederick Hopkins impersonated Ernestine Hill', *The Advertiser* (Adelaide, SA), 11 September 1933, p. 10.

121 'there were many more con men out there': EH, 'Outback confidence men', *Sunday Mail* (Brisbane, Qld), 2 April 1933, p. 18.

122 'definitely a force of evil': Letter, EH to Mary Durack, January 1943, J S Battye Library of West Australian History, Private Archives, MN 0071 Acc 7273A.

124 'Too much fellowship': Letter, EH to Mary Durack, February 1946, J S Battye Library of West Australian History, Private Archives, MN 0071 Acc 7273A.

124 'I like quiet natures': Letter, EH to Coy Bateson, 1941, Fryer Library, University of Queensland Library, UQFL18.

125 'Ewers told her not to worry': J.K. Ewers, 'Australian bookman', *The Daily News* (Perth, WA), 1 April 1933, p. 18.

17   The *Silver Gull*, 1934

127   'Beatrice Grey was a dark-haired, slender and active
woman': 'The woman and the yacht', *Sydney Morning
Herald* (Sydney, NSW), 17 May 1934, p. 11.

129   'an excellent cook': EH, 'Scouts on *Silver Gull*', *Sunday
Mail* (Brisbane, Qld), 18 March 1934, p. 25.

129   'brave and wonderful': EH, 'Thrilling voyage of
Sea Scouts', *The Advertiser* (Adelaide, SA), 12 March 1934,
p. 18.

131   'Rugs, mattresses, pillows': Sea Scout Reg Thompson, 'Oil
poured on sea', *The West Australian* (Perth, WA), 9 May
1934.

131   'they were feared dead': 'Where is the *Silver Gull*?', *The
Daily News* (Perth, WA), 9 March 1934, p. 5.

18   Adelaide

133   'she never named Robert Packer': Email, Louise Campbell
to author, 10 October 2005.

134   'the love of her life': Ibid.

134   'No record remains': Ibid.

137   'poor as wood': 'Mrs Daisy Bates helps Aboriginals', *The
News* (Adelaide, SA), 24 May 1934, p. 12.

19   From Alice to Dumas

141   'Ernestine found the courtroom crowded': EH, 'Alice
Springs Court today', *The Advertiser* (Adelaide, SA),
6 February 1935, p. 17.

143   'The bush was alight': EH, *Kabbarli: A personal memoir of
Daisy Bates*, Angus & Robertson, Sydney, 1973, p. 134.

143   'expressing her concerns': Ibid.

144   'a prickly bush': Ibid., p. 137.

145 'He would be travelling from Melbourne': 'Utmost efforts: Mr Lyon's pledge', *Canberra Times* (Canberra, ACT), 22 February 1935.

146 'now Lyons might be willing': *Kabbarli*, p. 137.

147 'hidden herself from sight': Ibid.

147 'She believed that her work as the rescuer': Bob Reece, *Daisy Bates: Grand dame of the desert*, National Library of Australia, Canberra, 2007, p. 113.

147 'I want only the best': *Kabbarli*, p. 138.

148 'the morality of native and half-caste women': Daisy Bates, *The Passing of the Aborigines*, John Murray, London, 1938, p. 93.

148 'It must be your book': *Daisy Bates: Grand dame of the desert*, p. 115.

148 'all expenses the move incurred would be paid for': *Kabbarli*, p. 136.

149 'joyous little interruptions from my own kind': Elizabeth Salter, *Daisy Bates*, Coward, McCann & Geoghegan Inc, New York, 1972, p. 198.

150 'the manual labour of typing': *Kabbarli*, p. 142.

150 'method and manner of writing': Ibid., p. 141.

151 'My Natives and I': *The Advertiser* (Adelaide, SA), 4 January 1936, p. 8.

20 Writing books

152 'a springboard for the future': 'Heard here and there by Mayfair', *Sydney Morning Herald* (Sydney, NSW), 4 March 1937, p. 19.

153 'onto a small canvas': Letter, EH to Mary Durack, 14 January 1940, J S Battye Library of West Australian History, Private Archives, MN 0071 Acc 7273A.

155 'To make unusual pictures': EH, 'Shooting big game with a camera', *The Advertiser* (Adelaide, SA), 24 July 1935, p. 20.

155 'two of them drowned': Ibid.

21 The silver river

158 'encouragement of innovation was paramount': EH, *Water into Gold*, Robertson & Mullens, Melbourne, 1937, p. 65.

159 'graphically written': 'About books', *Cairns Post* (Cairns, Qld), 8 April 1937, p. 2.

160 'He is completely suburban': Letter, EH to Coy Bateson, 1941, Fryer Library, University of Queensland Library, UQFL18.

161 'charred and rusted plane rudder': 'Charred rudder of plane found on beach', *Morning Bulletin* (Rockhampton, Qld), 29 November 1937.

161 'his only loyalty': Letter, EH to Beatrice Davis, A&R Files, State Library of NSW, ML MSS 3269.

161 'It has all been nothing but woe': Letter, EH to Henrietta Drake-Brockman, National Library of Australia, MS 1634.

162 'free of "the English affair"': Ibid.

162 'shed its grisly jacket': Letter, EH to Beatrice Davis, April 1940, A&R Files, State Library of NSW, ML MSS 3269.

22 Radio star

164 'gay exhibitionist': Letter, EH to Coy Bateson, 1941, Fryer Library, University of Queensland Library, UQFL18.

164 'like a skeleton in the dark': Ibid.

165 'best Australian novel': Jacqueline Kent, *A Certain Style: Beatrice Davis, a literary life*, Viking, Melbourne, 2001, p. 77.

165 'Cousins called her bluff': Ibid., p. 78.

165 'Ernestine sent Ingleton a gracious letter': Ibid.

166 'Five of my own kind': Letter, EH to Henrietta Drake-Brockman, June 1940, National Library of Australia, MS 1634.

167 'The lack of music': 'Radio in the Outback', *The Land* (Sydney, NSW), 24 July 1942, p. 11.

167 'now, when the postman comes in': Ibid.

168 'remember the vowels of the King's English': 'Ernestine Hill knows what the Outback needs', *Border Watch* (Mount Gambier, Vic), 11 July 1942, p. 5.

168 'she wasn't even political': 'A woman of mark', *The Telegraph* (Brisbane, Qld), 30 June 1942, p. 6.

169 'Ernestine had always argued': EH, 'The tragic Territory', *The Chronicle* (Adelaide, SA), 21 June 1934, p. 49.

169 'Ernestine had previously written of the hospitality of the Japanese': *The Great Australian Loneliness*, Jarrolds, London, 1937, p. 72.

170 'He has a great sense of drama': Letter, EH to Henrietta Drake-Brockman, 1940, National Library of Australia, MS 1634.

170 'I hope there are no politics': 'A woman of mark'.

171 'droving cattle across the country': 'Droving with a typewriter', *The Argus* (Melbourne, Vic), 25 June 1942, p. 5.

171 'stockwhips cracking': Ibid.

23   Exemption

172 'most neurotic women': 'Authoress seeks son's exemption', *The News* (Adelaide, SA), 5 October 1943, p. 3.

172 'After suffering a stroke': Letter, EH to Henrietta Drake-Brockman, August 1943, National Library of Australia, MS 1634.

173 'taking him from her would have a disastrous effect on her health': 'Authoress seeks son's exemption'.

173 'could not continue this work': Letter, EH to Prime Minister Curtin, 9 November 1942, National Archives of Australia, NAA: A42, W16168.

173 'During the past year she had earned': 'Authoress seeks son's exemption'.

174 'her income was grossly overstated': Letter, EH to PM Curtin, 15 January 1943, National Archives of Australia, M1415, 431.

174 'Bob's help was of no less than national importance': Letter, EH to PM Curtin, 9 November 1942, National Archives of Australia, NAA: A42, W16168.

174 'he appreciated the importance of her work': Letter, PM Curtin to EH, 24 January 1943, National Archives of Australia, M1415, 431.

174 'advised her to take whatever legal steps': Letter, PM Curtin to EH, 15 January 1943, Papers of Prime Minister John Curtin, National Archives of Australia, M1415, 431.

174 'the merchant navy': Letter, EH to PM Curtin, 18 November 1943, National Archives of Australia, M1415, 431.

175 'The decision must be left to the authorities': Ibid.

175 'no way a party to the events': Letter, Attorney-general to state secretary, 24 December 1943, National Archives of Australia, NAA: A42, W16168.

175 'most harmful and untrue': Letter, EH to PM Curtin, 18 December 1943, National Archives of Australia, M1415, 431.

176   'the boy has done nothing wrong': Letter, EH to PM Curtin, 18 December 1943, National Archives of Australia, M1415, 431.

176   'Bob was happy at Cordillo': Letter, EH to Mary Durack, 16 December 1943, J S Battye Library of West Australian History, Private Archives, MN 0071 Acc 7273A.

176   'the pale white sun for company': Ibid.

176   'listed as fugitives': 'Flying Doctor helps authoress,' *Western Grazier* (Wilcannia, NSW), 14 January 1944, p. 3.

177   'a clear and confident mind': Letter, EH to PM Curtin, February 1943, National Archives of Australia, M1415, 431.

177   'I thought I could help': Letter, EH to Mary Durack, 9 November 1944, J S Battye Library of West Australian History, Private Archives, MN 0071 Acc 7273A.

178   'God must have sent the intervention': Ibid.

179   'It's a grand thing': 'Authoress in Perth', *The West Australian* (Perth, WA), 6 August 1946.

179   'She later forwarded a copy': Letter, EH to PM Curtin, 19 January 1943, National Archives of Australia, M1415, 431.

180   'I am writing a book about the Flying Doctors': Letter, EH to Coy Bateson, 7 January 1945, Fryer Library, University of Queensland Library, UQFL18.

180   'Bob returned to his mother': Letter, EH to Coy Bateson, 1945, Fryer Library, University of Queensland Library, UQFL18.

180   'life in the saddle too harsh': Robert Hill Notes, Fryer Library, University of Queensland Library, UQFL18.

24 Travels with Bob

182 'you won't find better quality': Letter, EH to Wirlie Moore', undated, Papers of Mrs W. Moore, John Oxley Library, State Library of Queensland, M296.

183 'she often hated all the travelling': Letter, EH to Beatrice Davis, 1945, A&R Files, State Library of NSW, ML MSS 3269.

183 'I never seem to have time to settle': Letter, EH to Henrietta Drake-Brockman, 2 February 1947, National Library of Australia, MS 1634.

184 'She had overheard them': 'An epic account of a Territory police family', *Citation* (Berrimah, NT), Newsletter of the Northern Territory Police Museum and Historical Society, May 2010.

184 'All right, Mother!': Ibid.

185 'poor Bob was embarrassed': Ibid.

186 'Go back to sleep, Mother': Joan Pilgrim, 'Across the Bight with Ernestine Hill', *The Land* (Sydney, NSW), 24 October 1947, p. 7.

186 'They meant no harm': Ibid.

186 'She felt both sorrow and admiration': Ibid.

187 'powerful tired': Letter, EH to Mary Durack, 26 January 1946, J S Battye Library of West Australian History, Private Archives, MN 0071 Acc 7273A.

25 Henrietta Drake-Brockman

188 'Henrietta is a brick': Letters, EH to Beatrice Davis, 1948, A&R Files, State Library of NSW, ML MSS 3269.

188 'one of the most endearing and dashing people': Letter, EH to Coy Bateson, Fryer Library, University of Queensland Library, UQFL18.

189 'I am suffering from one of the trials': Letter, Henrietta Drake-Brockman to Beatrice Davis, A&R Files, State Library of NSW, ML MSS 3269.

190 'Breezing about in his utility': Letter, EH to Henrietta Drake-Brockman, 1947, National Library of Australia, MS 1634.

191 'I realise that the complication': Patricia Kotai-Ewers, The Fellowship of Australian Writers (WA) from 1938 to 1980 and its role in the cultural life of Perth, Thesis, Murdoch University, November 2013.

192 'Eleanor Smith would soon be leaving for Sydney': 'About people', *Sydney Morning Herald* (Sydney, NSW), 12 December 1946, p. 15.

192 'readers describe it as "too solid" ': Letter, EH to Beatrice Davis, 1951, A&R Files, State Library of NSW, ML MSS 3269.

192 'rumoured to be four figures': 'My Love Must Wait', *The Argus* (Melbourne, Vic), 20 May 1946, p. 1.

192 'surrender the screen rights': 'Olivier as Flinders?', *Sunday Times* (Perth, WA), 12 September 1948.

192 'Sir Laurence': 'Choice of Olivier pleases author', *The Daily News* (Perth, WA), 2 September 1948, p. 8.

193 'no longer interested': Letter, EH to Beatrice Davis, 14 June 1950, A&R Files, State Library of NSW, ML MSS 3269.

193 'any reasonable proposition by Chauvel': Ibid.

193 'mother and son could let any amount of money disappear': Letter, Henrietta Drake-Brockman to Beatrice Davis, 1951, A&R Files, State Library of NSW, ML MSS 3269.

193 'she managed to write novels': Ibid.

194 'her friend had been able to capture the magnificent spirit': Henrietta Drake-Brockman, 'An epic of the air', *Northern Times* (Carnarvon, WA), 24 December 1947, p. 2.

194 'insisting on grammatical purity': Letter, EH to Beatrice Davis, December 1946, A&R Files, State Library of NSW, ML MSS 3269.

194 'Living is the strain': Letter, EH to Henrietta Drake-Brockman, National Library of Australia, MS 1634.

195 'strange otherwhereish creature': Tom Griffiths, *Hunters and Collectors: The antiquarian imagination in Australia*, Cambridge University Press, Cambridge, UK, 1996, p. 190.

26   A dog and a caravan, 1947–48

196 'if Ernestine would be up for the job': EH, *Kabbarli: A personal memoir of Daisy Bates*, Angus & Robertson, Sydney, 1973, p. 167.

198 'queerly difficult woman': Letter, EH to Coy Bateson, undated, Fryer Library, University of Queensland Library, UQFL18.

198 'Ernestine also arranged for Daisy's allowance': *Kabbarli*, p. 167.

198 'inimitable brilliantly sympathetic manner': Henrietta Drake-Brockman, 'An epic of the air', *Northern Times* (Carnarvon, WA), 24 December 1947, p. 2.

199 'I'm now looking for that fable': Letter, EH to Mary Durack, 1949, J S Battye Library of West Australian History, Private Archives, MN 0071 Acc 7273A.

199 'a strange note arrived': *Kabbarli*, p. 170.

200 'demanding the immediate return': Ibid.

200 'he totters about all day': Letter, EH to Mary Durack, April 1948, J S Battye Library of West Australian History, Private Archives, MN 0071 Acc 7273A.

200 'Mostly I'm confused': Letter, EH to Bess Durack, J S Battye Library of West Australian History, Private Archives, MN 0071 Acc 7273A.

201 'Yes, Mother, but *that's* the point': Letter, EH to Henrietta Drake-Brockman, 1948, National Library of Australia, MS 1634.

201 'he had criticised Nora Heysen's 1938 Archibald win': 'Women and art', *The Evening News* (Rockhampton, Qld), 27 January 1939, p. 10.

201 'she genuinely enjoyed reading them': Letter, Beatrice Davis to EH, 15 March 1949, Fryer Library, University of Queensland Library, UQFL18.

202 'new suburbs were springing up': 'Authoress visits Deviot', *The Examiner* (Launceston, Tas), 29 December 1948, p. 6.

27 *The Territory*

203 'ruler of doggie kingdom': Letter, EH to Mary Durack, 1950, J S Battye Library of West Australian History, Private Archives, MN 0071 Acc 7273A.

203 'he was finally developing his own talent': Letter, EH to Beatrice Davis, A&R Files, State Library of NSW, ML MSS 3269.

204 'unassuming visitor': 'Interesting visitor': *Albany Advertiser* (Albany, WA), 24 January 1949.

204 'Sydney had become a horror': Letter, EH to Beatrice Davis, 30 July 1949, A&R Files, State Library of NSW, ML MSS 3269.

205 'She was regarded as a social lass': 'Leaping Lena on last legs', *The Examiner* (Launceston, Tas), 24 April 1942, p. 5.

206 'Civilisation has clothed her': EH, *The Great Australian Loneliness*, Jarrolds, London, 1937, p. 331.

206 'Durack was the last of his kind': EH, 'A figure in history', *The West Australian* (Perth, WA), 16 September 1950, p. 21.

207 'two stone rooms and very picturesque': Letter, EH to Tully family, 1954, J S Battye Library of West Australian History, Private Archives, MN 0071 Acc 7273A.

207 'He dropped in from the sky': Brenda Niall, *True North: The story of Mary and Elizabeth Durack*, Text Publishing, Melbourne, 2012, p. 66.

208 'a little party with Mary's bunnies': Letter, EH to Ann Tully, March 1950, J S Battye Library of West Australian History, Private Archives, MN 0071 Acc 7273A.

208 'She manages five babies': Letter, EH to Bess Durack, 1950, J S Battye Library of West Australian History, Private Archives, MN 0071 Acc 7273A.

208 'time was running out': Letter, EH to Beatrice Davis, 1951, A&R Files, State Library of NSW, ML MSS 3269.

210 'publishing it in two volumes': Jacqueline Kent, *A Certain Style: Beatrice Davis, a literary life*, Viking, Melbourne, 2001, p. 82.

210 'recurrent headaches': Letter, Bob Hill to EH, 1951, Fryer Library, University of Queensland Library, UQFL18.

211 'I hope you are not being a trouble': Letter, EH to Bob, 1953, Fryer Library, University of Queensland Library, UQFL18.

211 'working like a woodpecker': Letter, EH to Beatrice Davis, A&R Files, State Library of NSW, ML MSS 3269.

211 'Betty's bright and interesting pics': Letter, EH to Beatrice
Davis, A&R Files, State Library of NSW, ML MSS 3269.

212 'bush narratives': 'Australian literature', *The West Australian*
(Perth, WA), 18 July 1953, p. 29.

28 Eleanor Smith, 1952

This chapter has been realised with the kind help of Eleanor Smith's
daughter, Sally Hinks, and Steve Howell of the J S Battye Library.

213 'who encouraged me to write it': Eleanor Smith, *Isle of
Girls*, Paterson, Perth, 1953, Foreword.

213 'Gair-brand tents': Letter, EH to Wirlie Moore, 1954,
Papers of Mrs W. Moore, John Oxley Library, State Library
of Queensland, M296.

214 'Ernestine had asked A&R for an advance': Letter, EH to
A&R, February 1952, A&R Files, State Library of NSW,
ML MSS 3269.

214 'elderly prospectors trying to live on a small pension': EH,
'A home for the old folks of gold', *The West Australian*
(Perth, WA), 25 October 1952, p. 2.

216 'always eager to learn': Robert Hill Notes, Ernestine Hill
Collection, Fryer Library, University of Queensland Library,
UQFL18.

216 'a fascinating little recreation': Letter, EH to Ann Tully,
February 1954, J S Battye Library of West Australian
History, Private Archives, MN 0071 Acc 7273A.

216 'Eleanor thought that an anonymous article': 'Daisy Bates:
Passing of a remarkable woman', *The Advertiser* (Adelaide,
SA), 20 April 1951, p. 2.

217 'She had succeeded': EH, 'Australian literature', *The West
Australian* (Perth, WA), 18 July 1953, p. 29.

217 'Were they afraid to try?': Ibid.

217 'Mary Durack, commenting on this article': Mary Durack, 'Writers don't spring from the soil', *The West Australian* (Perth, WA), 11 July 1953.

218 'My mother, in urging young writers to write': Robert Hill, 'In the open air life lie most of our classics', *The West Australian* (Perth, WA), 25 July 1953, p. 32.

29   Art and age

220 'a special child': Letter, Henrietta Drake-Brockman to Beatrice Davis, A&R Files, State Library of NSW, ML MSS 3269.

221 'I thought art had gone truly mad': Letter, EH to Ann Tully, 1950, J S Battye Library of West Australian History, Private Archives, MN 0071 Acc 7273A.

221 'I am skinny and sinister': Letter, EH to Henrietta Drake-Brockman, 1952, National Library of Australia, MS 1634.

221 'Ernestine felt disheartened': 'Twenty-one again', *The Western Australian* (Perth, WA), 16 June 1954.

223 'right up his particular little street': Letter, EH to Tully family, J S Battye Library of West Australian History, Private Archives, MN 0071 Acc 7273A.

223 'Ernestine inspected the cairn': 'Keeping alive the memory of a remarkable woman', *The Advertiser* (Adelaide, SA), 16 November 1954, p. 2.

223 'Ernestine told the reporter how she had met Daisy': Ibid.

224 'I am working away': Letter, EH to Bob Hill, 1953, Fryer Library, University of Queensland Library, UQFL18.

224 'just waiting to surface': Letter, EH to Beatrice Davis, 1955, A&R Files, State Library of NSW, ML MSS 3269.

224 'The story of an aboriginal': Flyer announcing the release of Johnnie Wise-Cap, A&R, September 1955.

30 Mary Durack

227 'certain obligations': 'Mary Durack's plan to help the natives', *The Daily News* (Perth, WA), 4 March 1944, p. 7.

227 'fly for free': Letter, EH to Henrietta Drake-Brockman, 1942, National Library of Australia, MS 1634.

228 'Bob was always dreaming up schemes': Letter, Patsy Durack to Louise Campbell, 2003, Fryer Library, University of Queensland Library, UQFL18.

228 'Children are such wonders': Letter, EH to Mary Durack, 1955, J S Battye Library of West Australian History, Private Archives, MN 0071 Acc 7273A.

229 'Ernestine and Bob kept their distance': Email, John Miller to author, 19 November 2007.

230 'I wouldn't have had any money left': Letter, EH to Bob Hill, 1955, Fryer Library, University of Queensland Library, UQFL18.

230 'I cannot afford to stay where I am now living': Letter, EH to Beatrice Davis, 1957, A&R Files, State Library of NSW, ML MSS 3269.

230 'I work, work and work': Letter, EH to Bob Hill, August 1955, Fryer Library, University of Queensland Library, UQFL18.

230 'Why stay in a room': Letter, EH to Bill Moore, Papers of Mrs W. Moore, John Oxley Library, State Library of Queensland, M296.

31 Bob

231 'He looked really wild': Robert Hill Notes, Fryer Library, University of Queensland Library, UQFL18.

232 'how he was getting on': Letters, EH to Bob Hill, 1956–57, Fryer Library, University of Queensland Library, UQFL18.

232 'It was she who preached [the] "romance" of the Australian Outback': Robert Hill Notes, Fryer Library, University of Queensland Library, UQFL18.

232 'her 61st birthday': Robert Hill Notes, Fryer Library, University of Queensland Library, UQFL18.

233 'All that travelling around': Robert Hill Notes, Fryer Library, University of Queensland Library, UQFL18.

233 'an alternating wail': Ibid.

233 'my life is getting out of hand': Letter, EH to Beatrice Davis, December 1959, A&R Files, State Library of NSW, ML MSS 3269.

233 'I have been working away': Letter, EH to Beatrice Davis, 1960, A&R Files, State Library of NSW, ML MSS 3269.

233 'All dressed up': Letter, EH to Bob Hill, 1958, Fryer Library, University of Queensland Library, UQFL18.

234 'a good and earnest little girl': Letter, EH to Henrietta Drake-Brockman, 1961, National Library of Australia, MS 1634.

235 'Australia has changed before our eyes': Letter, EH to Bob Hill, 1960, Fryer Library, University of Queensland Library, UQFL18.

235 'the drunks singing down stairs': Ibid.

235 'My mother's people were Irish': Letter, EH to Wirlie Moore, undated, Papers of Mrs W. Moore, John Oxley Library, State Library of Queensland, M296.

235 'she insisted on having her typewriter': Letter, Bob Hill to Beatrice Davis, 1960, A&R Files, State Library of NSW, ML MSS 3269.

236 'if Beatrice could help': Ibid.

236 'Sydney has never made her happy': Letter, Beatrice Davis to Bob Hill, Fryer Library, University of Queensland Library, UQFL18.

236 'Archibald would moan': Letter, EH to Bob Hill, 1961, Fryer Library, University of Queensland Library, UQFL18.

236 'I don't want to be connected to the new management': Ibid.

237 'everyone at A&R': Jacqueline Kent, *A Certain Style: Beatrice Davis, a literary life*, Viking, Melbourne, 2001, p. 85.

237 'The British promised': Richard Walsh, personal recollection.

237 'of course I won't leave them': Letter, EH to Wirlie Moore, 1963, Papers of Mrs W. Moore, John Oxley Library, State Library of Queensland, M296.

32 Disasters and grandchildren

238 'Most family arguments were very Irish': Letter, EH to Henrietta Drake-Brockman, National Library of Australia, MS 1634.

238 'my second wind': Letter, EH to Wirlie Moore, November 1963, Papers of Mrs W. Moore, John Oxley Library, State Library of Queensland, M296.

239 'still drinking': Letter, EH to Beatrice Davis, 1963, A&R Files, State Library of NSW, ML MSS 3269.

239 'There is no question of alcohol neurosis': Letter, EH to Beatrice Davis, 1959, A&R Files, State Library of NSW, ML MSS 3269.

239 'New Space Age': Letter, EH to Ann Tully, 1964, J S Battye Library of West Australian History, Private Archives, MN 0071 Acc 7273A.

240 ‘Bob and Jacky’: Bob Hill and Jacqueline Scrivener were married on 22 February 1962.

240 ‘a little car for the beaches’: Letter, EH to Wirlie Moore, 1962, Papers of Mrs W. Moore, John Oxley Library, State Library of Queensland, M296.

240 ‘He wears a cross’: Letter, EH to Coy Bateson, 1961, Fryer Library, University of Queensland Library, UQFL18.

241 ‘The photos could earns us hundreds’: Letter, EH to Bob Hill, Fryer Library, University of Queensland Library, UQFL18.

242 ‘Although the publisher had just contracted Elizabeth Salter’: Jacqueline Kent, *A Certain Style: Beatrice Davis, a literary life*, Viking, Melbourne, 2001, p. 86.

242 ‘with big pop-eyes’: Letter, EH to Bill Moore, Papers of Mrs W. Moore, John Oxley Library, State Library of Queensland, M296.

242 ‘Ernestine, however, remained adamant’: Robert Hill Notes, Fryer Library, University of Queensland Library, UQFL18.

243 ‘he turned to A&R in 1969’: Letter, Bob Hill to Beatrice Davis, March 1969, A&R Files, State Library of NSW, ML MSS 3269.

243 ‘Beatrice Davis did not think’: Letter, Beatrice Davis to Bob Hill, 14 March 1969, A&R Files, State Library of NSW, ML MSS 3269.

243 ‘Found living in Adelaide too cold’: Letter, EH to Wirlie Moore, Papers of Mrs W. Moore, John Oxley Library, State Library of Queensland, M296.

246 ‘an old harpy actress’: Letter, EH to Bob Hill, Fryer Library, University of Queensland Library, UQFL18.

246 ‘Sir John Kerr was rejected’: Carolyn Webb, ‘Sam Fullbrook dies’, *The Age* (Melbourne, Vic), 5 February 2004.

246   '**Katharine Hepburn**': 'Hepburn and Helpmann to make a film,' *Sydney Morning Herald* (Sydney, NSW), 25 November 1969, p. 3.

The lady in the blue dress

251   '**I did forget to put the drunks in**': Email, Louise Campbell to author, 2006.

253   '**women are as rare as roses**': EH, *The Great Australian Loneliness*, Jarrolds, London, 1937, p. 208.

Epilogue

254   '**Just under a tree**': Robert Hill Notes, Fryer Library, University of Queensland Library, UQFL18.

254   '**Olivetti typewriter and a camera**': Letter, Charles Bateson to A&R, 1972, A&R Files, State Library of NSW, ML MSS 3269.

254   '**Her executor, Charles Bateson**': Letter, Charles Bateson to A&R, 1972, A&R Files, State Library of NSW, ML MSS 3269.

255   '**the great secret**': Email, John Miller to author, 23 November 2007.

255   '**bit of a gambling problem**': Ibid.

255   '**obsessive about the considerable Packer legacy**': Ibid.

255   '**would waste all his earnings**': Ibid.

255   '**Bob was always putting himself down**': Ibid.

255   '**quite a fretful person**': Email, Louise Campbell to author, 9 May 2006.

Bibliography

PRIMARY SOURCES

Works by Ernestine Hill

Books

Australia: Land of Contrasts, edited by Sydney Ure Smith, John Sands Pty Ltd, Sydney, 1943.

Flying Doctor Calling: *The Flying Doctor Service of Australia*, Angus & Robertson, Sydney, 1947.

Kabbarli: A personal memoir of Daisy Bates, Angus & Robertson, Sydney, 1973.

My Love Must Wait: The story of Matthew Flinders, Angus & Robertson, Sydney, 1941.

Paul Johns' Statement about Lasseter, as Told to Ernestine Hill, Scrivener Press, Adelaide, 1968.

Peter Pan Land and Other Poems, Hibernian Newspaper Co., Brisbane, 1916.

'Story of the state', in *The Centenary Chronicle*, Advertiser Newspapers Limited, Adelaide, 1936.

The Great Australian Loneliness, Jarrolds, London, 1937.

The Territory, Angus & Robertson, Sydney, 1951.

Water into Gold, Robertson & Mullens, Melbourne, 1937.

Magazine and newspaper articles

1930

'A Cossack "graveyard" ', *The West Australian* (Perth, WA),
    25 October 1930.

'Race carnival', *Sydney Sun* (Sydney, NSW), 8 November 1930.

'Scorching days in the nor'west', *The Mail* (Adelaide, SA),
    13 December 1930.

1931

'The tragedy of Henry Lee', *Sunday Times* (Perth, WA), 4 January
    1931.

'Savage Arnhemland', *The West Australian* (Perth, WA),
    6 February 1931.

'A swaggie in the Kimberley', *The West Australian* (Perth, WA),
    13 June 1931.

'Gordon and Kendall', *The West Australian* (Perth, WA),
    7 October 1931.

1932

'The woman of Ooldea', *The West Australian* (Perth, WA), 25 June
    1932.

'Where Australians bow to Allah', *Northern Standard* (Darwin,
    NT), 7 October 1932.

'Granites is gold city in embryo', *The Mail* (Adelaide, SA),
    15 October 1932.

'Man with the green umbrella', *The Mail* (Adelaide, SA),
    22 October 1932.

'Bank for Granites gold', *The News* (Adelaide, SA), 31 October
    1932.

'The strange case of Mrs Widgety', *The Sun* (Sydney, NSW),
    18 December 1932.

1933

'New township', *The Advertiser* (Adelaide, SA), 4 February 1933.

'Six days on a camel', *The West Australian* (Perth, WA),
    25 February 1933.

'Outback confidence men', *Sunday Mail* (Brisbane, Qld), 2 April
    1933.

'Darwin', *Queensland Times* (Ipswich, Qld), 18 April 1933.

'Gallant voyagers of the north', *The Sunday Mail* (Brisbane, Qld),
    3 September 1933.

'Disgrace', *The West Australian* (Perth, WA), 30 September 1933.

'Library hidden in jungle', *The Chronicle* (Adelaide, SA),
    2 November 1933.

'Trek from Granites begging lifts', *The News* (Adelaide, SA),
    22 November 1933.

'Human moles of Cooper Pedy', *The Advertiser* (Adelaide, SA),
    16 December 1933.

1934

'Thrilling voyage of Sea Scouts', *The Advertiser* (Adelaide, SA),
    12 March 1934.

'Scouts on *Silver Gull*', *Sunday Mail* (Brisbane, Qld), 18 March 1934.

'Glory of the gardens', *The Advertiser* (Adelaide, SA), 31 May 1934.

'Reading with fingers', *The Advertiser* (Adelaide, SA), 8 June 1934.

'The tragic Territory', *The Chronicle* (Adelaide, SA), 21 June 1934.

'Pies and pioneers', *The Advertiser* (Adelaide, SA), 26 June 1934.

'Woman who loves children: Mrs Lydia Longmore', *The Advertiser*
    (Adelaide, SA), 5 July 1934.

'Parakeet and lorikeet', *The Advertiser* (Adelaide, SA), 23 July 1934.

'Coffee as we ought to know it', *The Advertiser* (Adelaide, SA),
    17 November 1934.

'Our cup of tea', *The Advertiser* (Adelaide, SA), 22 November 1934.

1935

'Big event for Alice Springs', *The Advertiser* (Adelaide, SA),
24 January 1935.

'Visit to Winnecke Goldfield', *The Advertiser* (Adelaide, SA),
25 January 1935.

'Need for hospital', *The Advertiser* (Adelaide, SA), 26 January
1935.

'Criminal sittings at Alice Springs', *The Advertiser* (Adelaide, SA),
1 February 1935.

'Alice Springs Court today', *The Advertiser* (Adelaide, SA),
6 February 1935.

'A town goes west', *The Advertiser* (Adelaide, SA), 9 March 1935.

'Shooting big game with a camera', *The Advertiser* (Adelaide, SA),
24 July 1935.

1948

'After twenty years', *The Examiner* (Launceston, Tas), 28 January
1948.

1950

'A figure in history', *The West Australian* (Perth, WA),
16 September 1950.

1952

'There is gold on the goldfields', *The West Australian* (Perth, WA),
27 September 1952.

'A home for the old folks of gold', *The West Australian* (Perth,
WA), 25 October 1952.

1953

'Australian literature', *The West Australian* (Perth, WA), 18 July
1953.

Archives and manuscripts

Private Archives, J S Battye Library of West Australian History, Perth
Papers of the Durack Family, MN 0071 Acc 7273A
Papers of William Robert Easton, MN 1826 Acc 5408A
Papers of John Keith Ewers, MN 1870 Acc 5340A, 5459A

Fryer Library, University of Queensland Library
Ernestine Hill Collection, UQFL18
Louise Campbell Collection, UQFL120

The Heritage Collections of the State Library of Queensland
Papers of Mrs W. Moore, John Oxley Library, M296
Papers of Timothy Keleher, OM 73-73

National Archives of Australia, Canberra
Papers of Prime Minister John Curtin, M1415, 431
Ernestine Hill, re exemption of son from military service,
    NAA: A472, W16168

National Library of Australia, Canberra
Papers of Henrietta Drake-Brockman, MS 1634

State Library of NSW
Correspondence between A&R/Beatrice Davis and
    writer Henrietta Drake-Brockman; and between A&R/
    Beatrice Davis and Ernestine Hill, A&R Files,
    ML MSS 3269

SECONDARY SOURCES

Books, essays and lectures

Bates, Daisy, *The Passing of the Aborigines*, John Murray, London, 1938.

Baume, F.E., *Tragedy Track: The story of the Granites*, F.C. Johnson, Sydney, 1933.

Berrington, Minnie, *Stones of Fire*, Robertson & Mullens, Melbourne, 1958.

Blackburn, Julia, *Daisy Bates in the Desert*, Martin Secker & Warburg Ltd, 1994.

Boland, T.P., *James Duhig*, University of Queensland Press, St Lucia (Qld), 1987.

Brockwell, Sally & Tom Gara, Sarah Colley & Scott Cane, *The History and Archaeology of Ooldea Soak and Mission*, Australian Archaeological Association Inc., 2011.

Drake-Brockman, Henrietta, *Sheba Lane*, Angus & Robertson, Sydney, 1936.

Dudley Edwards, Ruth & Bridget Hourican, *An Atlas of Irish History*, Routledge, London and New York, 2005.

Durack, Mary, *Kings in Grass Castles*, Constable and Company Ltd, London, 1959.

——, *Sons in the Saddle*, Constable, Hutchinson, London, 1983.

Francis, Rae Professor, *Women in White Australia*, lecture given at Monash University, 24 September 2013.

Griffen-Foley, Bridget, *Sir Frank Packer: A biography*, Sydney University Press, Sydney, 2014.

Griffiths, Tom, *Hunters and Collectors: The antiquarian imagination in Australia*, Cambridge University Press, Cambridge, UK, 1996.

Inglis, Kenneth S., *This Is the ABC: The Australian Broadcasting Commission 1932–1983*, Melbourne University Press, Melbourne, 1983.

Isaacs, Victor & Rod Kirkpatrick, *Two Hundred Years of Sydney Newspapers: A short history*, Rural Press Ltd, NSW, 2003.

Kenneally, Kevin, *Exploration and Botany: The W.R. Easton 1921 Expedition*, Kimberley Society, Broome, 2013.

Kent, Jacqueline, *A Certain Style: Beatrice Davis, a literary life*, Viking, Melbourne, 2001.

Kotai-Ewers, Patricia, The Fellowship of Australian Writers (WA) from 1938 to 1980 and its role in the cultural life of Perth, Thesis, Murdoch University, November 2013.

Laugesen, Amanda, *Writing the North-West Past and Present: The 1930s fiction and drama of Henrietta Drake-Brockman*, History Australia, vol. 8, no. 1 (2011), pp. 109–26.

Lea, Tess, *Darwin*, New South Books, Sydney, 2014.

MacDonald, Lorna, *Rockhampton: History of a city and district*, University of Queensland Press, Brisbane, 1981.

Manning, Arthur, *Larger Than Life: The story of Eric Baume*, A.H. & A.W. Reed, Sydney, 1967.

Mayne, Alan & Stephen Atkinson, *Outside Country: A history of inland Australia*, Wakefield Press, Kent Town, SA, 2011.

Morris, Meaghan, *Identity Anecdotes: Translation and media culture*, Sage Publications, London, 2006.

Murch, Ria, *Arthur Murch: An artist's life 1902–1989*, Ruskin Rowe Press, Avalon Beach, 1997.

Niall, Brenda, *True North: The story of Mary and Elizabeth Durack*, Text Publishing, Melbourne, 2012.

Norman, John E. De Burgh & Verity Norman, *Journey of a Master Pearler 1886–1942*, Kimberley Society, Broome, 2006.

O'Connor, Desmond, *Helping People Has Been My Happiness: The contribution of Elena Rubero to the Italian community in South Australia*, in Sue Williams et al (eds), *The Regenerative Spirit*, vol. 2, *(Un)settling, (Dis)locations, (Post-)colonial, (Re) presentations—Australian Post-Colonial Reflections*, Lythrum Press, Adelaide, 2003, pp. 93–101.

Olsten, Rob, *Farina: From gibbers to ghost town*, Bundinyabba Publications, Lake Wendouree, Vic, 2009.

Reece, Bob, *Daisy Bates: Grand dame of the desert*, National Library of Australia, Canberra, 2007.

Reid, Richard, *The Irish in Australia*, National Museum of Australia. www.nma.gov.au/exhibitions/irish_in_australia/irish_in_australia

Salter, Elizabeth, *Daisy Bates*, Coward, McCann & Geoghegan Inc, New York, 1972.

Sheahan-Bright, Robyn & Craig Munro, *Paper Empires 1946–2005*, University of Queensland Press, Brisbane, 2006.

Smith, Eleanor, *Isle of Girls*, Paterson, Perth, 1953.

Speake, Jennifer, *Literature of Travel and Exploration: An encyclopaedia*, Routledge, New York, 2003.

Stephens, Phil & Matt, *The Flood of 1929*, Launceston Historical Society Inc (Flood), Launceston, 1929.

Strehlow, T.G.H., *Journey to Horseshoe Bend*, Angus & Robertson, Sydney, 1969.

Radio plays, TV interviews and sound recordings

Hill, Ernestine, *Santa Clause of Christmas Creek* in *Australian Radio Plays*, 5AN (ABC Radio), Adelaide, 28 December 1938.

Denton, Andrew, interview with Ted Egan on *Enough Rope*, ABC TV, 2 August 2004.

Mascall, Sharon, *BBC One Minute World News: The Women Who Dig for Opal*, 20 October 2005.

Treagus, Aileen, 'We remember Daisy Bates', State Library of South Australia OH541/11 Margaret Kelsh, 5 October 1999.

——, 'We remember Daisy Bates', State Library of South Australia OH541/10 Rae Brewster, 5 October 1999.

Sources, written communication and interviews

Flight of Ducks, an online documentary developed by Simon Pockley in 1995 that revolves around the 1933 journal of Simon's father, John Antill Pockley: www.duckdigital.net/FOD/

Libby Allen: Email correspondence with author as well as personal files on the Foster-Lynam Family.

Sally Hinks, daughter of Eleanor Smith: Email and telephone correspondence with author.

Email and letter correspondence between author and Louise Campbell.

Email correspondence between author and John Miller.

Newspaper, magazine and journal articles

The Advertiser (Adelaide, SA)

Byrne, Bob, 'Remember the South Australian Hotel?', 24 June 2014.

'Daisy Bates: The passing of a remarkable woman', 20 April 1951.

'Defrauded persons who befriended him: How Frederick Hopkins impersonated Ernestine Hill', 11 September 1933.

'Doctors to study Aborigines', 4 January 1933.

'Great interest in new goldfield', 16 September 1932.

'Keeping alive the memory of a remarkable woman', 16 November 1954.

' "My Natives and I": Publication to begin tomorrow', 3 January 1936.

'My Natives and I', 4 January 1936, p. 8.

'650 miles to receive honour', 23 May 1934.

'Social notes: Ernestine Hill will speak on the problem of Aborigines', 9 July 1934.

'Speculation in the Granites: Melbourne brokers view it with disfavour', 17 September 1932.

'The beauty of the new art gallery', 6 August 1937.

Advocate (**Melbourne, Vic**)

'Ernestine Hemmings', 2 September 1916.

The Age (**Melbourne, Vic**)

'New books', 23 September 1916.

Webb, Carolyn, 'Sam Fullbrook dies', 5 February 2004.

Albany Advertiser (**Albany, WA**)

'Interesting visitor', 24 January 1949.

The Argus (**Melbourne, Vic**)

'Droving with a typewriter, 25 June 1942.

'My Love Must Wait', 20 May 1946.

'The founding of Mildura', 21 August 1937.

'Training brings a job', 7 January 1935.

'Women's Commissioner Ernestine Hill resigns', 11 July 1942.

Australian Journalism Monographs

Vine, Josie, 'If I must die, let me die drinking at an inn', vol. 12, 2010.

Australian Worker (**Sydney, NSW**)
'Sea Thoughts by Ernestine Hemmings', 19 September 1918.

Barrier Daily Truth (**Broken Hill, NSW**)
'Exemption application withdrawn', 12 May 1944.
'Military exemption application', 25 April 1944.

Barrier Miner (**Broken Hill, NSW**)
'Flying Doctor busy at Cordillo Downs', 13 January 1944.
'Granites gold hardy men', 26 September 1932.
'Madigan Party', 2 November 1932.
Special Correspondent, 'Gold discovery near Granites',
    14 September 1932.
'The Granites boom', 19 September 1932.

Border Watch (**Mount Gambier, Vic**)
'Ernestine Hill knows what the Outback needs', 11 July 1942.

Cairns Post (**Cairns, Qld**)
'About books', 8 April 1937.
'Appointment of youthful sub-editor', 18 October 1919.
'Death of Mr Hemmings', 3 October 1910.
'Tour of the state', 5 April 1949.

Canberra Times (**Canberra, ACT**)
'Utmost efforts: Mr Lyon's pledge', 22 February 1935.

The Chronicle (**Adelaide, SA**)
Beetee (Alys Truman), 'Of interest to women', 23 May 1935.
'The tragic Territory', 21 June 1934.

Citation (**Newsletter of the Northern Territory Police Museum and Historical Society, Berrimah, NT**)
'An epic account of a Territory police family', May 2010.

City Views (**Armidale, NSW**)
'Heritage Preserved at Darjeeling', vol. 40, 2012.

Coober Pedy Regional Times (**Coober Pedy, Qld**)
Britt, Sue, 'Coober Pedy street and road names: Santing Drive',
    20 December 2012.

The Daily News (**Perth, WA**)
'Author's son paints beauty spots', 16 February 1949.
Baume, Eric, 'Loneliest goldfield', 19 November 1932.
'Chit chat', 2 September 1948.
'Choice of Olivier pleases author', 2 September 1948.
Ewers, J.K., 'Australian Bookman', 1 April 1933.
'*Koolinda*'s passengers', 3 May 1934.
'Lover of the outback', 2 September 1933.
'Mary Durack's plan to help the natives', 4 March 1944.
'*Silver Gull* sails soon', 8 January 1934.
'Transport for two', 16 February 1949.
'Where is the *Silver Gull*?', 9 March 1934.

The Daily Telegraph (**Sydney, NSW**)
'Desert gold or Granites mirage', 12 October 1932.

The Evening News (**Rockhampton, Qld**)
'Women and art', 27 January 1939.

The Examiner (**Launceston, Tas**)
'Authoress visits Deviot', 29 December 1948.

'Holidaying at Nandana', 29 December 1948.
'Leaping Lena on last legs', 24 April 1942.
'Woman's world to women readers', May–November 1927.

The Farm and Settler (**Sydney, NSW**)
Blight, Malcolm, 'When white loves black', 11 November 1955.

The Guardian (**Australia edition**)
Wolff, Sharne, 'Sam Fullbrook: Delicate Beauty review', 9 April 2014.

Journal of Australian Studies (**UNSW Press, Sydney, NSW**)
Duncan Owen, June, 'Mixed matches: Interracial marriage in
    Australia', 2002.
Spencer, Tracy, ' "White woman lives as a lubra in native camp", in
    *Sharing Spaces: Indigenous and Non-indigenous Responses to
    Story, Country and Rights*, API Network, Perth, 2006,
    pp. 217–31.

Kalgoorlie Western Argus (**Kalgoorlie, WA**)
'The marriage ceremony', 11 June 1907.

The Land (**Sydney, NSW**)
Pilgrim, Joan, 'Across the Bight with Ernestine Hill', 24 October
    1947.
——, 'Around Australia with Ernestine Hill', 24 October 1947.
'Radio in the Outback', 24 July 1942.

Maryborough Chronicle, Wide Bay and Burnett Advertiser (**Qld**)
'Granites reef six miles long', 26 September 1932.

Morning Bulletin (**Rockhampton, Qld**)
'Charred rudder of plane found on beach', 29 November 1937.

The News (Adelaide, SA)
'Authoress seeks son's exemption', 5 October 1943.
'Mrs Daisy Bates helps Aboriginals', 24 May 1934.
'Natives' four month walk to attend pictures', 29 March 1937.
'Women's Council', 14 July 1934.

Northern Standard (Darwin, NT)
'Round about: Mrs Hill is in Katherine', 14 February 1933.

Northern Times (Carnarvon, WA)
Drake-Brockman, Henrietta, 'An epic of the air', 24 December 1947.
'Social afternoon', 27 July 1950.

The Queenslander (Brisbane, Qld)
'Blind Tom', 17 July 1897.

Recorder (Port Pirie, SA)
'Gold boom: Granites field trading at fever pitch', 4 October 1932.

Science
Laves, Gerhardt, 'Words among Australian Aborigines', *Science* n.s. 70, no. 1823, supplement, xiv, 1929.

The Sunday Herald (Sydney, NSW)
McKay, Claude, 'A living legend', [date unknown] 1919.

Sunday Mail (Brisbane, Qld)
'Town wiped out', 15 April 1934.

Sunday Sun (Sydney, NSW)
'Letters to the editor', 2 February 1931.
'The Madigan Report', 4 December 1932.

***Sunday Times* (Perth, WA)**
'Olivier as Flinders?', 12 September 1948.

***Sunday Times* (Sydney, NSW)**
'Genius unspoilt', 3 February 1918.
'Girl poet as legal librarian', 3 February 1918.
'Engagements', 27 January 1919.

***Sydney Morning Herald* (Sydney, NSW)**
'About people', 12 December 1946.
Bisset, Lady, 'Humped her bluey outback', 7 July 1951.
'Heard here and there by Mayfair', 4 March 1937.
'Hepburn and Helpmann to make a film', 25 November 1969.
'The woman and the yacht', 17 May 1934.

***The Telegraph* (Brisbane, Qld)**
'A woman of mark', 30 June 1942.

***Townsville Daily Bulletin* (Townsville, Qld)**
'Authoress in Mackay', 11 July 1953.
'Granites gold: A note of caution', 26 September 1932.

***Tribune* (Melbourne, Vic)**
Hemmings, E., 'Poem', 31 May 1917.

***Weekly Times* (Melbourne, Vic)**
'New star hailed: Queensland's girl poet', 2 February 1918.

***The West Australian* (Perth, WA)**
'A figure in Australian history: E. Hill', 16 September 1950.
'APH and a mackerel: "Three days in very fine place" ', 15 January
    1951.

'Authoress in Perth', 6 August 1946.

Carey, W.J., 'Letter to the editor', 3 September 1931.

'Death of Daisy's husband, 79 years old', 15 April 1935.

Durack, Mary, 'Writers don't spring from the soil', 11 July 1953.

'In the mailbag', 2 May 1946.

'Shipping news', 27 March 1931.

Taylor, A.R., 'In the open air life lie most of our classics', 25 July 1953.

Thompson, Sea Scout Reg, 'Oil poured on sea', 9 May 1934.

The Western Argus (**Kalgoorlie, WA**)

'The marriage ceremony of Gool and Adrienne', 11 June 1907.

The Western Australian (**Perth, WA**)

'Twenty-one again', 16 June 1954.

Western Grazier (**Wilcannia, NSW**)

'Flying doctor helps authoress', 14 January 1944.

Western Mail (**Perth, WA**)

'People', 18 March 1955.

'This week's best tale: The background', 6 February 1930.

The Winthrop Review (**University of Western Australia Arts Union, Perth, WA**)

Hill, Robert D., 'Thoroughfare', vol. 2, no. 1, 1954, p. 29.

Hill, Robert D., 'Sonnet on a flying saucer', Ibid., p. 37.

Acknowledgements

Thank you to:

Richard Walsh, whose knowledge of the time and the people was invaluable. His patient guidance, editing, suggestions and questions led me through the mountains and kept me from falling off the cliffs.

Bob and Kasper, for their loving support.

The staff of Allen & Unwin, especially Louise Thurtell, Sarah Baker, Lisa White and Aziza Kuypers for all their help and dedicated work.

Nicola Young, for her great editing.

Libby Allen, who supplied the documents for the early Foster-Lynam family history.

Sally Hinks, daughter of Eleanor Smith, for her valuable comments and suggestions.

Steve Howell of the J S Battye Library, for his aid with the Eleanor Smith story.

John Miller, for his comments, frankness, humour and help.

The wonderful staff of the J S Battye Library of West Australian History, Perth; the Fryer Library, University of Queensland Library; The Heritage Collections of the State

Library of Queensland; Women's Historical Society in Alice Springs; National Library of Australia, Canberra; and the State Library of NSW for their patience and help during my research.

George Karloff, for introducing me to people who mattered.

Marty, Saskia and Bryn, for their enthusiasm and support.

Silvana Sodde, who managed to float the marooned boat.

Antoinne Tai Chi, who taught me patience.